# The Psalms

## ESSENTIALS OF BIBLICAL STUDIES

THE PSALMS
Keith Bodner

EARLY JEWISH WRITINGS AND NEW TESTAMENT INTERPRETATION
C. D. Elledge

AN INVITATION TO BIBLICAL POETRY
Elaine James

ANCIENT ISRAEL'S NEIGHBORS
Brian R. Doak

SIN IN THE NEW TESTAMENT
Jeffrey Siker

READING HEBREW BIBLE NARRATIVES
J. Andrew Dearman

THE HISTORY OF BRONZE AND IRON AGE ISRAEL
Victor H. Matthews

NEW TESTAMENT CHRISTIANITY IN THE ROMAN WORLD
Harry O. Maier

WOMEN IN THE NEW TESTAMENT WORLD
Susan E. Hylen

# The Psalms

KEITH BODNER

# OXFORD
UNIVERSITY PRESS

Oxford University Press is a department of the University of Oxford. It furthers the University's objective of excellence in research, scholarship, and education by publishing worldwide. Oxford is a registered trade mark of Oxford University Press in the UK and certain other countries.

Published in the United States of America by Oxford University Press
198 Madison Avenue, New York, NY 10016, United States of America.

© Oxford University Press 2024

All rights reserved. No part of this publication may be reproduced, stored in a retrieval system, or transmitted, in any form or by any means, without the prior permission in writing of Oxford University Press, or as expressly permitted by law, by license, or under terms agreed with the appropriate reproduction rights organization. Inquiries concerning reproduction outside the scope of the above should be sent to the Rights Department, Oxford University Press, at the address above.

You must not circulate this work in any other form
and you must impose this same condition on any acquirer.

Library of Congress Cataloging-in-Publication Data
Names: Bodner, Keith, 1967– author.
Title: The Psalms / Keith Bodner.
Description: New York, NY, United States of America : Oxford University Press, [2024] | Series: Essentials of biblical studies series | Includes bibliographical references and index.
Identifiers: LCCN 2023025011 (print) | LCCN 2023025012 (ebook) | ISBN 9780190916879 (paperback) | ISBN 9780190916862 (hardback)| ISBN 9780190916893 (epub) | ISBN 9780190916886 (updf) | ISBN 9780190916909 (online)
Subjects: LCSH: Bible. Psalms—Criticism, interpretation, etc.
Classification: LCC BS1430.52 .B626 2024 (print) |
LCC BS1430.52 (ebook) | DDC 223/.206—dc23/eng/20230819
LC record available at https://lccn.loc.gov/2023025011
LC ebook record available at https://lccn.loc.gov/2023025012

DOI: 10.1093/oso/9780190916862.001.0001

*Dedicated to the memory of
Evelyn Bodner (1998-2018)
Your eyes saw my unformed body;
all the days ordained for me were written in your book
before one of them came to be. (Psalm 139:16, NIV)*

# Contents

| | |
|---|---|
| *List of Abbreviations* | ix |
| *Series Introduction* | xi |
| 1. Entering the Psalms | 1 |
| 2. The Psalms in the Ancient Near East | 23 |
| 3. The Variety of Psalms | 43 |
| 4. Israel's Story in the Psalms | 74 |
| 5. Psalm Titles and Collections | 100 |
| 6. The Fivefold Symphony of the Psalter | 133 |
| *Bibliography* | 173 |
| *Index* | 183 |

# Abbreviations

| | |
|---|---|
| AB | Anchor Bible |
| ACCS | Ancient Christian Commentary on Scripture |
| AOTC | Abingdon Old Testament Commentaries |
| BBR | Bulletin for Biblical Research |
| BCBC | Believers Church Bible Commentary |
| BCOTWP | Baker Commentary on the Old Testament Wisdom and Psalms |
| BTB | Biblical Theology Bulletin |
| BTCB | Brazos Theological Commentary on the Bible |
| EJ | European Judaism |
| ESV | English Standard Version |
| FOTL | Forms of the Old Testament Literature |
| HBT | Horizons in Biblical Theology |
| HUCA | Hebrew Union College Annual |
| ICC | International Critical Commentary |
| JBL | Journal of Biblical Literature |
| JNSL | Journal of Northwest Semitic Languages |
| JSOT | Journal for the Study of the Old Testament |
| JSOTSup | Journal for the Study of the Old Testament: Supplement Series |
| LHBOTS | The Library of Hebrew Bible/Old Testament Studies |
| LNST | The Library of New Testament Studies |
| NCBC | New Cambridge Biblical Commentary |
| NIBC | New International Biblical Commentary |
| NICOT | New International Commentary on the Old Testament |
| NIV | New International Version |
| NIVAC | New International Version Application Commentary |
| NJPS | Tanakh: The Holy Scriptures: The New JPS Translation according to the Traditional Hebrew Text |
| NRSV | New Revised Standard Version |
| OS | Oudtestamentische Studiën |
| OTE | Old Testament Essays |
| OTG | Old Testament Guides |
| SBET | Scottish Bulletin of Evangelical Theology |

SSN     Studia Semitica Neerlandica
TOTC    Tyndale Old Testament Commentaries
VT      *Vetus Testamentum*
VTSup   Supplements to *Vetus Testamentum*
WBC     Word Biblical Commentary
ZAW     *Zeitschrift für die alttestamentliche Wissenschaft*

# Series Introduction

The past three decades have seen an explosion of approaches to study of the Bible, as older exegetical methods have been joined by a variety of literary, anthropological, and social models. Interfaith collaboration has helped change the field, and the advent of more cultural diversity among biblical scholars in the West and around the world has broadened our reading and interpretation of the Bible. These changes have also fueled interest in Scripture's past: both the ancient Near Eastern and Mediterranean worlds out of which Scripture came and the millennia of premodern interpretation through which it traveled to our day. The explosion of information and perspectives is so vast that no one textbook can any longer address the many needs of seminaries and colleges where the Bible is studied.

In addition to these developments in the field itself are changes in the students. Traditionally the domain of seminaries, graduate schools, and college and university religion classes, now biblical study also takes place in a host of alternative venues. As lay leadership in local churches develops, nontraditional, weekend, and online preparatory classes have mushroomed. As seminaries in Africa, Asia, and Latin America grow, a particular need for inexpensive, easily available materials is clear. As religious controversies over the Bible's origins and norms continue to dominate the airwaves, congregation members and even curious nonreligious folk seek reliable paths into particular topics. And teachers themselves continue to seek guidance in areas of the ever-expanding field of scriptural study with which they may be less than familiar.

A third wave of changes also makes this series timely: shifts in the publishing industry itself. Technologies and knowledge are shifting so rapidly that large books are out of date almost before they are in print. The internet and the growing popularity of eBooks call for flexibility and accessibility in marketing and sales. If the days when one expert can sum up the field in a textbook are gone, also gone are the days when large, expensive multi-authored tomes are attractive to students, teachers, and other readers.

During my own years of seminary teaching, I have tried to find just the right book or books for just the right price, at just the right reading level for my students, with just enough information to orient them without drowning them in excess reading. For all the reasons stated above, this search was all too often less than successful. So I was excited to be asked to help Oxford University Press assemble a select crew of leading scholars to create a series that would respond to such classroom challenges. Essentials of Biblical Studies comprises freestanding, relatively brief, accessibly written books that provide orientation to the Bible's contents, its ancient contexts, its interpretive methods and history, and its themes and figures. Rather than a one-size-had-better-fit-all approach, these books may be mixed and matched to suit the objectives of a variety of classroom venues as well as the needs of individuals wishing to find their way into unfamiliar topics.

I am confident that our book authors will join me in returning enthusiastic thanks to the editorial staff at Oxford University Press for their support and guidance, especially Theo Calderara, who shepherded the project in its early days, and Dr. Steve Wiggins, who has been a most wise and steady partner in this work since joining OUP in 2013.

*Patricia K. Tull*
Louisville Presbyterian Theological Seminary

# 1
# Entering the Psalms

Within the library of the world's classics, the book of Psalms occupies a unique place. Few books were composed over a longer period of time and have exercised more cultural and religious influence than the Psalms, the longest and most complex collection in the Hebrew Bible and arguably one of the most illustrious and durable texts in history. Nearly one thousand years in the making, with dozens of contributors, this ancient anthology includes 150 prayers and poems for a host of public occasions and private exigencies, and altogether exhibits a sprawling array of historical memories and theological reflections. Not only is the book of Psalms the most quoted book of the Hebrew Bible in the New Testament, but for more than two millennia these lyrics have been variously interpreted by assorted religious groups and artists, musicians and poets, and even politicians and rock stars, and altogether ranks among the most translated and transcribed books in world literature.

This study is an introduction to the world of the Psalms that focuses on the content and the poetic forms that are encountered in the collection, guiding the reader toward an appreciation of the purposes of the Psalms and their contribution to the Hebrew Bible. Along with background discussion on the development of the Psalms and an overview of the variety and genres of these poetic texts, there is also some consideration of why the book contains some of the most famously comforting lines in history ("Though I walk through the valley of the shadow of death," Ps 23:4) and some of the most violent imprecations ("O daughter of Babylon," writes the poet of Psalm 137, "blessed is the one who seizes and shatters your little ones against the rock"). Rather than abstract theorizing, this study features close readings of numerous psalms so that the reader can explore the theological performance and poetically framed questions raised in the Psalms, ranging from the problem of evil and the silence of God to issues of philosophical speculation, practical atheism ("the fool says in his heart, 'There is no God!,'" Ps 14:1), and even life after death.

## Reading the Psalms in "4-D": A Multidimensional Approach

The goal of my opening chapter is to outline a fourfold approach for studying the Psalms that considers the historical background of ancient Israel, central features of Hebrew poetry, some core theological elements, and the overall literary shape and structure of the book of Psalms. I will start with a discussion of the Psalms in their historical context. Here a basic sketch of key moments in the story of Israel's national journey is provided, along with several remarks about the place of the book of Psalms within the Hebrew Bible. Second, an overview of biblical poetry is presented, with an explanation of *parallelism* as a foundational stylistic feature of the Psalms. Besides parallelism, at various points later in this book other formal features may be mentioned in passing, such as metaphor, wordplay, irony, modulations in point of view, deliberate ambiguity, acrostic structures, temporal compression, allusion, inner monologue, and quoted direct speech, as well as issues of characterization of the people of Israel as a collective, the presentation of various enemies and adversaries, and the towering figure of the king. Third, I will offer a brief discussion of distinctive theological beliefs held by ancient Israelites that contemporary readers may overlook, and some of their basic assumptions about God and humanity that are useful to bear in mind when analyzing the Psalms (along with several key terms, such as *creation*, *Torah*, *salvation*, and *Zion*). Fourth, I will suggest that this larger collection of psalms is finally shaped as a book with an overarching structure and a plot, and introduce the notion that "the Psalter" can be read as a five-act drama that traces God's promise to David and moves from *petition* and cries for help to unencumbered *praise* over the course of its 150 compositions.

## Israel's Story

The book of Psalms is ideally understood with some appreciation for the story of Israel, a story that scarcely has an equal, as a childless couple is given a promise that their descendants will bless every neighborhood on earth: "The books of the Hebrew Bible from Genesis to 2 Kings tell how in the space of a thousand years or more a small family of ancient Semites, the descendants of Israel, grew from humblest beginnings as wandering shepherds on the fringes of the civilizations of the ancient Near East to become a nation, a kingdom and even an empire before tragically succumbing to division, dissolution and the loss of the land that had made their nationhood possible."[1]

It should be noted that by *historical context* I do not have in mind an objective and rigorous inquiry by the standards of modern scholars. Instead, I am referring to the people of Israel's own account of their past as recorded in their sacred texts, recognizing that in general the Psalms draw on many of the main events over the thousand-year period reflected in these memories.

Since the biblical story begins with the creation of the universe, the account of Israel as God's chosen people is woven from the outset into the tapestry of the created order. Indeed, stories such as the two trees in the garden function not as isolated episodes but as an overture to the forthcoming drama: just as the man and the woman have the choice to accept God's word or reject it in favor of autonomy, so the people of Israel—along with every other human being—continually face the same options in the theater of everyday life. So, when Psalm 1 compares the blessed person to a flourishing tree along the banks of a nourishing stream, it is quite likely that the poet is drawing on a fund of early images in the story.

An early turning point in the Genesis narrative—after an escalation in scope and scale of violence that is hardly assuaged even by a cataclysmic flood—is the astonishing *promise* to Abraham and

---

[1] William Johnstone, *Exodus,* Old Testament Guides (Sheffield: Sheffield Academic Press, 1990), 12. For a standard overview, see J. Maxwell Miller and John H. Hayes, *A History of Ancient Israel and Judah,* 2nd edition (Louisville, KY: Westminster John Knox, 2006).

Sarah: through the offspring of a childless couple, God promises to bless every family on earth. Though that guarantee is often imperiled and threatened, by the end of Genesis there *is* a people of Israel (Abraham's grandson), who multiply by the thousands in the land of Egypt as a most pivotal installment of their history is about to be set in motion. At numerous points in the Psalter the promise to Abraham and the sojourn in Egypt hover in the background.

Life in Canaan is fraught with its own difficulties of climate, terrain, and hostility, but in Egypt—the land of the Nile—the fruitful Israelites are confronted with the bitterest of fates: the onset of slavery commandeered by an oppressive new king. Yet the covenant with the ancestors is not abandoned, for God dramatically rescues the Israelites in the unparalleled event of the *exodus*. After the tenth plague, the people are led through the waters of the Red Sea with a startling ironic reversal: just as Pharaoh and the Egyptians attempted to destroy Israel through drowning, so now the Egyptian army is drowned and destroyed. The people of Israel journey to Sinai, where the covenant is ratified and sealed with the Torah, before undertaking a long journey of discipleship in the wilderness and eventually entering the land of their inheritance in the early chapters of Joshua.

Occupancy of Canaan is tenuous for the Israelites and vacillates between moments of obedience offset by lengthy periods of neglect and spiritual lethargy. It may have been thought that the advent of kingship would usher in a new political stability, but any such hopes are quickly dashed, and the books of Samuel illustrate that monarchy carries its own share of problems. Even so, the theological center of the books of Samuel—and a major moment in all of biblical history—is the divine promise to David in 2 Sam 7:12–16 that a descendant would always reign on the throne of Israel, and even though this promise is sorely tested in the book of Kings and beyond, its durability becomes a significant touchstone of hope.[2]

The Solomonic Empire is unrivaled in wealth and architecture, but the cost of corruption is high: Solomon—David's immediate

---

[2] See Patricia K. Tull, "1 and 2 Samuel," in *Theological Bible Commentary*, ed. Gail R. O'Day and David L. Petersen (Louisville, KY: Westminster John Knox Press, 2009), 111–112.

successor—has a divided *heart*, and the consequence is a divided *kingdom* in 1 Kings 12. The nation is now split in two, with "Israel" in the north and "Judah" in the south. Although both kingdoms are fraught with turmoil throughout their respective histories, the south has the advantage of Jerusalem as a stable capital and a Davidic scion continuously in power. The north is larger and more powerful, but ultimately succumbs to the Assyrians in 2 Kings 17 (~722 BCE) after a long and sordid history of disobedience and covenant neglect. Jerusalem seems poised for the same demolition, but at the eleventh hour there is a divine intervention that strikes the Assyrians and allows Jerusalem to survive.

For the next century and a half, the southern kingdom of Judah is alone. Although Jerusalem miraculously withstands the Assyrian offensive during the reign of Hezekiah, the last stretch of 2 Kings narrates the city's demise at the hands of the next superpower in the ancient Near East, the Babylonians. Indeed, the eventual Babylonian conquest is foreshadowed in 2 Kings 20, when ambassadors for the king of Babylon carry gifts and letters to Hezekiah (who recently recovered from serious illness). But Isaiah the prophet lectures the king for showing lavish hospitality to these diplomats, even though he had previously announced Jerusalem's rescue from the Assyrians in a multilevel oracle of salvation. Isaiah's potent words are an ominous cloud that grows into a tempest with the Babylonians edging closer to Jerusalem, until the invasion of the city in 2 Kings 25 (~586 BCE) results in the demolition of the temple and exile, an ironic reversal of Abraham's journey from Chaldean territory at the outset of the story. Yet, another chapter soon begins, and the story continues with the edict of Cyrus the Persian (~538 BCE; see Ezra 1) that invites the dislocated citizens to return from exile and rebuild the ruined city and ravaged nation, thus inaugurating the second temple period in the era of restoration.

By way of summary, some salient moments of Israel's story to keep in mind when studying the Psalms are creation and the promise to Abraham, the exodus from Egypt and receiving the gift of the law at Sinai, the arrival of kingship and the dynastic guarantee granted to David, the long sequence of disobedience that culminates in the exile and the destruction of the temple, and the era of restoration that is inaugurated by the edict of Cyrus that results in the rebuilding of the temple during the Persian and Greek periods, when emerging Judaism takes root.

At this point, it should also be noted that there are three parts to the Hebrew Bible: the Law, the Prophets, and the Writings. Located in the last third, referred to as the Writings (*Ketuvim*), the Psalms provide a kind of commentary or response to the history of Israel. Creation, exodus, kingship, and exile are all variously refracted in the book of Psalms. While the majority of biblical books describe a specific period or persona (such as Judges and the premonarchic period, Jeremiah and the Babylonian invasion, Lamentations and the fall of the city of Jerusalem, or Esther and the Persian Empire), the book of Psalms spans a much larger time frame, with compositions that stem at least from the dawn of the monarchy all the way through to the second temple period. Rather than a description or straight narration of Israel's royal history as such, the Psalms provide voices and prayers throughout the various stages of the story, including reflections on creation, ruminations on the exodus, the theology of kingship, laments for the exile, and hopes for restoration. Such expansive historical meditations probably explain why "Protestant writers, following Luther, often see the book of Psalms as a 'little Bible,' reflecting the larger canon and thus expect the Psalter to reflect a biblical theology in miniature."[3]

## Poetic Features

Most readers would probably agree that *poetry* is a form of literary expression that utilizes the artistic qualities of language—sound and syntax, meter and metaphor, tone and tenor, rhyme and rhythm, wordplay, spatiality, image, and temporal sequencing—crafted into a meaningful composition of varying length and purpose. As one writer puts it, "[P]oetry is language brought to its most scorching, most succinct, most pellucid purity, like a Bunsen burner, where we want, not

---

[3] Mark Zvi Brettler, "Jewish Theology of the Psalms," in *The Oxford Handbook of the Psalms*, ed. William P. Brown (New York: Oxford University Press, 2014), 488, citing Hans-Joachim Kraus, *Theology of the Psalms* (Minneapolis. MN: Augsburg, 1986), 12.

a bonfire, but a small prick of blue flame."[4] Often considered to be the highest and most sophisticated of literary genres, poetry is attested throughout human history from the ancient Sumerians to postmodern experimentalists, across many hundreds of languages and on every continent. Consider the following example, taken almost at random:

> Two households, both alike in dignity,
> In fair Verona, where we lay our scene,
> From ancient grudge break to new mutiny,
> Where civil blood makes civil hands unclean.
> From forth the fatal loins of these two foes
> A pair of star-cross'd lovers take their life;
> Whose misadventur'd piteous overthrows
> Doth with their death bury their parents' strife.
> The fearful passage of their death-mark'd love,
> And the continuance of their parents' rage,
> Which, but their children's end, naught could remove,
> Is now the two hours' traffic of our stage;
> > The which if you with patient ears attend,
> > What here shall miss, our toil shall strive to mend.

The prologue to Shakespeare's *Romeo & Juliet* is a highly ornate example with which to begin, as its fourteen lines follow the formal rules and structural conventions of the sonnet even as it is spoken by the Chorus and functions as an introduction to the play. The point here, however, is not to examine this composition as a sonnet or even as the preface to a theatrical production, but rather to make a basic observation about the features of poetry: for most readers, the first element that distinguishes this writing as poetry is the presence of *rhyme*. Apart from the syllable counts or any other formal components, the rhyme is the most familiar feature for the majority of the audience (especially those reared in or acquainted with the English tradition).

For Hebrew poetry, the basic equivalent to rhyme is *parallelism*, but rather than a rhyme of sounds (such as *life* and *strife* or *scene* and

---

[4] Thomas Howard, *Dove Descending: A Journey into T. S. Eliot's Four Quartets* (San Francisco, CA: Ignatius Press, 2006), 21.

*unclean*, as in the Shakespearean example), Hebrew poetry in general tends to "rhyme" images or pictures or ideas, often with a dynamic intensity that is heightened from line to line.[5] Consider the following example, taken from early in Psalm 18, usually classified as a thanksgiving song, where the poet celebrates a spectacular deliverance from dire straits. The psalm begins with effusive praise as God is variously described as, among other things, a *shield* and a *fortress*. The introduction is followed by a lengthy retrospective, describing the poet facing insurmountable odds, crying out for rescue, and being met with an incendiary divine response:

> [4] Ropes of death entwined me,
>    Torrents of the underworld terrified me;
> [5] Cords of the grave surrounded me,
>    Snares of death confronted me,
> [6] In my distress I called to the Lord,
>    To my God I cried for help,
>    From his palace he heard my voice,
>    My cry for help came before his ears.
> [7] Then the earth reeled and quaked,
>    Foundations of the mountains rocked,
>    They trembled because of his anger.
> [8] Smoke rose from his nostrils,
>    Consuming fire from his mouth,
>    Burning coals flamed forth.
> [9] He bent the heavens and descended,
>    Thick darkness beneath his feet.
> [10] He mounted a cherub and flew,
>    Soared on the wings of the wind.[6]

---

[5] Note the helpful treatment of F. W. Dobbs-Allsopp, *On Biblical Poetry* (New York: Oxford University Press, 2015). Although I am stressing the interplay of ideas and word-pictures, there also can be an acoustic element in Hebrew poetry; for example, in Ps 140:3 ("They sharpen their tongue like a snake") there is a sequence of *sh* sounds in the Hebrew language that imitates the hissing of a serpent. For the onomatopoeia, see James H. Charlesworth, *The Good and Evil Serpent: How a Universal Symbol Became Christianized* (New Haven, CT: Yale University Press, 2010), 437.

[6] Unless otherwise indicated, biblical translations are my own. I am also following the English verse numbering and hope that Hebrew readers will make the necessary adjustments.

*Parallelism* is a broad term, and under its umbrella are a variety of subcategories. For instance, in these lines from Psalm 18 there are several useful examples of *semantic* parallelism, as the phrase *ropes of death* in the first half-line of v. 4 corresponds to the phrase in the next half-line, *torrents of the underworld*. Moreover, the verb *entwined* is parallel to the next verb, *terrified*; along with the surrounding images, these verbs combine sequentially to create a claustrophobic feeling in the reader, thus identifying with the poet's plight and cry for help in the absence of any other options. Furthermore, the divine response is likewise presented with rich parallelism, as God *soars* and *flies* to the rescue of the embattled poet. Generally speaking, this example from Psalm 18 gives credence to the following assertion: "The lines of biblical poetry are informed by an often fierce or mesmerizing energy of assertion that sweeps from one part of the line to its parallel member and, frequently, from the line to a whole sequence within the poem."[7] The poetic technique of parallelism can thus be used to create an experience and tell a story of a spectacular divine intervention. As we will see, examples of parallelism are found across the entire Psalter:

> Kings are not delivered by a large force,
> > Warriors are not saved by great strength. (Ps 33:16)

> You have set me in the lowest pit,
> > In the darkest places of the depths. (Ps 88:6)

> May there be well-being within your ramparts,
> > Peace in your citadels. (Ps 122:7)

Other varieties of parallelism in biblical poetry can include *antithetical* (the second line negates or describes a situation opposite to that of the first line), *elliptical* (a verb or another part of speech is omitted, compelling the reader to finds its completion in the previous line), *syntactic* (the sentence structure of the first line is replicated in the next), or parallelism of *intensification* (the enhancing or magnifying of an image in the next line). Altogether, parallelism is a poetic technique

---

[7] Robert Alter, *The Art of Biblical Poetry*, revised and updated edition (New York: Basic Books, 2011), xi.

that remarkably survives the process of translation and can work effectively when rendered into other languages. As C. S. Lewis once remarked, "It is (according to one's point of view) either a wonderful piece of luck or a wise provision of God's, that poetry which was to be turned into all languages should have as its chief formal characteristic one that does not disappear (as mere metre does) in translation."[8]

Another poetic feature that should be outlined briefly here is the use of *metaphor* in Hebrew poetry. While among the more difficult literary concepts in terms of theoretical discussion, in essence a metaphor is a figure of speech whereby a word (or even a phrase) is used to evoke a comparison with another object or term that creates a new meaning in the mind of the reader/hearer because of the analogy. Common examples might be "life is a highway" or "time is a thief," whereby the horizon of meaning is expanded through comparison. In a wide-ranging study of metaphors in the Psalms, the comments of a leading scholar merit some reflection: "In the metaphor, 'seeing as' and 'saying' converge in powerful ways to stimulate reflection and emotion. The term originally denoted 'transference' or 'carrying across' (metafora: *meta* 'trans' + *pherein* 'to carry'), particularly of property. As chief among the tropes, the metaphor signals the transference of meaning from something familiar to something new; it describes one thing in terms of another."[9] In Psalm 18, for instance, God is described as a *shield*, perhaps suggesting the divine capacity to defend the people of Israel or deflect the assaults of an adversary. Consider also the remarks in the following influential theoretical work:

> The metaphor is that figure of speech whereby we speak about one thing in terms [that] are seen to be suggestive of another. . . . The purpose of the metaphor is both to cast up and organize a network of associations. A good metaphor . . . [is] a new vision, the birth of a new understanding, a new referential access. A strong metaphor compels new possibilities of vision.[10]

---

[8] C. S. Lewis, *Reflections on the Psalms* (New York: Harcourt, Brace, 1958), 4–5.
[9] William P. Brown, *Seeing the Psalms: A Theology of Metaphor* (Louisville, KY: Westminster John Knox Press, 2002), 5.
[10] Janet Martin Soskice, *Metaphor and Religious Language* (New York: Oxford University Press, 1985), 15, 57–58.

Metaphors in the book of Psalms that frequently occur include *refuge* (divine protection extended in a multitude of ways) and *pathway* (often referring to how one lives and where one is going in life), and we will have occasion to discuss these and other examples of metaphorical language as they arise in the course of our study. Furthermore, as mentioned above, we will also explore other poetic elements (such as irony, point of view, and deliberate ambiguity) in order to appreciate the literary dynamics of the Psalter in its context. Indeed, as a psalm unfolds, various poetic features are often combined to create vivid examples of *characterization*, as can be illustrated in the portrait of a gang of villains who are attacking the poet in Psalm 64:2–6, not with physical weapons but with toxic words:

> Conceal me from the secret schemes of the wicked,
>     from the raging plots of workers of iniquity;
> Who sharpen their tongues like swords,
>     who have armed their bow: their arrows are bitter words,
> To shoot from the shadows at the upright,
>     quickly they shoot, and without fear,
> They strengthen themselves in their evil deed,
>     they talk of laying snares secretly, thinking:
>         "Who can see them?"
> They devise evil acts:
>     "We have perfected a well-devised plan,
>         and deep is the human heart and mind!"

Across the breadth of the Psalter there are a plethora of characters, from the mention of a legendary potentate such as Og king of Bashan, to more extended constructions of the "fool" and the "righteous person," to the collective portrait of Israel as a people, and perhaps most comprehensively (apart from God), the figure of the king. But in this example of Psalm 64, the psalmist asks God for protection from a company of miscreants, who evidently have formed a conspiracy that poses a significant threat. There are two formal features of characterization that can be noted. First, the poet describes the group as *verbally vicious*, with an array of terms to underscore the subversive nature of their lethal discourse. Second, the actual *direct speech* of the conspirators themselves is an important component of their portrait, and their words are quoted in order to reveal a bloated sense of confidence and their seemingly unassailable position of strength.

The concluding lines of the example above feature some Hebrew phrasing that is difficult to render in English. Although some interpret it as the psalmist's personal summary, I am assuming it is the conspirators' own villainous speech, and it might be paraphrased as follows: "We have devised a cunning plot that nobody can possibly detect or uncover, because it is safely hidden in the deepest recesses of our own minds, and so it can never be revealed."[11] And yet right after this swaggering utterance, the concluding lines of Psalm 64 describe a most unexpected outcome: with a deft recycling of language and imagery, God unmasks the conspirators and sets an ambush against them. Taking a page from their script, God shoots a divine arrow at this band of rogues; they are suddenly wounded, as their own words ricochet back against them and become the cause of their ruin. So, despite their malicious boasting, the poet of Psalm 64 affirms with ample irony that evidently God *is* able to read their minds and uncover this maliciousness. More could be said about this particular example, but our point here is that the poetic medium is used to portray even formulaic characters with a certain depth and subtlety, and other instances will be cited as our study continues.

## Theological Probing

In this introduction I have emphasized that interpretation of the Psalms ideally takes place while attending to the larger *historical* presentation of Israel, including major events such as exodus and exile, significant figures such as the king, and dominant spatial settings such as the temple in Jerusalem. Moreover, I am underscoring that the psalms need to be appreciated and read as *poetry*, that is, as works of literary art that operate within formal structures and conventions, with key

---

[11] See Allen P. Ross, *A Commentary on the Psalms,* vol. 2: *42–89* (Grand Rapids, MI: Kregel, 2013), 401; note also Robert Alter, *The Book of Psalms: A Translation with Commentary* (New York: W. W. Norton, 2009), 220.

features such as parallelism and the deployment of metaphor. A third lens through which the interpreter should view the Psalms is *theology*. Here one makes inquiries about the core beliefs, religious practices, spiritual life, and thinking patterns of the Israelites in the biblical period.

Biblical theology is a growing field of research, and there are numerous ways one could proceed and a host of sources that can be considered: both the internal documents of the Hebrew Bible and external data such as inscriptions on monuments and other ancient Near Eastern texts. It also makes a difference whether one wants to consider a systematic outline or a diachronic cross-section of Israel's ideological development. For our purposes, it might be useful to frame this study with some help from a recent essay by John Goldingay that variously considers the divine character, the people of Israel as a covenant community, and the threats to Israel's theological beliefs from both inside *and* outside. We will review two paragraphs; here is the first:

> A fundamental Old Testament challenge is, "Acknowledge that Yhwh is God" (Ps 100:2). While the Old Testament can use the generic Hebrew word *'ĕlōhîm* to refer to supernatural beings other than Yhwh, it is clear that Yhwh is God *par excellence*. "Yhwh is the great king over all gods" (Ps 95:3). Yhwh is not just one god among gods but *the* "God of gods" (Deut 10:17). Yhwh's relationship to other deities is traditionally formulated in terms of the development of monotheism (or belief in only one God), but this way of framing the question imposes a perspective from the later history of Christian thought. The Old Testament question was not "how many gods are there" (one or three or a thousand), but "who is God" (Baal or Marduk or Yhwh). And the Old Testament's attitude towards the "gods" that other nations worshiped was not to deny their existence, but to demote them to Yhwh's servants. Only Yhwh is truly God.[12]

---

[12] John Goldingay, "The Theology of the Hebrew Bible/Old Testament," in *The Cambridge Companion to the Hebrew Bible/Old Testament*, ed. Stephen B. Chapman and Marvin A. Sweeney (New York: Cambridge University Press, 2016), 468.

In Exod 12:12, on the brink of Passover, God made a startling announcement to a beleaguered group of slaves: "For I will pass through the land of Egypt that night, and I will strike all the firstborn in the land of Egypt, both man and beast; and on all the gods of Egypt I will execute judgments: I am the Lord." After Israel is brought out of Egypt through the waters of the Red Sea, they likewise sing in celebration: "Who is like you, O Lord, among the gods? Who is like you, majestic in holiness, awesome in glorious deeds, doing wonders?" (Exod 15:11). The point in these texts from Exodus is not an outright refutation of the existence of other deities as such. Rather, there is an issue of supremacy in the first instance: the God of Israel has no palpable rivals in the land of Egypt, a nation that was a major player in the panoply of ancient superpowers.

Using the imperative form of the verb *yada'* (to know), *acknowledging* that Yahweh is God seems to be a straightforward enough directive from the psalmist. However, even the most efficient survey of the Torah and the Former Prophets indicates that such *acknowledgment* was far from the norm, as illustrated in events such as the golden calf debacle (Exodus 32), Gideon's call to demolish his father's Baal installation prior to his confrontation with the Midianites (Judges 6), or even the veneration of the bronze snake (Nehushtan) in the days of Hezekiah (2 Kings 18:4). When the psalmist implores Israel to *acknowledge* that the Lord is God, therefore, it is a cry that could have been uttered in many periods and needed to be pronounced on a continual basis. To further this point, God's supremacy is dramatically underscored in Psalm 82, a composition that poetically unfolds a *trial of the gods* where judgment is rendered on the gods of other nations (*'ĕlōhîm*) for abject failure to defend the marginalized and afflicted citizens:

> *An Asaph psalm*
> [1] God takes position in the divine council,
>   In the midst of the gods, he pronounces judgment:
> [2] "How long will you carry out injustice,
>   Show preference for the wicked? *Selah*
> [3] Provide justice for the weak and the fatherless,
>   For the oppressed and the poor, do what is right.

⁴ Rescue the weak and the needy,
    Deliver them from the hand of the wicked.
⁵ They do not know, they do not understand,
    They walk around in darkness,
        All the foundations of the earth are reeling.
⁶ I had said: 'You are all gods,
    All of you are sons of the Most High.'
⁷ Nevertheless, like a mortal you *will* die,
    Like any of the leaders you *will* fall."
⁸ Arise, O God, judge the earth,
    For *you* are the one who possesses all the nations!

While scholars have no agreement on the date or provenance of Psalm 82, there is a general sense that this psalm presents the God of Israel as *qualitatively* better than any competitor because of integrity and concern for social justice. Consequently, the other gods have been weighed and found wanting, and are thus worthy of a death sentence. Although, as one scholar notes, the story is not quite over: "[I]n Psalm 82, the ʾĕlōhîm are understood to be existent as gods; it is only their failure to respond to Elohim's questioning about their crimes that leads to the loss of their divinity—but even then, it is a *sentence* of loss; we do not actually witness its *execution*."[13] Most crucial, therefore, is the prayer at the end of the psalm—calling on God to arise and judge the earth—because in the mind of the psalmist the gods of the nations have not yet been silenced, even if their days are numbered. So, as we move to the second quote from Goldingay's essay, it should be recognized that both Ps 100:2 ("Acknowledge that Yhwh is God") and Psalm 82 reveal a wider set of implications beyond the borders of Israel:

> In a variety of ways, the Old Testament makes clear that putting Israel in a special position does not mean Yhwh has written off the rest of the world. Israel exists within the context of Yhwh's intention so to

---

[13] Peter Machinist, "How Gods Die, Biblically and Otherwise: A Problem of Cosmic Restructuring," in *Reconsidering the Concept of Revolutionary Monotheism*, ed. Beate Pongratz-Leisten (Winona Lake, IN: Eisenbrauns, 2014), 230.

bless Abraham that all earth's families will make that blessing the paradigm for the blessing they seek (Gen 12:1–3). While this affirmation highlights what Yhwh will do for Abraham, it appears in the setting of a narrative that presupposes Yhwh's concern for all the nations. Thus, it also indicates what Yhwh will do for them. Indeed, all the Old Testament's talk of what Yhwh will do for Israel links to Yhwh's intentions for the world. That psalm urging acknowledgement of Yhwh as God actually addresses all the earth, and like many psalms, it makes the assumption that what Yhwh has done for Israel is good news for the world.[14]

Studying the Psalms from a theological angle thus involves an understanding of how the nations are configured in the various psalms and how God responds to the nations and Israel's various entanglements. Furthermore, we will observe in the Psalms that numerous facets of the divine character are memorialized in these poetic works, not restricted to God's supremacy and sovereignty, but also other aspects such as anger, patience, mercy, mystery, advocacy for the poor, opposition to the corrupt, and much else. Similarly, theological interpretation also attends to the human side of the equation: how to live a faithful life that is not swayed by the crowd or attendant temptations, avoiding despair in times of adversity and suffering, along with managing material prosperity (or lack thereof) and navigating family and political life. These and other matters we will pursue as our study continues.

To draw together our short theological discussion in this introduction, consider the following four definition of key terms that recur in our study: *creation*, *Torah*, *salvation*, and *Zion*. First, **creation** should be appreciated as an ongoing action and not limited to God's activity in Genesis 1; while God certainly creates the heavens and the earth at the outset, creation is a dynamic and often present-tense reality, as Ps 104:30–31 articulates: "When you send forth your Spirit, they are created, and you renew the face of the ground. May the glory of the

---

[14] Goldingay, "The Theology of the Hebrew Bible/Old Testament," 472.

Lord endure forever; may the Lord rejoice in his works." The world is teeming with biodiversity, from the smallest fish of the sea to the greatest animals on land: "O Lord, how manifold are your works! In wisdom have you made them all; the earth is full of your creatures" (Ps 104:24). Second, **Torah** (law) can be confusing for some modern readers, because it sounds (potentially) negative and a limitation on individuality. But it might be noted that the Hebrew term *tôrāh* "refers to the story of God's actions to create a people and guide them into the future, as described in Genesis and the first chapters of Exodus. Likewise it refers to the obligations, precepts and guidelines that shape the people's life, as in the rest of the first five books of the Bible, the Torah."[15] Third, **salvation** is an expansive idea in the Psalms that utilizes a number of different terms, but a common thread is personal or corporate *rescue* (from a predicament wherein no other options are available except for divine intervention), and can also include a future dimension. The first sense can be perceived in Ps 38:22 ("Make haste to help me, O Lord, my salvation!"), while the future is at stake in Ps 53:6 ("Oh, that the salvation of Israel would come out of Zion!"). Fourth, and on that note, **Zion** is a hill located in Jerusalem that is first mentioned in 2 Sam 5:7 ("David captured the stronghold of Zion"). But as Ps 53:6 illustrates, Zion increasingly became a metaphor for Jerusalem as the refuge of the people of God under the aegis of God's promises, a place for restored captives and those who are objects of divine favor. Along with Psalm 2, there are a number of "Zion songs" (46, 48, 76, 84, 87, 122, 132, 137) found in the book of Psalms. Other theological terms and ideas will be explored as we continue, but these four are a convenient starting point for this study.

## Reading for the Plot

Attentiveness to Israel's major historical movements, poetic crafting, and theological contours is significant in the interpretation of the

---

[15] Konrad Schaefer, *Psalms,* Berit Olam (Collegeville, MN: Michael Glazier, 2001), 3.

Psalms. A fourth way of approaching the Psalms involves considering it as a *book with a plot*.[16] For many readers, the Psalms is an assortment of poems that are often considered as individual compositions and as 150 fairly discrete units; while connections between adjacent psalms were sometimes identified, most scholars devoted more energy to reconstructions of liturgical setting or questions about the origins of particular psalms rather than the organization or structure of the book's final form. But far from a strictly recent concern, the question of the Psalter's shape has been pondered for some time, as even careful theologians such as Augustine (354–430 CE) wrestled with the matter: "The arrangement of the Psalms, which seems to me to contain a secret of great mystery, has not yet been revealed to me."[17]

Recent years have witnessed a surge in interest regarding the shape of the book of Psalms, with some intriguing advancements: "To what extent might the Psalter as a whole be read as a five-part drama, the development of a story, with each individual psalm playing its particular part?" writes one leading researcher. "There are many ways of reading this story, but one way of reading it is to see it as a testimony, perhaps even a drama in five acts, to the rise and fall of the Davidic monarchy."[18] As it stands, the Psalter is divided into five books—perhaps configured as a kind of poetic antiphon to the five books of the Pentateuch—and just as the Pentateuch traces the narrative development of God's promise to Abraham, so the Psalter reflects on the divine promise to David and his descendants: A longer discussion of the five-book design can be found in the last chapter of this book, but since we refer to this structure over the

---

[16] The subheading for this section is taken from Peter Brooks, *Reading for the Plot: Design and Intention in Narrative* (Cambridge, MA: Harvard University Press, 1984).
[17] Cited in Ian J. Vaillancourt, "Formed in the Crucible of Messianic Angst: The Eschatological Shape of the Hebrew Psalter's Final Form," *Scottish Bulletin of Evangelical Theology* 31 (2013): 127.
[18] Susan Gillingham, "Psalms 90–106: Book Four and the Covenant with David," *European Judaism* 48 (2015): 83–101.

course of our study—and include a few remarks here—the following chart can be referred to:

| BOOK 1 | BOOK 2 | BOOK 3 | BOOK 4 | BOOK 5 |
|---|---|---|---|---|
| 1-41 | 42-72 | 73-89 | 90-106 | 107-150 |
| Closing words (Doxology): "Blessed be the LORD, the God of Israel, from everlasting to everlasting. Amen and Amen" Ps 41:13 | Closing words (Doxology): "... Amen and Amen. The prayers of David son of Jesse are ended" Ps 72:19-20 | Closing words (Doxology): "Blessed be the LORD forever. Amen and Amen" Ps 89:52 | Closing words (Doxology): "Blessed be the LORD, the God of Israel, from everlasting to everlasting. Let all the people say 'Amen'! Praise the LORD" Ps 106:48 | Closing words (Doxology): "Let everything that breathes praise the LORD! Praise the LORD!" Ps 150:6 |

While most modern English versions of the Bible have, for instance, "Book II" as a major heading just before Psalm 42, the heading is not found as such in the Hebrew Masoretic text. So how is the collection divided into the five-book structure? At critical junctures, there is a concluding doxology—perhaps appended as the Psalter was reaching its final form—that seems to signal the close of one unit (or book) and the beginning of another. Such doxologies characteristically include a formal blessing or a closing *amen* (e.g., 41:13, "Blessed be the Lord, the God of Israel, from everlasting to everlasting, amen and amen"). How, then, do the five books of the Psalter cohere? One prominent scholar argues that the divine covenant with David (as initially articulated in 2 Samuel 7) is the focus of the first three books of the Psalter: "its introduction in divine grace (Ps. 2), its transmission to David's successors with hope (Ps. 72), and its collapse in the destruction and despair of the Exile (Ps. 89)."[19] The last two books of the Psalter, to further this view, aim to deflect Israel's attention away from trust in "human princes" toward the character of God: "YHWH is *eternal* king, only *he* is ultimately worthy of trust. Human 'princes' will wither and fade like the grass, but the steadfast love of YHWH endures for ever."[20] A host of studies over the past twenty years have extended this scholarly conversation, variously refining and modulating the emphases but with an essential agreement that the Psalter has a shape and a purpose.[21]

As one example, we can consider the following convenient summary found in a new multi-authored commentary, where it is argued that the organization of the Psalter chiefly corresponds to the monarchic history of Israel, from the reigns of David and Solomon through the murkiness of the divided kingdom, followed by the travail of exile and subsequent restoration to the land:

> The Psalter begins with the story of the reign of King David in Book One, moves to the reign of Solomon in Book Two, and on to the divided kingdom and destruction of the northern kingdom by the Assyrians and the southern kingdom by the Babylonians in Book Three; Book Four recounts the struggle of the exiles in Babylon to find identity and meaning, and Book Five celebrates the return to Jerusalem and the establishment of a new Israel with God as sovereign.[22]

---

[19] Gerald H. Wilson, "The Shape of the Book of Psalms," *Interpretation* 46 (1992): 133.
[20] Gerald H. Wilson, *The Editing of the Hebrew Psalter* (Chico, CA: Scholars Press, 1985).
[21] For examples and bibliographies, see David C. Mitchell, *The Message of the Psalter: An Eschatological Programme in the Book of Psalms,* JSOTSup 252 (Sheffield: Sheffield Academic Press, 1997); Robert E. Wallace, *The Narrative Effect of Book IV of the Hebrew Psalter* (New York: Peter Lang, 2007); Erich Zenger, "The Composition and Theology of the Fifth Book of Psalms, Psalms 107–145," *JSOT* 80 (1998): 77–102.
[22] Nancy J. DeClaissé-Walford, Rolf A. Jacobson, and Beth LaNeel Tanner, *The Book of Psalms*, NICOT (Grand Rapids, MI: Eerdmans, 2014), 16.

Despite some dissenting voices, the number of scholars researching the final form of the Psalms has been trending upward of late, and the position adopted in this present study is that the Psalter is a *poetic drama in five acts* that traces the rise and fall of Israel's monarchy with an overarching plotline.[23] It will be suggested that Psalms 1 and 2 form an overture to the entire book and outline the struggle between two ways—the path of the righteous and the ultimate doom of the wicked—and the clash between the kingship of God and the raging of the nations. A drawback, it seems to me, of tying the five books too closely to the careers of recognized figures such as David and Solomon is that many psalms then fit rather awkwardly and require a more linear timeline.

While the modest proposal that I will sketch in this study is certainly not the last word, it could be maintained that appreciating the five books as more general rhythms that illustrate a broader period and provide a series of poetic snapshots allows for more thematic flexibility within a given book. Roughly speaking, Book I represents the establishment and early travails of Israel's kingship; Book II reflects experiences both in Jerusalem and northern Israel; Book III traces the failure and collapse of Israel's royal leadership; Book IV encourages a chastened return from exile and call to fall back on the covenant; and Book V gives perspective on the restoration to the land and new horizons of divine kingship.

If it can be suggested that the five-book structure has a larger metanarrative, then what implications emerge for a more substantial theological message of the Psalter? We will further inquire if there is an overall movement between Psalm 1 and Psalm 150 from lament and petition to unfettered orchestral praise, and, at the social level, if there

---

[23] For example, Norman Whybray, *Reading the Psalms as a Book*, JSOTSup 222 (Sheffield: Sheffield Academic Press, 1996); Erhard S. Gerstenberger, *Psalms, Part 2, and Lamentations*, FOTL 15 (Grand Rapids, MI: Eerdmans, 2001). Note also the constructive survey of David M. Howard Jr., "The Psalms and Current Study," in *Interpreting the Psalms: Issues and. Approaches*, ed. David Firth and Philip S. Johnston (Downers Grove, IL: InterVarsity Press, 2005), 23–40, and the proposal of a broad movement from *petition* to *praise* in Walter Brueggemann, "Bounded by Obedience and Praise: The Psalms as Canon," *JSOT* 50 (1991): 63–92.

is a general movement from more individual cries for help to corporate worship with a symphony of instruments and grand chorus of voices. The Psalms have long been treasured as a resource for spiritual direction and appreciated for their poetic poignancy, and I would submit that the notion of an overarching plot or movement (rather than just a random assortment) is a reading strategy that recent scholars are increasingly commending.

# 2
# The Psalms in the Ancient Near East

A *psalm* can be defined as a spiritual poem or song that has been preserved and recited over time, and has a long association with music and performance in ancient Israel's historical memory. Often composed for a ceremonial occasion or in response to a private or public event, a psalm can be framed as a desperate prayer, a patient musing, a voluble complaint, or a paean of praise and awe, frequently including reflections about the intersection between the human and divine realms. For more than two millennia the Psalms have been a spiritual resource for different kinds of believers, as they are poetic works of art that nurture the imagination and explore a world where human beings *matter*; as one reads the Psalms, it appears that God is not easily manipulated yet is highly involved and passionate about creation, dissatisfied with religious cliché, and willing to push the limits of language. The following general remarks merit some consideration as we move forward in our study:

> Through the ages, Psalms has been the most urgently, personally present of all the books of the Bible in the lives of many readers. Both Jewish and Christian tradition made it part of the daily and weekly liturgy. Untold numbers have repeatedly turned to Psalms for encouragement and comfort in moments of crisis or despair. The inner world of major Western writers from Augustine, Judah Halevi, and George Herbert to Emily Dickinson and Paul Celan was inflected by the reading of Psalms. But for all the power of these Hebrew poems to speak with great immediacy in many tongues to readers of different eras, they are in their origins intricately rooted in an ancient Near Eastern world that goes back to the late Bronze Age (1600–1200 BCE) and that in certain respects is quite alien to modern people.[1]

[1] Alter, *The Book of Psalms*, xiii; note also William Holladay, *The Psalms through Three Thousand Years: Prayerbook of a Cloud of Witnesses* (Minneapolis, MN: Fortress, 1993).

Building on the last point about the world of the late Bronze Age from which the Psalms emerged, the goal of this chapter is to discuss how the world of the ancient Near East is reflected or hovers in the background of various psalms, and how considering such contextual data might lead to a richer experience when reading the Psalter. To that end, three samples are explored in this chapter: the presentation of the divine voice in Psalm 29, the figure of Leviathan in Psalm 74, and the enthronement images of Psalm 93. Altogether, these examples illustrate that there are similarities between Israelite psalms and other literature from the ancient Near East but also some significant points of departure.

From the outset it should be noted that the kinds of poetic deliberations that are characteristic of the book of Psalms were not limited to the people of Israel nor any particular region or ethnicity. Virtually every known major people group composed songs and poems that addressed matters of national and universal concern, and such compositions were standard fixtures in the religious landscape of the ancient world. The connection between poetry and religion gave rise to numerous genres of incantation, thanksgiving, petition, enthronement rituals, and sacrificial rites. Furthermore, a variety of topics can be perceived within the corpus of ancient Near Eastern religious lyrics, ranging from exalting a deity to complaining about a perceived injustice. Consider the following examples from three different lyrical compositions:

Look faithfully upon me and listen to my prayer.

He makes waves on the mountains like the sea.

He will sound his voice in the clouds, flash his lightning to the earth.

While it may appear that these lines are lifted directly from the book of Psalms in the Hebrew Bible, that is not the case. In fact, all three poetic examples are from the neighbors of ancient Israel, and all three are arguably older than most, if not all, of the biblical psalms.[2] The

---

[2] The first two examples are taken from Anna Elise Zernecke, "Mesopotamian Parallels to the Psalms," and Bernd U. Schipper, "Egyptian Backgrounds to the Psalms,"

first is a Mesopotamian plea addressed to the goddess Ishtar, and the second is part of the Egyptian "Great Hymn to the Aten" from the era of Pharaoh Akhenaten in the fourteenth century BCE.[3] The third example, most intriguingly, refers to Baal (lord), a prominent deity in ancient Canaan and mentioned nearly one hundred times in the Hebrew Bible. Although the terms *Canaan* and *Canaanite* need to be carefully defined, for the purposes of this study we will understand the region of Canaan to include parts of modern-day Lebanon, Syria, Israel, and Jordan, while *Canaanite* is basically an ethnographic catch-all term for numerous people groups who inhabited the area.

As the god of the storm that brings fertility to earth by means of rain, Baal is a major player in the Canaanite pantheon. References to Baal are found across the entire biblical corpus (e.g., Num 25:3, Judg 2:11, 2 Kgs 23:5, Jer 2:8), but among the notable archaeological discoveries in the previous century at Ugarit in modern Syria was a trove of clay tablets written using a cuneiform script in a Semitic language closely related to classical Hebrew. The third line in the three examples quoted above—"He will sound his voice in the clouds, flash his lightning to the earth"—is found in the six-tablet Baal cycle that was unearthed at Ugarit. Although fragmentary in places, the Baal cycle remains an indispensable source of extrabiblical perspective on this deity. The association of Baal with rain sheds further light on why this Canaanite god was a primary competitor with Yahweh in nascent Israel and, as we will see, also provides insight into numerous aspects of the book of Psalms.

---

both in *The Oxford Handbook of the Psalms*, ed. William P. Brown (New York: Oxford University Press, 2014), 27–42 and 57–75. The third example is taken from Michael D. Coogan and Mark S. Smith, eds. and trans., *Stories from Ancient Canaan*, 2nd edition (Louisville, KY: Westminster John Knox Press, 2012), 132.

[3] Further details and other examples can be found in James B. Pritchard, ed., *Ancient Near Eastern Texts Relating to the Old Testament*, 3rd edition (Princeton, NJ: Princeton University Press, 1969); William W. Hallo and K. Lawson Younger Jr., eds., *The Context of Scripture*, 3 vols. (Leiden: Brill, 1997–2003); Michael D. Coogan, *A Reader of Ancient Near Eastern Texts: Sources for the Study of the Old Testament* (Oxford: Oxford University Press, 2013).

## The Backbeat of Psalm 29

Regarding the three examples taken from Mesopotamian, Egyptian, and Canaanite literature, much more could be said. But the central point here is that psalms in the Hebrew Bible share a number of attributes common to other kinds of ancient religious poetry. Whether in terms of poetic form or similar subject matter, the affinities between Hebrew psalms and the poems of other nations are not surprising because they emerge from similar worlds. Nonetheless, while the wealth of common features can be appreciated and is worthy of every consideration, it can also be argued that Hebrew psalms have a series of distinguishing features, and on this score it might be helpful to explore a more extended illustration. An instructive example is Psalm 29, often thought by scholars to be an adaptation of the Canaanite hymn because of the repeated references to thunderstorms and the opening address to a council of divine beings. As a case study, this psalm is attractive because whatever the theorized origins—either an adapted hymn or one that draws on standard ancient Near Eastern images and tropes—the poem is unmistakably Israelite in tone and testimony. Indeed, Samuel Terrien labels Psalm 29 "the canticle of seven thunders" because *the voice of God* echoes seven times, and the poem as a whole celebrates God's supremacy even over the fiercest storms of nature.[4] Psalm 29 is not overly long, and after the superscription ("A psalm of David"), transports the reader to a lofty setting:

> [1] Give to the Lord, O sons of God,
>   Give to the Lord glory and strength.
> [2] Give to the Lordthe glory of his name,
>   Bow down to the Lord in the splendor of his holiness.
> [3] The voice of the Lord over the waters,
>   The God of glory thunders,
>   The Lord over the mighty waters.
> [4] The voice of the Lord is powerful,
>   The voice of the Lord is majestic.

---

[4] Samuel L. Terrien, *The Psalms: Strophic Structure and Theological Commentary* (Grand Rapids, MI: Eerdmans, 2003), 275–276.

⁵ The voice of the Lord breaks the cedars,
   The Lord breaks the cedars of Lebanon.
⁶ He makes Lebanon skip like a calf,
   Sirion like a young wild ox.
⁷ The voice of the Lord strikes with flames of fire.
⁸ The voice of the Lord shakes the desert,
   The Lord shakes the desert of Kadesh.
⁹ The voice of the Lord causes deer to calve,
   Lays bare the forest,
      So that in his palace all say, "Glory!"
¹⁰ Over the flood the Lord is seated,
   The Lord is seated as the eternal king.
¹¹ May the Lord give strength to his people,
   May the Lord bless his people with peace.

Notions of *competition* and *combat* among the gods may seem remote for many contemporary readers, but they were a common feature within the intellectual framework of the ancient world. Even in the single line of Canaanite poetry quoted earlier ("He will sound his voice in the clouds, flash his lightning to the earth") certain impressions about Baal are formed: identification of thunder with the god's voice, and divine activity connected with storms and related weather phenomena. Furthermore, when another text from the Baal cycle is considered, other qualities emerge: "But our king is Baal the Conqueror, our judge higher than all."[5] In this context it is a goddess who is praising Baal, thus drawing attention to a pair of related ideas: the notion of supremacy among the gods of the Canaanite pantheon and the forum of a council or meeting among the gods. After comparing Psalm 29 to the Baal cycle, one perceives a number of similarities, such as the awe-inspiring storm, the divine voice thundering, an assembly of divine beings, and mention of the storming floodwaters. No doubt this is why some commentators have advocated the theory that Psalm 29 was originally a Canaanite hymn with the name of Israel's God *Yahweh* substituted.[6] Other scholars may not go

---

[5] Coogan and Smith, *Stories from Ancient Canaan*, 124.
[6] Note the bibliography and discussion in Gianni Barbiero, "The Two Structures of Psalm 29," *VT* 66 (2016): 378–392.

as far as arguing for a straightforward replacement of the divine name, but do acknowledge that the psalm draws on a host of standard images and thought patterns from the ancient world of Israel's neighbors. One interpreter helpfully summarizes the background of Psalm 29 and how early Israelite audiences would have perceived the major images in the poem:

> Modern readers need to be reminded of the narrative implied in this hymn: the combat myth telling of the origin of religio-political authority in the universe. According to the myth, there was a threat to the stability of the world, which the gods could not defeat. An outsider god was selected to go out to battle, and he defeated the monster, restored order, and was given ultimate authority by the divine assembly. The myth is attested in Mesopotamian and Canaanite literature and in the Bible. This psalm concentrates on only one moment of the story: the acclamation by the heavenly beings of Yahweh's sole divinity.[7]

There are reasonable grounds for suggesting that Psalm 29 arose in Israelite circles as a response to the prevailing notions of combat among deities, an invitation to the audience to envision an alternative to Baal's ascendancy. The opening imperative of the psalm is often translated "ascribe" and implies the handing over of something to its lawful owner. A comparable example of the verb is found in Gen 47:16, when Joseph—the prime minister of Egypt who was responsible for selling grain during the severe famine—implores the people to *give* or

---

[7] Richard J. Clifford, *Psalms 1-72*, AOTC (Nashville, TN: Abingdon, 2002) 153. In the judgment of John Day, *Psalms* (Sheffield: JSOT Press, 1990), 43 it is "preferable to regard Psalm 29 as modelled on Baal prototypes rather than simply reproducing a Baal psalm verbatim, with the mere substitution of Yahweh for Baal." Cf. Benjamin D. Sommer, "A Little Higher Than Angels: Psalm 29 and the Genre of Heavenly Praise," in *Built by Wisdom, Established by Understanding: Essays on Biblical and Near Eastern Literature in Honor of Adele Berlin*, ed. Maxine L. Grossman (Bethesda: University Press of Maryland, 2013), 147: "In the end, this psalm provides a banner example of the closeness of Canaanite and Israelite literary cultures, but we cannot conclude that the psalm was originally composed by the former for the god Baal. The extreme frequency of the elements that recall the high god of the Canaanites is probably deliberate: the poem may use a great deal of this imagery in order to demonstrate that YHWH, and not Baal, is the lord of nature."

*hand over* their livestock in return for food to survive the emergency. Notably, in Ps 29:1 it is "the sons of God" (*beney 'elim*), usually understood as supernatural beings and members of the divine court who do God's bidding and carry out their duties as directed, who are ordered to *hand over* glory to the Lord, using the same verb.[8] Among other biblical scenes that feature the heavenly court, the most famous is Job 1–2, where the sons of God (*beney ha'elohim*) are gathered before the divine throne room awaiting instructions that are issued from the council of God. Not only is this heavenly collective ordered to give glory to God in Ps 29:1, but they are also told to *bow down* in verse 2, thus acknowledging a superior and paying deference to a king. Moreover, the same verb is used in 2 Sam 9:6 when Mephibosheth (son of Jonathan and grandson of Saul) is summoned to David and bows low in honor, and also in 1 Kgs 1:53 when the vanquished Adonijah pays homage to the triumphant Solomon. Bowing down implies a certain physicality, and the celestial entourage is commanded to fall face down while ascribing honor to God. Most striking, however, is the fact that *humanity* is ordering the heavenly host to prostrate themselves in God's presence, and thus unfolding a particular anthropology and vision of human beings in the universe.[9] Even while drawing on conventional images in ancient Near Eastern religion, Psalm 29 moves in a different direction as far as the value of human participation in worship: "While its poetic images stress YHWH's absolute power over nature, the psalm's use of the conventions of heavenly worship intimate an extraordinarily exalted view of humanity."[10]

Other elements of Psalm 29 utilize standard images from the ancient Near East but likewise feature a substantial departure. The voice of God is a further case in point. The psalm is evidently highlighting the voice of Israel's God over against the voice of Baal (or any other

---

[8] Walter Brueggemann and William H. Bellinger Jr., *Psalms*, New Cambridge Biblical Commentary (New York: Cambridge University Press, 2014), 147. The authors note the alternative view of J. Clinton McCann Jr., "The Book of Psalms: Introduction, Commentary, and Reflection," in *The New Interpreter's Bible*, ed. Leander E. Keck (Nashville, TN: Abingdon, 1996), 4:792, who argues that *the sons of the gods* refers to "the deposed gods of the Canaanite pantheon."
[9] Cf. John Goldingay, *Psalms*, vol. 1: *Psalms 1–41*, Baker Commentary on the Old Testament Wisdom and Psalms (Grand Rapids, MI: Baker, 2006), 413.
[10] Sommer, "A Little Higher Than Angels," 153.

competing deity). In this canticle of seven thunders, the divine voice is capable of powerful feats while covering a vast amount of land and sea.[11] Reference to *waters* in verse 3 is probably an allusion to the primordial chaos, as reflected in Gen 1:2: "Now the earth was confused and empty [*tōhû vabōhû*], with darkness over the face of the deep, but the spirit of God was hovering over the face of the waters." Those dark and unruly waters were subdued by God's voice at the outset of creation, so now Psalm 29 is declaring that God's voice remains in control despite ongoing threats by the forces of chaos, and God's kingship is not imperiled by disturbances in the heavens or on the earth.[12] In the poetic configuration of Psalm 29, the mighty waters represent various kinds of disorder that threaten to inundate the community; the Israelites are thus encouraged to believe that just as God's power extends over every aspect of the natural world and its fearful tempests, so by extension every storm faced by God's people can be faced with equanimity. Such a message is punctuated by a reference to the flood in verse 10, and it can be assumed that the flood in the days of Noah (Genesis 6–9) is referenced here. The flood allusion operates as a reminder that God's enthronement was not affected even by the tumultuous floodwaters of chaos. Furthermore, God's voice *continues* to thunder from the northern mountains of Lebanon to the southern desert of Kadesh, with tremors that cause deer to give birth and shakes the forest.[13]

On the one hand, it could be the same human speakers describing the voice of God as in verses 1–2—the crowd who enjoin the sons

---

[11] On *thunder* here and elsewhere in the Psalter, see Steve A. Wiggins, *Weathering the Psalms: A Meteorotheological Survey* (Eugene, OR: Cascade Books, 2014), 34–35.

[12] Note also James L. Mays, *Psalms*, (Louisville, KY: John Knox, 1994), 137: "Where in Canaan's myth sea and river were the opponents of Baal in his battle to gain kingship, in the psalm the mighty waters and the flood are simply subject to the Lord's power as symbols of his everlasting reign."

[13] For the geographical issue of Kadesh's location, see Pieter M. Venter, "Spatiality in Psalm 29," in *Psalms and Liturgy*, ed. Dirk J. Human and Cas J. A. Vos, JSOTSup 410 (London: T & T Clark, 2004), 235–250. On the translation controversy, see Jeffrey H. Tigay, "'The Voice of Yhwh Causes Hinds to Calve' (Psalm 29:9)," in *Birkat Shalom: Studies in the Bible, Ancient Near Eastern Literature, and Postbiblical Judaism Presented to Shalom M. Paul on the Occasion of His Seventieth Birthday*, ed. Chaim Cohen, Victor Avigdor Hurowitz, Avi Hurvitz, Yochanan Muffs, Baruch J. Schwartz, and Jeffrey H. Tigay (Winona Lake, IN: Eisenbrauns, 2008), 399–411.

of God to ascribe glory and honor—enhancing their argument for bowing on the basis of the incomparable divine voice. On the other hand, verses 3 and following could be spoken as a response by the sons of God themselves, and part of the way they acknowledge and render honor to God is by testifying to the majestic qualities and efficacy of the divine voice. As with many issues in the Psalms, interpreters are challenged to discern what best suits the context as a whole. There are advantages to both readings, but maintaining that the human chorus is speaking throughout the poem makes the concluding prayer in v. 11 easier to construe: the community is asking for peace to come from the God whose voice brooks no rivals. Here there may be a clue as to the psalm's origins and the reason(s) for its composition. Dating the individual psalms is notoriously difficult, but Psalm 29 at least offers some prospects, albeit limited. Scholars have offered a number of proposals, often suggesting that the fund of Canaanite images points to an earlier rather than a later date in Israelite history.

While recognizing the paucity of data, one scholar has observed that there are some affinities between the theological concerns of the psalm and the era of Hosea: "Viewed from a purely biblical perspective, this poem should respond to the issues raised in the Book of Hosea, where the conflict between Baal and YHWH is depicted as a living issue."[14] A northern prophet active during the reign of Jeroboam II (and a contemporary of Isaiah, a counterpart in southern Jerusalem), Hosea portrays the eighth century BCE as a divided era in Israelite history. A main component of the book is an elaborate parable about abandoning God for other deities, with Hosea himself taking an unfaithful wife who is meant to exemplify national infidelities. The focus of Psalm 29—where divine beings are implored to bow in recognition of God's sovereignty—may well have spoken to the kind of situation depicted in Hosea. The psalm may have been recited or performed as a way of combating the seductive allure of fertility religions through an innovative recasting of traditional combat-myth images, thus nurturing the community through its vision of celestial worship and

---

[14] Dennis Pardee, "On Psalm 29: Structure and Meaning," in *The Book of Psalms: Composition and Reception*, ed. Peter W. Flint and Patrick D. Miller, with the assistance of Aaron Brunell and Ryan Roberts, VTSup 99 (Leiden: Brill, 2005), 177–178.

the thundering of the divine voice. Psalm 29 is thus an example of a psalm that quite possibly arose as a response to prevailing worldviews, drawing on familiar images yet thoroughly reconfigured as a distinctively Israelite composition.

## How to Tame Your Dragon

As a second example to illustrate how Israel's psalms draw on familiar images from the ancient Near East and yet take them in startlingly different directions, I would like to briefly discuss the dreadful and mysterious Leviathan as this creature appears in the book of Psalms. Featured in both the literature of the ancient world and a number of times in various biblical texts, Leviathan is usually described as a primordial sea beast with multiple heads, a figure of chaos and destruction.[15] In the same Baal cycle mentioned earlier, there is a reference to the defeat of Litan (the equivalent of Leviathan), Baal's enemy: "Didn't I snare the Dragon and destroy him? I demolished the Twisting Serpent, the seven-headed monster."[16] The book of Job has references to Leviathan (3:8 and 41:1), while Isaiah 27:1 poetically describes the future fate of the chaos monster: "On that day the Lord will wield his hard and great and strong sword against Leviathan the fugitive serpent, against Leviathan the twisted serpent, and he will kill the dragon who is in the sea." In the context of Isaiah 27, God's victory over Leviathan ("the great sea monster who embodies the autonomous, recalcitrant force of evil that lies beneath the surface of the earth and that endlessly threatens the stability of creation") may symbolize the defeat of Babylon—the superpower responsible for Israel's destruction—and thus an end to the chaos of captivity.[17]

---

[15] Cf. John Day, *God's Conflict with the Dragon and the Sea: Echoes of a Canaanite Myth in the Old Testament* (Cambridge: Cambridge University Press, 1985) and Debra Scoggins Ballentine, *The Conflict Myth and the Biblical Tradition* (New York: Oxford University Press, 2015).

[16] Coogan and Smith, *Stories from Ancient Canaan*, 120.

[17] Walter Brueggemann, *Isaiah 1–39* (Louisville, KY: Westminster John Knox Press, 1998), 210. On the identity of Israel's foe as, e.g., Egypt, Babylon, or Persia, see John T. Willis, "Yahweh Regenerates His Vineyard: Isaiah 27," in *Formation and Intertextuality in Isaiah 24–27*, ed. J. Todd Hibbard and Hyun Chul Paul Kim, Ancient Israel and Its Literature 17 (Atlanta, GA: Society of Biblical Literature, 2013), 201–207.

The foul and crooked Leviathan has an intriguing cameo in Psalm 74, a composition that is usually categorized as a communal lament that implores God to act in light of the desecration of the sanctuary and consider the cry of distress: "Why, O God, do you reject us forever? . . . Direct your footsteps toward the lasting ruins, the enemy has ravaged everything in the holy place." Most plausibly, the event described is the destruction of Jerusalem in 586 BCE, a traumatic invasion that is narrated in 2 Kings 25 when the temple was razed by the Babylonians and many citizens deported into exile. In Psalm 74 the weapons of the attackers are vividly described (axes, hatchets, and hammers), as is the ransacking of other meeting places in the land with an appetite for violence akin to the Vandals who invaded Rome in the fifth century and looted the city. The psalm also features the inner direct speech of the foreign invaders, although the group is barely articulate and only thinks, "[W]e will oppress them" (v. 7). After a complaint that God's name is being reviled, the middle section of the poem (vv. 12–15) remembers past divine actions that brought order and life out of chaos and confusion, and thus the poet beseeches God to deal with the Babylonians in the same way that God imposed order at creation and during the events of the exodus from Egypt:

> $^{12}$ But God is my king from ancient days,
> Working deeds of salvation in the midst of the land.
> $^{13}$ You split the sea in your strength,
> You broke the heads of the monsters on the waters.
> $^{14}$ You crushed the heads of Leviathan,
> You gave him as food for an army of wild creatures.
> $^{15}$ You broke open springs and torrents,
> You dried up the ever-flowing rivers.

The psalmist complained in v. 11 that God's right hand is pocketed and idle, but such present inactivity is then contrasted with powerful deeds in the past when God was actively involved in rescuing the people. There are several ways to understand the images in vv. 12–15, and scholars often perceive in these lines references to divine kingship that was asserted over the forces of chaos in the act of creation. Furthermore, the images are fused to the events in the story of the exodus and afterward.[18] For the Israelites, a paradigmatic example of salvation was the rescue from Egypt after years of slavery and hopelessness. In Psalm 74 the waters of the Red Sea are driven back and the monsters' (*tanninim*) heads are shattered; in Exod 7:9–12 the staff of Aaron that had turned into a sea monster (*tannin*) swallowed up the staffs of the Egyptian magicians, foreshadowing the victory over Pharaoh's army at the Red Sea. In the case of Ps 74:14, Leviathan becomes an image of the oppression of Egypt and the evil of slavery, yet God crushes the (seven?) heads of this beast and feeds the animals with the slain Egyptian soldiers who were pursuing Israel through the parted waters. The same God who split the waters of the Red Sea also proceeds to break open springs of water in the desert to sustain the people (v. 15) and allows the miraculous traversing of the Jordan River on dry ground in order for the Israelites to cross into the land of Canaan.

For the poet of Psalm 74, God's victories of old are the fulcrum of the plea for God to take action in the present moment and regard the people's plight by silencing the mocking voice of a fierce enemy who desecrated the sanctuary and gloats in triumph. Consequently, Babylon is configured as a new Leviathan, and the poet cries out for rescue from the chaos inflicted by this agent of confusion. When God creates (as in Genesis 1), chaos is replaced with order, and so if Leviathan is an embodiment of unstable forces of resistance to God, then the head-crushing of this monster results in stability and order. The placement of Psalm 74 thus needs to be considered, as it is located early in Book III of the Psalter. As we recall, the psalms of Book III variously reflect the perspective of exile after the destruction of Jerusalem; in this case, the poet of Psalm 74 recalls that God acted with saving deeds in the past—such as the defeat of the superpower Egypt—and implores God to do so again and subdue a foe that has destroyed the land and again enslaved the people. Psalm 74 thus provides a helpful example of how a familiar image from the world of the ancient Near East is poetically appropriated in the context of a communal lament

---

[18] Details and bibliography can be found in Jeremy M. Hutton, "Isaiah 51:9–11 and the Rhetorical Appropriation and Subversion of Hostile Theologies," *JBL* 126 (2007): 271–303.

after the fall of Jerusalem: Leviathan is used to activate memories of God's supremacy over the dark and menacing powers of chaos in days of old, and forms the basis of a cry for help in the new and forlorn circumstances of Babylonian captivity.

Leviathan makes one more appearance later in the Psalter that is worth mentioning, although there it has a quite different poetic effect than Psalm 74. Leviathan in Ps 74:14 is crushed and eviscerated, whereas a seemingly antithetical picture is developed in Psalm 104. The context of this psalm is less somber and more celebratory of divine creation in its richness and diversity, perhaps in keeping with its position in Book IV as the people of God are encouraged to rebuild their community after the exile. It is regrettable that our discussion of Psalm 104 is here limited to a single verse, as it obscures the richness of this expansive composition that has a number of points of contact with and departure from the Egyptian *Hymn to the Aten*. But focus here is restricted to the startling appearance of Leviathan, and if any reader is hoping for another battle with blood and evisceration, such hopes will be disappointed. In Ps 104:25 the poet meditates on the sea that teems with living creatures, and it forms a transition to v. 26: "There the ships travel about; Leviathan is there, that you formed to sport with." The contrast with Psalm 74 could hardly be greater; in that psalm, which reflects the turbulence of exile, Leviathan was presented as a multiheaded monster destroyed in a great act of divine salvation. But in 104:26, rather than an instrument of chaos that needs to be crushed, Leviathan is described surprisingly with the verb "sport" or "play" (*śaḥaq*). In Psalm 74 there is a shattering of heads, but in Psalm 104 God sports with Leviathan like a rubber ducky in the bathtub (as Jon Levenson famously quipped), or like a Pixar film franchise about training dragons. Of course, regardless of the antithesis, in both psalms the God of Israel is presented as clearly triumphant over Leviathan, and so in different ways this image of a chaotic beast is subverted to the same effect and becomes an affirmation of divine control over an unruly and disruptive force.

There is an interesting translation issue in Ps 104:26. The issue can be recognized by readers of an English version such as the NRSV, where verse 26 is rendered "There go the ships, and Leviathan that you formed to sport in it." The NRSV interprets Leviathan as playing in the sea, implying that the threat of chaos has been subdued and the human-engineered ships can sail with reasonable safety on top of the waters. Although syntactically possible, my translation differs from the NRSV by interpreting God as the subject of the clause ("Leviathan is there, that you formed to sport with"), a reading that fits more naturally with the tenor of the psalm as a whole. The same sense is found in Job 41, when God asks Job if he can draw out Leviathan with a fishhook (v. 1) or play (śaḥaq) with him like a bird (v. 5). The notion of *sport* relegates Leviathan, far from the threatening chaos monster of murky origins, to midlevel status within the created order. Consequently, Psalm 104 provides another glimpse of how images from the ancient Near East were transformed in order to encourage new imaginative horizons for the audience.

## Navigating the Rivers of Psalm 93

In this chapter we have been exploring how various motifs in the religious landscape of the ancient Near East have been adapted to an Israelite worldview. Psalm 29 affords a good example of how images from Canaanite fertility religion hover in the background and yet are subverted, as the voice of Israel's God thunders over any rival; the psalm is less interested in monotheism than one may expect, and more interested in efficacy of the divine voice. Moreover, the disturbing figure of Leviathan appears in several biblical texts and is attested from literature elsewhere in the ancient world, but in Psalm 74 this creature is crushed decisively and given as food for the beasts, while presented as merely God's object for entertainment in Psalm 104. To extend our discussion of this crucial ideological question in the religious landscape of ancient Israel and the surrounding nations—*Who among the gods is worthy to be acclaimed as king and ruler of the world?*—a relevant example can again be found in one of the tablets from the episodic Baal cycle found at Ugarit in northern Syria. We will then observe how similar ideas are reconfigured in the enthronement hymn of Psalm 93. But first consider the Canaanite text:

> Let me tell you, Prince Baal,
>     let me repeat, Rider on the Clouds:

Now, your enemy, Baal,
   now you will kill your enemy,
      now you will annihilate your foe.
You will take your eternal kingship,
   your dominion forever and ever.[19]

It can readily be observed that there are some immediate stylistic similarities between this Canaanite literary work and the poetry of the psalms, ranging from the use of parallelism to the structure of formulaic phrasing from line to line. While Israelite poets may have been keen to differentiate their God from the deities of the surrounding peoples, they often seemed quite content to use various cultural expressions and poetic forms in order to make those points, including *climactic parallelism* that spans three lines with amplifying intensity.[20] As in the Baal text, the idea of a divine being proclaimed as king after some sort of victory has widespread attestation and is a typical motif in ancient religious literature. The Babylonian epic *Enuma Elish* likewise "celebrates Marduk's elevation to preeminent status in the pantheon; in the epic, the other gods agree to confer ultimate royal authority on him following his defeat of Tiamat, the goddess of salt water and chaos."[21] As mentioned earlier in this chapter, a *combat myth* usually features a battle against forces of chaos manifested by some sort of sea monster, with the god who is victorious over this chaotic creature proclaimed as king by members of a divine council and honored with a temple or palace. These images are given an interesting treatment in Psalm 93, a composition that occurs at the outset of a cluster of *enthronement hymns* (Psalms 93–99) in the heart of Book IV of the Psalter:

[1] The Lord reigns! Majestically clothed,
   Clothed is the Lord: equipped with power.
      Truly, the world stands firm, it will not collapse.

---

[19] Coogan and Smith, *Stories from Ancient Canaan*, 180.
[20] Stephen A. Geller, "Myth and Syntax in Psalm 93," in *Mishneh Todah: Studies in Deuteronomy and Its Cultural Environment in Honor of Jeffrey H. Tigay*, ed. Nili Sacher Fox, David A. Glatt-Gilad, and Michael J. Williams (Winona Lake, IN: Eisenbrauns, 2009), 322.
[21] David S. Vanderhooft, "Marduk," in *Eerdmans Dictionary of the Bible*, ed. D. N. Freedman (Grand Rapids, MI: Eerdmans, 2000), 856.

> ² From ancient times your throne stands firm,
> You are from everlasting.
> ³ Rivers are rising, O Lord,
> Rivers are raising their voice,
> Rivers are rising with their pounding waves!
> ⁴ More than the sounds of great waters,
> Or the mighty breakers of the sea,
> Mighty is the Lord on high.
> ⁵ Your testimonies have proven sure,
> For your house, holiness is befitting,
> O Lord, for days unceasing.

Earlier in the previous century it was fashionable to interpret Psalm 93 as part of an annual festival whereby God's kingship was (re)affirmed by the community. While there is no concrete evidence for such a ceremony in ancient Israel, the idea that Psalm 93 and related compositions originally emerged from some sort of liturgical gathering is not unreasonable. One particular aspect of this scholarly controversy that has not abated even in more recent days is the translation of the opening line: while most English versions have the rendering "The Lord reigns" or "The Lord is king," some scholars opt for "The Lord has become king" or "The Lord began to reign." At issue is the meaning of the phrase, and there are implications in the two options: "Does it stress the eternal kingship of Yahweh, affirming his everlasting authority over the whole creation and all other divine powers? Or does it communicate remembrances of old, when Yahweh used to assume supreme lordship annually, in the manner of dying and rising deities of the ancient Near East?"[22]

There are a number of ways that Psalm 93 can be interpreted, but a plausible account is as follows: this psalm utilizes images from the traditional ancient Near Eastern combat myth, but subverts these images as well. Such divergence begins with the opening line, and on balance the first phrase of the psalm is best rendered in its present-tense aspect: *The Lord reigns*. Unlike Marduk or Baal, there is no time when

---

[22] Erhard S. Gerstenberger, *Psalms, Part 2, and Lamentations*, FOTL 15 (Grand Rapids, MI: Eerdmans, 2001), 173.

God has not reigned, on a throne that has long been established; God is not a recent claimant, and consequently the world remains stable and secure. In contrast to the typical lineaments of the combat myth, Psalm 93 starts with an affirmation of enthronement, and there is no challenger in sight. Yet the opening verse also suggests that opposition may arise, for not only is God outfitted in regal apparel, but God is also armed and ready for battle, as though anticipating conflict. So even though no struggle or actual combat is presented in the opening phrases of Psalm 93, the text implies that God is poised to vanquish any foe or threat to the stability of the world. By way of Israelite analogy, after Solomon had dispatched his major rivals in a violent and cunning purge early in his career, his kingdom was "established" (1 Kgs 2:46), yet Psalm 93 declares that God's throne has *always* been established.

It turns out, however, that a threat emerges in v. 3, and although the key noun *neharot* is variously translated, it is repeated three times in a climactic parallelism. Many translators opt to render *neharot* as "floods," and one also finds "oceans" or "seas" in commentaries and English versions, especially by those interpreters who prefer to argue for the opening phrase as "The Lord began to reign." Accordingly, the *oceans* can then be understood as hostile primeval waters, and it may be noted that Tiamat (the rival mother goddess killed by Marduk in the *Enuma Elish*) bears a consonantal resemblance to the Hebrew term "deep" (*tehom*) in Genesis 1, and so Psalm 93 obliquely alludes to a primeval uprising when God subdued the dark waters and subsequently began to reign as king. Alternatively, the *floods* might be explained as underground currents or subsurface streams that periodically rise to water the earth or even burst their seams to overflow into the land.[23] Some scholars would further insist that these floods in Psalm 93 are erupting in a chorus of praise, in a kind of aquatic witness to the grandeur of God.[24] A neighboring enthronement psalm certainly presents this picture: "The Lord reigns! Truly the world is established, it will not be moved. He will judge the peoples with fairness. So let the heavens

---

[23] See Allen P. Ross, *A Commentary on the Psalms*, vol. 3: *90–150* (Grand Rapids, MI: Kregel, 2016), 76.

[24] For example, DeClaissé-Walford, Jacobson, and Tanner, *The Book of Psalms*, 419.

rejoice, let the earth be glad, let the sea and its fullness resound" (Ps 96:10–11).

In Psalm 96 the *sea* is exhorted to join a symphony of praise in creation, and the crashing waves are part of a global response to divine equity. But something quite different is happening in Psalm 93, for instead of a summons to praise, the waters are depicted as raging and hostile. Thus, I have retained the translation *rivers* because in this case they are symbolizing the various nations historically associated with the great rivers of the Nile, Tigris, and the Euphrates, and therefore the superpowers Egypt, Assyria, and Babylon. Comparing the hostility of the nations to surging waters occurs elsewhere in the Hebrew Bible; Isaiah 17:12 is a case in point: "Oh, the thundering of many peoples, who thunder like the thundering of the sea, and the roar of nations who roar like the roaring of mighty waters!"[25] Throughout Israel's history, the people were buffeted by such nations, as first Egypt, then Assyria and Babylon surged against the Israelites: the Egyptians tried to drown the hopes of Israel in the waters of the Nile, while Assyria and Babylon crossed the Tigris and Euphrates rivers with imperious armies capable of great destruction.

The ominous power of these hostile nations is poetically represented in Psalm 93 through the technique of *climactic parallelism*, as three compact lines are used in v. 3 to lyrically simulate an onrushing army that incrementally raises its voice like surging waves. But the increasing height of these waves generated by the rivers is poetically countered in v. 4 by another climactic parallelism, as the poet insists that God is greater than these seething waters: "Using terse and powerful language, the hymn rushes along like the roaring water of which it speaks. The subdued reminiscences of mythical ideas and images are outshone by the poet's powerful exultation of the majesty of God, to which all his thoughts are subordinated to form a forceful unity."[26] Climactic parallelism, as we noted above, is well attested in Canaanite poetry. In Psalm 93, this form is used by the poet to underscore an important theological affirmation: those superpowers from the Nile, Tigris, and the

---

[25] Goldingay, *Psalms*, 3:45.
[26] Artur Weiser, *The Psalms*, OTL (Philadelphia, PA: Westminster John Knox, 1962), 618.

Euphrates dealt crushing blows to the people of Israel but were never able to completely drown the people of God, and on each occasion God did not allow the people to be utterly consumed by chaos.

Psalm 93 can certainly be interpreted as a primordial picture of dark waters that are subdued by God at the dawn of creation in an act of divine majesty. But it is also compelling to view the psalm as an account of those nations ("rivers") that raged against Israel in events such as the exodus from Egyptian slavery, Assyrian aggression, or the Babylonian invasion. None of these destructive events was entirely successful, as every force of chaotic opposition eventually wilted and God's kingship was not overturned. On this reading, there is a nice segue to v. 5, a celebration of the *testimonies* and the beauty of the divine *house*. At first glance it may seem an awkward transition, but both Baal and Marduk in the respective combat myths are rewarded with a palace after their victories as "a proof of royal status."[27] In contrast, God's house has eternal schematics, and there is no report that it has been granted as a reward; in fact, the chief beneficiaries are the *people of God* who are granted access to the divine testimonies, and owing to God's mastery of the raging rivers, these decrees have a proven reliability and are thus dependable during times of crisis and conflict. For a community struggling with the uncertainties of exile and displacement, the notion of trustworthy divine words would be of considerable relevance.

To further that last point about the relevance of *testimonies* in v. 5 for an exilic community, the positioning of Psalm 93 in the heart of Book IV of the Psalter should also be considered. As we recall, the overarching structure of the Psalter tells the story of the rise and fall of the Davidic covenant—affirming that God has been faithful to the covenant despite the waywardness of the people—and the first three books reflect the establishment of Israel's monarchy and the calamity of exile. Book IV invites a complete reappraisal of the community's worldview, and just as there are seventeen psalms in Book III that bear witness to the demise of the monarchy, so there are seventeen psalms in Book IV that reaffirm the sovereign reign of God.[28] Psalm 93 is the first in a

---

[27] Coogan and Smith, *Stories from Ancient Canaan*, 165.
[28] Susan Gillingham, "Psalms 90–106: Book Four and the Covenant with David," *European Judaism* 48 (2015): 87.

sequence of kingship psalms that occupy a strategic position in Book IV and probably utilizes the motifs of an ancient enthronement ceremony to underscore that God's throne has never been toppled, despite the surging rivers of the great superpowers. After forty-two kings in the monarchies of Israel and Judah—each with varying levels of failure—Psalm 93 invites the nation to remember a different kind of royalty. "The kings may have vanished," as one writer paraphrases, "but 'The Lord is king!'"[29] For a community that has experienced the trauma of exile, such reimaging turns their focus away from typical accouterments of worldly power and focuses instead on new forms of loyalty to God.

To conclude this chapter, we have observed that some Israelite psalms take advantage of common tropes from the religious poetry of the ancient world, but then proceed to take such images in a quite different direction. In both Psalm 29 and the images of Leviathan in Psalms 74 and 104, the Israelite poets are drawing from the religious landscape of the surrounding nations and even in some cases adopting similar artistic forms, but they shaped these forms to their particular worldview. Likewise with Psalm 93; a previous generation of scholars variously argued that Psalm 93 was one of a number of compositions that trace their origins to part of a fall festival that celebrated the kingship of God. As with the other "enthronement psalms" (93–100), these compositions collectively testify to divine kingship. Regardless of the theorized origins, Psalm 93 now stands at the head of the enthronement psalms early in Book IV, a book—as we earlier noted—that is concerned with returning to the covenant granted to Israel by the true king long before any monarchy arose. Ancient images were rebooted with a present-tense vitality for a new generation facing different threats after the return from exile, and perhaps a new and more powerful perspective was gained in the process. The next chapter explores other genres that can be found in Israel's collection of psalms and further attempts to discern how the collection was finally assembled.

---

[29] Terrien, *The Psalms*, 660.

# 3
# The Variety of Psalms

Within the symphony of 150 psalms composed over the course of numerous centuries and that variously refract events from the heights of the monarchy to the depths of exile and promising days of the restoration, there is a great diversity of subject matter and poetic material. Just as there are different kinds of songs nowadays (ballads, anthems, hymns, folk tunes) and assorted musical genres (classical, jazz, country, hip-hop), so there are numerous categories and styles of psalms in ancient Israel. I have already commented on the difficulty of assigning specific dates of composition to most of the psalms, and caution is highly recommended: "The dating of individual psalms has long been a region of treacherous scholarly quicksand. The one safe conclusion is that the writing of psalms was a persistent activity over many centuries."[1] Fortunately, it is ostensibly easier to identify a particular genre of a psalm than to posit a date of composition, if nothing else because there is at least measurable data and poetic patterns for the interpreter to assess. Moreover, if the reader is acquainted with the genre of a poetic text, then the reader roughly knows what to expect and when to be surprised.

There is not an outright consensus on the various genres of the Psalms nor of individual compositions, but there are at least broad swaths of agreement among scholars. From the outset, however, it should be kept in mind that genres are *not* fixed in stone, and one should hesitate before over-pressing individual psalms (or even sections of psalms) into certain molds. For instance, there are a number of psalms that resist categorization and preserve the voice of an outsider, perhaps even someone excluded from temple worship.

---

[1] Alter, *The Book of Psalms*, xv.

In many cases the poetic medium was also utilized to explore important topics such as alienation and suffering, child-rearing woes and vocational anxieties, fear of the future and situations of deep distress, in addition to the seemingly mundane circumstances of everyday routine as opportunities to experience the divine presence, and poetic works such as these do not always fit easily into categories.

Having discussed the context of the psalms in the cultural and religious milieu of the ancient Near East, I will survey some of the main genres of Israel's psalms, with at least one extended example of each. There is a certain fluidity among the boundaries of genre, and so five of the more popular varieties that are attested across the Psalter are included here: *royal* (with the figure of the earthly king as a main subject), *creation* (the natural world as a central focus), *lament* (both individual and corporate cries of complaint and petition), *trust* (declaration of assurance usually amid crisis or a troublesome situation), and *wisdom* (where instruction is at the forefront or the voice of a sage within Israel's tradition can be discerned). Perhaps these assorted kinds of psalms are distributed randomly throughout the five books. Alternatively, it could be maintained that there is a more strategic deployment and an intentional placement of a particular genre of psalm in the unfolding story one traces in the larger work. For this study, I will suggest the latter approach, inviting the reader to consider not only the particular features of the various genres of psalms but also *where* they are positioned in the overall arrangement of the Psalter.

## The Scepter's Shadow

Earlier in this study several lines were quoted from Psalm 18, a dramatic composition wherein the poet celebrates a supernatural divine rescue in the midst of harrowing circumstances. Replete with *chaos* and *cosmic battle* imagery, the first half of Psalm 18 narrates the main character's desperation and subsequent response from God, while the second half commemorates the faithfulness and integrity of the poet who is divinely rewarded. By all estimates, Psalm 18—with its parallel version in 2 Samuel 22 and close connections to the career of David—is categorized by scholars as a *royal* psalm, and in this case features a positive portrait of the king who faithfully calls out in distress and is delivered from calamity.[2]

What are the standard features of royal psalms, and what role do they play in the story of the Psalter? From the outset it should be noted that *human* (rather than divine) kingship is the interest of a royal psalm. There are numerous examples of psalms that exalt God's enthronement or kingship over Israel and the world (e.g., Psalms 93–99), but they typically represent a different genre. For a majority of commentators, the list of royal psalms include the following: 2, 18, 20, 21, 45, 72, 89, 101, 110, 132, and 144. Allowing for margins of error, this is not a long list, and given the importance of the monarchy in Israel's political history, the fact that royal psalms comprise less than 15 percent of the Psalter is surprising. In light of the overwhelming failure of Israel's kings—an active prayer life is rarely glimpsed in Israel's historical literature about the monarchs—maybe the paucity of royal psalms is intentional and underscores one of the reasons *why* the monarchy failed.

Moreover, considerable diversity can be found within these royal psalms. Even though a psalm may mention or invoke the king, it is not necessarily classified as a royal psalm, for even Psalm 84, discussed above, mentions the king as part of the pilgrimage to Jerusalem but is not included in the list. Instead, there is a common set of shared characteristics. According to the authors of a recent commentary, royal psalms "are thematically related rather than related according to formal similarities. They are poems that were composed for specific events in the king's life or for other reasons related to the monarchy. The events may have included the king's coronation, marriage, or an impending military campaign. Other possibilities are prayers for the king to pray himself or to be prayed on his behalf."[3]

Turning back to Psalm 18, it is clear that the central topic of this expansive poem revolves around a military crisis in the king's life. The combination of victory motifs from "darkness of waters" (v. 12) and

---

[2] On the comparisons between Psalm 18 and 2 Samuel 22, see the classic study F. M. Cross Jr., and D. N. Freedman, "A Royal Song of Thanksgiving: II Samuel 22 = Psalm 18," *JBL* 72 (1953): 15–34.

[3] Nancy J. DeClaissé-Walford, Rolf A. Jacobson, and Beth LaNeel Tanner, *The Book of Psalms*, NICOT (Grand Rapids, MI: Eerdmans, 2014), 11.

fearsome enemies (augmented by the instructional exhortations later in vv. 25–30) envisions an audience that spans numerous spectrums of life in ancient Israel, all of whom can benefit from the experience of the poet. Certainly the most overt feature of Psalm 18 that categorizes it as a royal psalm is a reference to the *anointed* in v. 50 at the poem's climactic finish. The term *anointed* (*māšîaḥ*), from which the term *messiah* ("anointed one") is derived, is most commonly a reference to priestly or monarchial ceremonies where someone is set apart for a unique task or vocation. In the book of Psalms it is first used in 2:2, and in that context refers to the earthly king's successor. Similarly, in Ps 18:50 the *anointed* is a reference to David's successor, a future leader or even a group of leaders, who here receive encouragement to believe and act a certain way: an early king like David was rescued by God and resolved to respond with a life of faithfulness, and so those successors are encouraged to follow this model. As a royal composition, Psalm 18 testifies to God's active involvement in the affairs of national life and the person of the king, and in this case recounts the events of a king in distress who is answered by God and brings relief to a beleaguered population.

Psalm 20 is another example of a royal psalm, a compact poem that is positioned after Psalm 18 (where the king cries for help in the midst of battle) and prior to Psalm 21 (a prayer of thanks by the king for God's gift of success in battle: "In your strength the king rejoices, O Lord, and in your help how greatly he exults! You have given him his heart's desire, and have not withheld the request of his lips"). Appropriately, then, Psalm 20 is a prayer *before* battle, and so a certain logic can be observed in the sequential organization of these psalms. Compared to Psalm 18, Psalm 20 is quite compact, but a quick reading reveals that standard features of royal psalms are apparent, especially mention of *his anointed* and a plea for God to give *salvation* or *victory* to the king:

> [1] May the Lord answer you in the day of distress,
>     may the name of the God of Jacob lift you safely on high.
> [2] May he send you help from the holy place,
>     and sustain you from Zion.
> [3] May he remember all your gift offerings,
>     and your burnt sacrifices consider with favor.

> ⁴ May he grant everything in your heart,
>    and fulfill all your plans.
> ⁵ May we sing for joy in your victory,
>    and in the name of our God raise our banner.
>       May the Lord answer all your requests!
> ⁶ Now I know that the Lord gives victory to his anointed:
>    he will answer him from his holy heaven,
>       with the saving power of his right hand.
> ⁷ Some trust in chariots, some in horses,
>    but we will invoke the name of the Lord our God.
> ⁸ They collapse at their knees and fall,
>    but we arise and stand together.
> ⁹ O Lord, give victory to the king,
>    answer us on the day we call!

As we consider the genre of royal psalms, there are several points that emerge from Psalm 20. First, this psalm is a *prayer*, that is, a request for God's help and intervention. Recognizing that an Israelite king was the military leader of the nation, Psalm 20 underscores the need for the king to be dependent on God in all circumstances. Second, it is *not* a celebration of violence but rather a reorientation of the king's perspective away from the typical accouterments of war and toward the character of God. Psalm 20 assumes that battles are a necessary reality of life in Israel's context, but this prayer encourages both king and people to appreciate the true source of their strength. Third, the climax of the psalm is the bold anticipation in v. 5 that God is willing to grant victory to Israel in a military crisis where the nation's borders are threatened or the security of the people needs to be safeguarded. By contrast, those opponents whose trust is limited to the conventional weapons of war—so the poet affirms—will eventually stagger and collapse, while those who depend on the capacity of God's strength are vindicated. Reading the books of Samuel and Kings, there is a significant tension that arises since the vast majority of monarchs invested more energy in military hardware than spiritual strength and often trusted in a large stable of horses. In Psalm 20 the national leader is challenged to depend on God rather than any other resources; *trust* in this case is not reckless lethargy but an active belief that Israel's military efforts are under the aegis of God's direction. More often than not

Israel was the underdog in such hostilities, as they faced stronger, more experienced, and better equipped opponents, and thus needed divine help for any hope of success. Given the frequency of conflict during most of the Israelite monarchy, one can imagine a prayer such as this would need to be offered on a regular (if not continual) basis. Psalm 20 maintains that as the king and the people recognize their dependence on God in a just cause, there are grounds for confidence that the divine name ultimately will prove stronger than any foe.

Scanning the royal psalms of Books I and II, the image of kingship is often positive and generally portrays the monarch as the nation's military captain, advocate for righteousness and social justice, and supporter of the temple. The "wedding song" of Psalm 45 is unique in the Psalter, and perhaps was used in the context of royal marriage and emphasizes the correct view of power and the role of the king as one entrusted with *the scepter of equity* (v. 7). Similarly, Psalm 72 appears to be a prayer with a specific context, a ceremony of succession ("Grant the king your justice, O God, and your righteousness to the royal son," v. 1). A key role of the king in Psalm 72 is to maintain justice and advocate for the poor and the marginalized, thus presenting a picture of the king as a champion for the Torah at every level of society. Nonetheless, these images stand in tension with most of the narrative in Samuel and Kings, where such priorities are rarely in the purview of Israel's leaders. Solomon himself has hundreds of wives—surely Psalm 45 was *not* performed at all of his weddings!—and he was certainly not a fair or impartial monarch. The royal psalms of Books I and II therefore carry an ironic edge when considered against the backdrop of Israel's actual experience, as the forty-two kings rarely came anywhere close to such ideals.[4]

---

[4] Such a tension causes John Day (*Psalms*, 97) to reflect further on how kingship is configured in the Psalter: "[T]hough originally relating to pre-exilic Israelite monarchs, the royal psalms depict the king in idealized language, e.g. he is promised universal rule and reigns with complete justice and righteousness. This reflects the traditional court style of the ancient near east and is attested also in Egypt and Mesopotamia. Clearly a kingly ideal is being set forth here that was not achieved in reality." Day proceeds to discuss the reformulations of kingship language in the psalms in the wake of the collapse of institutional monarchy after captivity, the hopes for an ideal ruler to arise in the days ahead, and the realization of the Davidic promise that may culminate with the arrival of the messiah.

The only royal psalm in Book III is Psalm 89, a long composition that compares God's lasting covenant with the house of David with the forlorn situation of exile, where the "crown is defiled in the ground" (v. 39) and the regal "splendor" has come to an end (v. 44). Rather than *the king* as a primary voice in Book III, one notices that Levite psalms dominate in this stretch of the Psalter, as the monarchs are displaced by the chorus of Asaph and Korah songs in exile. Statistically, the word *king* is also used differently: in the first three books it refers to all sorts of royal figures (including the kings of Israel and Judah), but in Books IV and V, the term is not used again with a present-tense reference to an Israelite king.[5] Consequently, there is a noticeable shift in tone for the remaining royal psalms in Books IV and V. Psalm 110, for example contains some textual difficulties but has thematic connections with Psalm 2 and underlines God's commitment to the nation's leadership even during the unpredictable circumstances of life after the exile. Psalm 144, the last of the royal psalms, has a retrospective tone that commemorates the divine preservation of Israel's kings in the past. The atmosphere of the royal psalms in Books IV and V are nicely encapsulated in Psalm 144, where the focus in not on the king's conquests or ambitions but rather on the saving power of God.[6] Instead of drawing attention to regal ambition, this composition stresses the value of fields, progeny, and safe public squares; at the end of the royal psalms, there is a tacit acknowledgment of the fleetingness of the monarchic enterprise and an emphasis on the blessing that flows from a community rooted in divine kingship.

Identifying the *genres* of psalms does not seem quite as popular nowadays among scholars as it was half a century ago, but as we can see from a brief survey of the royal psalms, there is nonetheless some value for the interpreter. When the royal psalms are considered as a

---

[5] Gerald H. Wilson, "The Structure of the Psalter," in *Interpreting the Psalms: Issues and Approaches*, ed. David G. Firth and Philip S. Johnston (Downers Grove, IL: InterVarsity Press, 2013), 236: "In Books I–III the Hebrew word for king [*melek*] is used to describe kingship in general, including non-Israelite kings, kings of Israel and Judah, as well as the YHWH as king. In Books IV and V, [*melek*] is never again used in relation to David or the kings of Israel and Judah."

[6] Cf. Brueggemann and Bellinger, *Psalms*, 600: "In verse 3 of the present psalm, it is as if the king in Jerusalem acknowledges the limit, if not the futility, of his own military capacity. Human (royal) capacity is fragile and vulnerable."

group, two concluding points can be made. First, if the overarching story of the Psalter traces the rise and fall of the Israelite monarchy, then the royal psalms make a significant (although understated) contribution to this story. Rather than being restricted to one section or cluster, the royal psalms are distributed throughout the five books of the Psalter, with a noticeable difference from start to finish. In Books I and II, the royal psalms are more positive toward the monarchy, but in Books III, IV, and V there is a different perspective that gradually emerges: "In both parts of the Psalms, this trajectory posits the king as starting off with high status and great power but descending by stages to a loss of status and power, even to the point of establishing the king's irrelevance to Israelite society and religion."[7] Second, the royal psalms incrementally point toward an alternative way of thinking about kingship and invite the community to consider new paradigms. Instead of typical models of power in the ancient world, scholars have suggested that the royal psalms toward the end of the Psalter nurture hopes of an ideal ruler from the line of David bringing the vision of Psalm 2 ("I will make the nations your heritage, and the ends of the earth your possession") to its fulfillment.[8] Recognizing the particular features and thematic emphases of the royal psalms, therefore, is helpful for appreciating the overarching storyline of the Psalter.

## Pillars of the Earth

Genesis 1 opens with the famous words "In the beginning God created the heavens and the earth," and while it is the first creation account in the Hebrew Bible, it is certainly not the only one (nor perhaps even the earliest one written). Other accounts of creation can be found in passages such as Job 38:9–10 ("who shut in the sea with doors when it

---

[7] Norman K. Gottwald, "Kingship in the Book of Psalms," in *The Oxford Handbook of the Psalms*, ed. William P. Brown (New York: Oxford University Press, 2014), 439.

[8] For example, Jamie A. Grant, "The Psalms and the King," in *Interpreting the Psalms: Issues and Approaches*, ed. David G. Firth and Philip S. Johnston (Downers Grove, IL: InterVarsity Press, 2013), 116: "The thoughts of the reader are not directed towards the best examples of kingship (David or Josiah), they are directed rather to the ideal of kingship. The coming king will be the one who keeps the kingship law, the ultimate exemplar of torah-piety lived out in reality."

burst out from the womb?—when I made the clouds its garment, and thick darkness its swaddling band, and prescribed bounds for it, and set bars and doors") and Proverbs 8:27–28 ("When he established the heavens, I was there, when he drew a circle on the face of the deep, when he made firm the skies above, when he established the fountains of the deep"). Since the biblical story begins with a creation account, the first of several throughout the Bible, it indicates the importance of the subject from the outset. The book of Psalms also contains a number of *creation* psalms, and although the total number is fewer than the royal psalms (commentators usually at least point to 8, 19, 65, 104 and 148 as examples of this genre), they nonetheless have several distinctive features and likewise contribute to the overarching storyline of the Psalter. A handful of lines from Psalm 8 provide a useful illustration of the lineaments of a creation psalm. The poet commences with the idea that the splendor of the divine name is radiated in the heavenly spheres, and takes a decidedly personal turn in the middle stanza of the poem:

> [3] As I look up at your heavens, the work of your fingers,
>   Moon and stars that you have established,
> [4] What is a human being that you would be so mindful,
>   Mortal offspring, that you would care so much?
> [5] You have made them just less than divine,
>   Yet crowned with glory and majesty!

In terms of placement, Psalm 8 occurs after a cluster of psalms (3–7) where there is complaint, pain, and affliction caused by various kinds of enemies and adversities. Psalm 8 thus immediately stands out from its surrounding context because there is no petition as such, but instead the poet's awestruck wonder is the primary focus. Furthermore, humanity is the subject of extended reflection in Psalm 8, and rather than oppressors or tyrants taking center stage, humanity in general is essentially celebrated. As one scholar points out, Psalm 8 "interrupts the sequence of prayers for salvation to say something very important about the God to whom the prayers are made: The Lord is the cosmic sovereign whose majesty is visible in the whole world. The psalm also discloses why the salvation of those who pray is so important for the reign of God: As human beings, they have an office in God's kingdom."[9] Consequently, to have a hymn of praise for the splendor of creation and Creator on the heels of these other psalms about desperate circumstances is surely intentional, and the placement draws further attention to the theological message in this psalm about the value and purpose of human life.

Many commentators suggest that the account of Genesis 1 is in view as Psalm 8 unfolds, with humanity created in the divine image and granted dominion (that is, responsibility) for the care and stewardship of the garden (as a microcosm of the world).[10] On the sixth day, human beings are created as the apex of God's activity in Genesis, activity that occurs because of God's word, and in contrast to other creation accounts in the ancient Near East, creation in Genesis 1 occurs without violence or competition. Rather than slaves or servants, in Genesis 1 human beings are *royal stewards*, and similar to Psalm 8, humanity enjoys a unique mandate:

> [6] You allow them to rule over the works of your hands,
>     All things you have set under their feet.
> [7] Sheep and oxen, all of them,
>     Every beast of the field.
> [8] Birds of the sky and fish of the sea,
>     Everything that passes through the paths of the waters.
> [9] O Lord, our master,
>     how majestic is your name in all the earth!

Ancient monarchs were renowned for their building projects, but in Psalm 8 the divine works are of a different order; rather than a fortress or a citadel, "the heavens" and "all creatures" carry the testimony of the divine fingerprint, far eclipsing the monuments of Solomon, Sargon,

---

[9] Mays, *Psalms*, 65. Note also the turning-point soliloquy of Hamlet as he apprehends an uncertain future: "Sure he that made us with such large discourse,/Looking before and after, gave us not/That capability and god-like reason/To fust in us unused" (*Hamlet*, Act 4, Scene 4).

[10] Adele Berlin, "The Wisdom of Creation in Psalm 104," in *Seeking Out the Wisdom of the Ancients: Essays Offered to Honor Michael V. Fox on the Occasion of his Sixty-Fifth Birthday*, ed. Ronald L. Troxel, Kelvin G. Friebel, and Dennis R. Magery (Winona Lake, IN: Eisenbrauns, 2005), 75.

or Sennacherib. When observing the moon and the stars, the psalmist does not see other gods in the heavens—as Israel's neighbors would assert—but rather limitless evidence of God's magnificence, even as the vastness of the cosmos prompts an inward turn with a question about the worth (or significance) of comparably small human beings. Psalm 8 declares that humanity has a central place in the organization of the world, and it is interesting that the psalmist stresses the importance of humanity in general rather than just Israel in particular, an emphasis that is apparent in the use of the phrase *sons of Adam* instead of *sons of Abraham* in v. 4. It is not simply the chosen people who are singled out, but all of humanity who are created slightly lower than God, with a recognition of mortality and connection of *adam(ah)* with dirt or ground: "Humans are dirt, shaped by the divine potter's dexterous hands, yet transformed into a little less than God, whose self-revelation in the universe enables us to acquire a right understanding of self, someone who receives God's particular attentions."[11] Instead of an overwhelming sense of loneliness and insignificance in the face of a vast indifferent universe, the human person has a crowning affirmation of importance and dignity.[12]

In short, *creation* psalms invite the reader to consider the grandeur of the natural world as a partial reflection of the character of the creator. The universe may be charged with a fearful symmetry, but it is also tempered with a need for respect and is far from mundane or predictable. These various psalms highlight the intricacy and wonder of the natural ecosystem, and particular attributes of the divine personality are emphasized at the same time. Since God is the creator of the natural world—with humanity at the apex endowed with considerable responsibility as stewards—God is therefore recognized as the rightful ruler and judge. Not only does God vanquish chaos with the event of creation, but as Psalms 65 and 104 stress at length, God is also the sustainer

---

[11] Schaefer, *Psalms*, 24.
[12] For a historical aside, see DeClaissé-Walford, Jacobson, and Tanner, *The Book of Psalms*, 84: "When the Apollo 11 spacecraft journeyed to the moon in 1969, the leaders of the nations of earth were each invited to compose a message to be included on a small disk that was to be left on that heavenly body. Pope Paul VI—who was devoted to God, felt responsible for creation, and was the political leader of the Vatican—sent along the text of Psalm 8."

54 THE PSALMS

and provider of both the human and animal realm who supervises the fish of the sea and names the stars in the sky (147:4). In the larger structure of the Psalter, the great works of creation are extended in God's acts of salvation, and divine care for the cosmos mirrors God's care for humanity. But it is striking that in Book III—Psalms 73–89 that unfold a bleak picture of exile and dislocation from the land—there are no obvious creation psalms, as though the majesty of the natural world has been eclipsed by the darkness of suffering and painful circumstance.

## Cries of Complaint

By far the most frequently used genre in the Psalter are psalms of *lament*, and although estimates vary between one-third and one-half of the entire collection, there are examples of lament psalms attested in all five books (albeit in differing concentrations). As with most issues in biblical studies, there is not complete agreement on the criteria for psalms of lament, but there are certain shared characteristics. A key idea is some sort of *complaint* that is lodged by the poet or the community, often a plea or a cry for help, perhaps followed by a life lesson or resolution that is subsequently passed on. *Lament*, therefore, is an expansive term that involves more than just sadness: most often, there is a situation of calamity and a prayer for God to act. Such calamities range from an individual crisis (whether involving health, family, slanderous accusations, death, or attendant miseries) to national disasters (famine or ecological threat, invasion or oppression by a tyrant, widespread corruption and injustice in society). In these psalms, it should be stressed, there is a specific calling out to God which presupposes that the poet and, by extension, the community of Israel believe that God hears and can do something about their plight and act to remedy their misery.[13] Psalms of lament are not necessarily expressions of grief

---

[13] While some scholars divide the lament psalms into groups according to whether or not there is divine responsibility for suffering, Day (*Psalms*, 24) prefers a different approach than bifurcation: "It is surely better to think of a continuum ranging from psalms in which Yahweh is blamed outright for suffering, through psalms in which he is regarded as passively standing back, to psalms in which God is not explicitly held responsible at all, rather than attempting to divide all the lament psalms neatly into two groups."

after the fact but can be an appeal in the midst of crisis for God to intervene and change the situation.[14]

Turning to Psalm 32 as an illustration, the reader immediately notices a complex composition. While categorized by many commentators as a lament, other elements (such as wisdom and instruction) also can be discerned in Psalm 32. So not only is there is a variety *of* psalms, but there can be variety *within* a single psalm as well. Psalm 32 dramatizes the poet's inner struggle: a crisis over unresolved sin.[15] The superscription of Psalm 32 identifies it as a *maskil*, and because the root meaning of the Hebrew term is "teach/have insight," many interpreters suggest that a *maskil* is a type of teaching psalm. Using the NRSV translation, here is a short reading of Psalm 32, starting with the opening lines:

> [1] Happy are those whose transgression is forgiven,
>    whose sin is covered.
> [2] Happy are those to whom the Lord imputes no iniquity,
>    and in whose spirit there is no deceit.

Psalm 32 begins with the word *blessed*, the same as in Psalm 1: blessed is the person whose delight is in the Torah, on which such a person meditates day and night. Psalm 32, however, is about that person who has strayed from Torah, and for whom the Torah has *not* been the source of endless delight: "[H]ow extraordinary that it declares the good fortune not of the faithful person (like Ps. 1) but of

---

[14] C. Hassell Bullock, *Encountering the Book of Psalms: A Literary and Theological Introduction*, 2nd edition (Grand Rapids, MI: Baker, 2018), 193: "The crisis from which the psalmist prays for deliverance is sometimes sickness, but rarely is it disassociated from spiritual or psychological anguish caused by the psalmist's own doubts and uncertainty, or the criticism of his friends and foes and the gloating of his enemies. These enemies, while they are national in the community laments, are often personal in the individual laments. Metaphorical language often picks up the imagery of war, hunting, and animals enraged by hunger and fear to express the terrible pain and suffering the psalmist undergoes."

[15] Note also Mays, *Psalms*, 145: "In Proverbs 28:13 the lesson is formulated as general instruction using the same terms as the psalm: 'He who conceals his transgressions will not prosper; he who confesses and forsakes them will obtain mercy.' In Psalm 32 the lesson is based on a case of experience reported in verses 3–5 where the psalmist tells about the torment he suffered when he was silent and the forgiveness he received when he acknowledged his sin to the Lord."

the faithless person, not of the torah-keeper but the torah-breaker."[16] The poetic parallelisms of the opening verses use three different terms for human failure (*transgression*, or rebellion; *sin*, or refusing to walk on the best pathway; *iniquity*, conscious activity that is wrong or distorted), counteracted by three different terms for divine beneficence (*forgive*, lifting off a burden; *cover*, clothing as with a new garment; *does not impute*, clearing the account or list of charges). If we had to render a lengthy and unpoetic paraphrase it might resemble something like this: How fortunate is anyone whose burdens of mistake and guilty miseries have been carried off by God, and how favored is that person who refuses to live a double life of deceitful cover-up by constantly hiding their failures with an exterior façade designed to impress and fool the world. Not only does Ps 32:1–2 express this much more artistically, but these lines are actually the prelude to a story that is dramatized in vv. 3–5:

> ³ While I kept silence, my body wasted away
>       through my groaning all day long.
> ⁴ For day and night your hand was heavy upon me;
>       my strength was dried up as by the heat of summer. *Selah*
> ⁵ Then I acknowledged my sin to you,
>       and I did not hide my iniquity;
>    I said, "I will confess my transgressions to the Lord,"
>       and you forgave the guilt of my sin. *Selah*

After the aphorisms (or proverbial expressions) that commence the psalm, a story unfolds wherein the poet experiences inner torment because of *silence*, which might mean giving God the silent treatment, or perhaps it connotes inactivity based on a meaning of the term elsewhere. Either way, the psalmist does not deal with the pressing issue of sin, and concealed guilt is proving unbearable. For the poet, there is a sense of God's *heavy hand*; as an example, the same expression is used to describe the discomfort of the Philistines after capturing the ark of the covenant in 1 Sam 5:11. So perhaps the poet suffers from a physical

---

[16] Goldingay, *Psalms,* vol. 1: *Psalms 1–41*, 299.

affliction brought on by guilt (as a number of commentators aver) or, in my view more likely, suffers from psychological distress stemming from a relentlessly tortured conscience. The key image in v. 4 is a picture of dehydration in the dry heat of the rainless season, with paralysis and depletion of energy. Notably, the nature of the offense(s) is not stated in Psalm 32, nor is a reason provided as to *why* the poet is silent (whether out of unbelief or shame). Consequently, the focus of the psalm is more on the character of God and openness to confession rather than any specific category of sin. When the period of silence ends, there is a turning point in the poet's life as sin is *acknowledged* (lit. "made known" or "announced") and the guilt of sin is lifted off by God.

> [6] Therefore let all who are faithful offer prayer to you;
> at a time of distress, the rush of mighty waters shall not
> reach them.
> [7] You are a hiding place for me;
> you preserve me from trouble;
> you surround me with glad cries of deliverance. *Selah*
> [8] I will instruct you and teach you the way you should go;
> I will counsel you with my eye upon you.
> [9] Do not be like a horse or a mule, without understanding,
> whose temper must be curbed with bit and bridle,
> else it will not stay near you.
> [10] Many are the torments of the wicked,
> but steadfast love surrounds those who trust in the Lord.
> [11] Be glad in the Lord and rejoice, O righteous,
> and shout for joy, all you upright in heart.

Two comments can be made about the second half of the psalm in vv. 6–11. First, there is a new mode of address and a movement from private anguish to public proclamation in the rest of Psalm 32. Furthermore, there is what appears to be a direct divine statement in v. 8: earlier the poet struggled with silence, yet once the silence is broken, it is notable that God speaks. As far as content, the words of v. 8 are remarkably intimate and involved, and a very committed picture of God's character emerges here. Second, the poet feels an obligation to teach others from this experience about the power of confession and a lifted burden, with an intentional move from "denial rooted in self-sufficiency" to a new focus on God and others.[17] A number of psalms of *lament* feature this kind of public exhortation, as the poet moves from an inward and lonely space to an expansive arena in the presence of God's people, or from isolation to community as the desperate circumstance is resolved and the mask of hypocrisy is exchanged for authenticity and relief. Lament psalms are not, therefore, wholly negative, but usually feature "expressions of confidence" or "vows of praise" and direct the community to discern divine beneficence even in the midst of suffering.[18]

Considerable range can be found within lament psalms, the genre that occurs most frequently in the Psalter and with a higher percentage found in the first three books. For instance, in Psalm 71 a cabal of enemies are speaking malicious words against the poet. Unlike Psalm 32—where the psalmist admits wrongdoing and some sort of secret sin that can be concealed from family and community—the poet of Psalm 71 seems to be innocent. There is often not an obvious connection between a person's deeds and suffering, and psalms of lament thus provide a voice for such complaints about injustice. Furthermore, it is not always clear who the enemy is; sometimes they are clearly outsiders (such as the catalogue of foreign nations in Psalm 83), but on other occasions the enemies are from the poet's own social circle (as is most likely the case in Psalm 3, as the words attributed to the enemies in v. 2 are surely from Israelite speakers). The sense of divine abandonment in Psalm 13 ("How long, O Lord? Will you forget me forever?") has a decidedly personal feel, while the outpouring in Psalm 44 ("You have made us the taunt of our neighbors, the derision and scorn of those around us") is a communal voice calling on God to respond on the

---

[17] Brueggemann and Bellinger, *Psalms*, 161–162.
[18] Carleen Mandolfo, "Language of Lament in the Psalms," in *The Oxford Handbook of the Psalms*, ed. William P. Brown (New York: Oxford University Press, 2014), 115–116. Mandolfo further notes, "The language of reassurance and that of complaint sit side by side in the lament psalms without either getting the final say. Within a single psalm one or the other position might receive more emphasis, but within the entire lament corpus one should note an unresolved tension between expressions of faith and doubt.... Together these two ideological positions—doubt and faith—offer a profound reflection on human experience. Faith without doubt is myopic; doubt without faith runs the danger of sliding into existential meaninglessness" (126).

basis of the covenant commitment to the people of Israel. In a similar vein, Psalm 102 ("I am like a lonely bird on the housetop, All day long my enemies taunt me") has an individual voice that seems to speak for a multitude. Among the various suggestions for interpreting this psalm, one interesting proposal is that the destroyed city of Jerusalem is the personified speaker; the superscription refers to Psalm 102 as a *prayer of the afflicted*, and the ruined city certainly meets that criteria.[19] On the basis of this small sample of lament psalms, we can appreciate the variations within the genre and why it is the most attested kind of poem in the Psalter.

Another specific kind of complaint is the *imprecation*, an unfiltered response to injustice that is jarring and raw. Numerous texts in the Hebrew Bible indicate that atrocities abound in the history of Israel. 1 Kings 8:9-13 narrates the interaction between Elisha and Hazael of Damascus, and when the latter asks about Elisha's tears, the prophet responds "Because I know what evil you will do to the Israelites: to their fortresses you will send fire, their choice young men you will kill with the sword, their infants you will smash, and their pregnant women you will rip open." Readers may well recoil at such language, but when one has been the victim of such violence, a rather different view might emerge. In Psalm 69:23 the poet rails against a group of malicious attackers ("May their eyes be darkened so they have no sight, may their loins constantly shake") while confessing deep pain (v. 29) and a confidence that God hears the needy (v. 33). The language of imprecation is also found in the New Testament, and Psalm 69 itself is quoted by Peter in Acts 1:20. No doubt it is difficult to lay aside the desire for revenge and instead call on God to respond to evil, but such belief is the challenge of this kind of psalm.[20]

---

[19] Note Leslie Allen's *Psalms 101–150*, WBC 21 (Waco, TX: Word Books, 1983), 7 comment: "A bewildering multiplicity of interpretations have been offered for this complex psalm."

[20] Pleas for divine intervention, says Gordon J. Wenham (*Psalms as Torah: Reading Biblical Song Ethically* [Grand Rapids: Baker Academic, 2012], 79) "are much more than curses parading as prayers. They are undergirded by the conviction that God is both sovereign and just, indeed that he cares about the injustice suffered by the poor and downtrodden. The psalmists cry out that God will treat wrongdoers as they have treated others. In situations where faith in God's goodness seems to be disproved, the psalmists reassert that faith and place their trust in God to vindicate them rather than take revenge themselves."

Within the larger structure of the Psalter, psalms of lament make an arresting contribution. As mentioned above, lament psalms are found in all five books, but with a higher frequency in the first three. Cries of complaint occur often in Books I and II but take a darker turn in Book III, where the bleakness of exile gives voice to compositions such as Psalms 79 ("How long, O Lord? Will you be angry forever? Will your jealous wrath burn like fire?") and 88 ("Your wrath lies heavy upon me, and you overwhelm me with all your waves"), where the pleas reach their lowest ebb. But there is a lower percentage of lament psalms in Books IV and V, and by the time the reader reaches the final section of the Psalter, laments are more difficult to find. Indeed, the last words of the Psalter are not laments but songs of praise, as all of creation is invited to join a universal chorus. So psalms of lament are the genre that gets the most words in the Psalter, but not the last words.

## A Question of Trust

In the midst of stressful circumstances and the maelstrom of life, trust in God can be a challenge for the community. Israel's history is fraught with difficult moments—whether wars, famines, or even the precariousness of existence in the ancient Near East—and so the invitation to trust in God was often repeated. As discussed above, there are statistically more psalms of lament than any other genre. More specifically, psalms of lament illustrate that the quality of faith was not so easy in practice; dissent was frequent, as was frustration and anger, for surely it is hard for anyone to trust God when surrounded by disease, tragedy, cruelty, or personal failure. Directed toward such uncertainties, a *psalm of trust* poetically aims to inculcate confidence in God based on promises, covenant reminders, or ruminations on the divine character. Consider the opening stanza of Psalm 27, where the poet makes several affirmations about trusting God in various kinds of adversities:

> The Lord is my light and my salvation;
>  whom shall I fear?
> The Lord is the stronghold of my life;
>  of whom shall I be afraid?

² When evildoers assail me to devour my flesh—
my adversaries and foes—they shall stumble and fall.
³ Though an army encamp against me, my heart shall not fear;
though war rise up against me, yet I will be confident.

There is some variation among commentators, but the list of psalms of *trust* usually include 4, 16, 23, 27, 62, 90, 115, 118, and 123–126, and feature both individual and collective voices. The most common elements of a psalm of trust are expressions of assurance in the midst of turmoil, replete with metaphors for God such as *fortress* or *refuge*, often an indication of the verbal assaults or looming invasions faced by these psalmists. A brief glance at Psalm 62 reveals each of these elements at work: God is referred to as "my rock" and a citadel, there is a rhetorical address to those miscreants who delight in falsehood and seek to assail their victims, and the poet concludes by imploring the community to invest their hope in God rather than be driven to despair by human schemes of duplicity, for in the end all people are judged according to their deeds (v. 12). In terms of the structure of the Psalter, Psalm 62 occurs in Book II, but there are no psalms of trust in Book III, which, as noted previously, has a higher proportion of laments as the community grapples with the darkness of exile.

The most famous example of a psalm of *trust* is Psalm 23, a useful illustration of the genre that evocatively affirms that even in the most fearful of places there can be guidance and direction through the *shepherd*. Alongside striking and memorable images is a more subtle shift from "he" to the highly personal "you" that is integral to the structure of Psalm 23: discourses *about* God in the first and third parts are offset in the middle with an address *to* God, adding an unmistakable dimension of individuality to the shepherd who cares about the needs of every sheep.[21] Well-known texts in the Hebrew Bible about *shepherds* include David's own oration in 1 Sam 17:34–35 about aggressive protection ("Your servant used to keep sheep for his father. And when there came a lion, or a bear, and took a lamb from the flock, I went after

---

[21] As Marc Brettler, *Jewish Study Bible*, 2nd edition (New York: Oxford University Press, 2014), 1307 remarks, "*Shepherd* is a frequent biblical and ancient Near Eastern metaphor for royalty (Isa. 40.11; Ezek. 34; Ps. 80). This is the case with David (and Moses); the Babylonian king Hammurabi is called 'the shepherd' (*ANET*, p. 164)."

him and struck him and delivered it out of his mouth. And if he arose against me, I caught him by his beard and struck him and killed him"), while Ezekiel 34:12 presents a vision of the shepherd as a leader who rescues and accompanies the flock ("As a shepherd seeks out his flock when he is among his sheep that have been scattered, so will I seek out my sheep, and I will rescue them from all places where they have been scattered on a day of clouds and thick darkness").[22] The superscription of Psalm 23 labels it a *mizmor* (perhaps "song" or "melody") in the David tradition:

> [1] The Lord is my shepherd,
>     I will not lack.
> [2] In fresh meadows he makes me recline,
>     Beside still waters he leads me.
> [3] My soul he restores,
>     He guides me along sure paths of righteousness,
>         for his name's sake.
> [4] Even though I walk through the valley of death's shadow,
>     I do not fear evil, because you are with me.
>         Your scepter and your staff, *they* give me courage.
> [5] You arrange a table before me in the presence of my adversaries,
>     You soothe my head with oil, my cup flows over.
> [6] Indeed, goodness and faithfulness will pursue after me,
>     all the days of my life.
>         For into the house of the Lord I can return forever.

For many contemporary readers, the idea of a *shepherd* evokes mental pictures that may or may not be in line with the poet's sensibility in

---

[22] Note the introduction to Psalm 23 in DeClaissé-Walford, Jacobson, and Tanner, *The Book of Psalms*, 138: "As with many psalms of trust, a striking feature is the psalm's tacit acknowledgment of the presence of danger. In Psalm 27, the threat of enemies is named. In Psalm 46, the threats of raging chaos and roaring nations are named. Here, the threatening presence of *the darkest valley* is named. But the fear-evoking danger of that presence is more than balanced by the courage-providing, fear-removing presence of the Lord. This is the true setting of the psalm: the existential space of being in the presence of something that is terrifying, a space in which every reflective human being finds himself or herself at some point, and a space in which, according to the witness of the poem, the Lord can also be found."

Psalm 23. Thus, numerous scholars default to the image of the shepherd as a powerful king, which is certainly plausible in this context. For one commentator, however, the poetry is straightforward and beautiful: "Although the likening of God or a ruler to a shepherd is a commonplace in this pastoral culture, this psalm is justly famous for the affecting simplicity and concreteness with which it realizes the metaphor. Thus, in the next line the shepherd leads his sheep to meadows where there is abundant grass and riverbanks and where quiet waters run that the sheep can drink."[23] In Psalm 23 the images combine to paint a picture of a shepherd who guides the sheep to a destination: even though the way might be perilous, the paths of righteousness are going somewhere. The endgame is an intact arrival at a place where a table is set, and eventually the destination is the safest and surest location in the cosmos—the sanctuary of the Lord—where the believer can dwell for a length of days without limit. So Psalm 23 is about a journey and how a reliable God enables the sojourner to arrive safely at the greatest place of rest.

Divine *leading* is a key movement in Psalm 23, as the flock is not abandoned nor reduced to aimless wandering: "The sheep are not left to their own devices but are led by God himself to take the correct path—the one that gets the sheep where they need to go."[24] The path, however, traverses a dark valley fraught with the specter of death. One can imagine that there are moments when the sheep are hardly even aware that they are being (capably) led, given the treacherousness of their journey. The spatial setting of the *valley* is debated by scholars, but a number suggest a new word is coined here, one that combines *shadow* with *death*. The fearfulness of the sojourn may well blind the flock to the character of the one who leads even through the darkness, and this psalm of trust provides a glimpse of the God who is present even if the sheep are oblivious.

In terms of a date of composition, some commentators suggest that Psalm 23 was written in the aftermath of the temple's destruction in 586 BCE (see 2 Kings 25) and poetically unfolds a kind of new exodus journey: in this interpretation, the "flock" is the remnant in Babylon

---

[23] Alter, *The Book of Psalms*, 78.
[24] Wilson, *Psalms Volume 1*, 433.

who are then led through the darkest valley in the long march back to Jerusalem, where they find repose in the rebuilt city of Jerusalem and the restored temple as the center of communal worship.[25] Such an interpretation does have some currency, but the images could just as well apply to the first exodus out of Egyptian slavery and eventually to the Jerusalem temple; after all, the same verbs for *lead* and *guide* occur in Exod 15:13 ("You have *led* in your steadfast love the people whom you have redeemed; you have *guided* them by your strength to your holy place"). In the end, the images are supple and powerful enough to apply to any individual's life journey. Perhaps the best interpretive strategy is to keep Psalm 23 versatile and open-ended, which may well account for its popularity as a classic even today in a wide variety of circles. As an example of a psalm of trust, its very suppleness allows for readers across the ages to be immersed in the same qualities of confidence in divine leading despite real obstacles and terrors. The fact that Psalm 23 occurs relatively early in the Psalter—at roughly the halfway point of Book I—suggests that such lessons need to be kept in mind throughout the entire sojourn of life.

## The Path of Wisdom

Early in his reign, the newly crowned King Solomon had an inimitable experience: God appeared to him in a dream and invited him to ask for whatever he wanted (1 Kings 3:5–15), and in the end God gave him a *wise and discerning mind*. No doubt many people in the same situation would opt for physical health (and long life) or material prosperity (with all the power that riches may bring), but Solomon's choice of wisdom is certainly the correct one in this context. This episode in 1 Kings illustrates that wisdom is a gift, but a gift that needs to be cultivated by the recipient. Throughout the ancient world wisdom was desired by citizens of all nations, and certainly among the people of

---

[25] For example, Michael L. Barré and John S. Kselman, "New Exodus, Covenant, and Restoration in Psalm 23," in *The Word of the Lord Shall Go Forth: D. N. Freedman Festschrift*, ed. Carol L. Meyers and M. O'Connor (Winona Lake, IN: Eisenbrauns, 1983), 97–127.

Israel as well. Wisdom (*hokmah*) includes not only technical expertise and administrative skill but also the ability to make the optimal moral choices and ethical decisions.

The book of Psalms is located in the third section of the Hebrew Bible, as part of the "Writings" and wisdom literature, and therefore it is not surprising that a number of psalms (the list usually includes 1, 32, 37, 49, 73, 112, 119, 127, 128, 133, and 139) address topics that are generally associated with the wisdom tradition in ancient Israel; that is, they are concerned with matters such as discernment, ethical living, exercising sound judgment in every area of life, and cultivating the fear of God and reverence for the Torah. Consider Psalm 139, as it starts with "O Lord, you have searched me and known me. You know when I sit down and when I rise up; you discern my thoughts from far away. You search out my path and my lying down, and are acquainted with all my ways." Near the middle is an oft-quoted line about being *fearfully and wonderfully made*, followed later by the not as oft-quoted line about desiring that God kill one's enemies, before Psalm 139 ends in v. 24 with the petition "See if there is any wicked way in me, and lead me in the way everlasting." It could be said that *wisdom psalms* poetically probe Israel's wisdom tradition and open doors of perception about the best way to live and the optimal pathways to pursue: "God created the world and life, and placed order in it, and God continues to sustain and govern that order. The task of humans is to seek and find that order and live into it."[26] The strategic disbursement of wisdom psalms throughout the Psalter and at such key junctures as the beginning of Book I and Book III suggests that every generation of God's people requires wisdom in order to live well.

The longest and most complex example of a psalm of instruction— indeed, the longest composition in the entire Psalter—is Psalm 119. Like a number of other poems in the book, Psalm 119 has an *acrostic* structure, and in this case each of the twenty-two eight-line stanzas begin with a successive letter of the Hebrew alphabet.[27] A dominant theme is the capacity of the law to direct readers to the good life, and as one scholar notes, Psalm 119 has a sonnet-like intricacy: "[T]he

---

[26] Brueggemann and Bellinger, *Psalms*, 584.
[27] Other acrostic psalms are 25, 34, 37, 111, 112, and 145.

66 THE PSALMS

skill of the poet in composing this tour de force has been appreciated. For example, there are eight main words used for 'torah' (their English translations include: word, law, commandment, rules, decree, precepts, teaching), corresponding to the eight-fold acrostic; approximately 176 of these synonyms are found in the 176 vv. of the psalm (noted as early as Ibn Ezra and Radak)."[28] Altogether the psalm is too long for us to consider in its entirety, but here is one stanza near the midpoint:

> [105] Your word is a lamp for my foot,
> A light for my pathway.
> [106] I swore an oath, then I confirmed it:
> To keep your righteous decisions.
> [107] I am so very weak,
> Revive my life, O Lord, according to your word.
> [108] Be pleased with the voluntary offerings of my mouth, O Lord,
> Teach me your decisions.
> [109] My life is always in my hands,
> But your law I do not forget.
> [110] The wicked set a trap for me,
> But I do not wander from your precepts.
> [111] I have inherited your testimonies forever,
> They really are my heart's joy.
> [112] I incline my heart to perform your statutes,
> Forever, to the very end.

Psalm 119 did not fare particularly well with a previous generation of commentators. Even a brief survey of secondary literature reveals several works that use the word *boring*, and one critic is particularly unsubtle in his evisceration of this longest of psalms: "Tedious repetitions, poor thought-sequence, apparent lack of inspiration reflect the artificiality of the composition."[29] It would be a stronger argument if Psalm 119 actually contained a series of legal disquisitions or references to the sacrificial system or dietary restrictions or clothing regulations, but such material is absent. Instead, there is a cascade

---

[28] Brettler, *Jewish Study Bible*, 1415.
[29] Cited in McCann, "Book of Psalms," 1166.

of internal struggles, desires, prayers, and nuanced descriptions of deep-seated opposition that the poet faces. To be sure there are some repetitions over the course of 176 lines, but a closer look at even the single stanza quoted above—where all eight lines begin with *nun*, the fourteenth letter of the Hebrew alphabet—reveals there is much more going on.

At least two general remarks can be made. First, the above stanza begins with one of the more famous lines in the Psalter, as the poet personally affirms that God's word is a light and a lamp on the pathway of life. Indeed, such guidance and illumination are sorely needed throughout the period of suffering that is mentioned in v. 107, so even in the darkest times of affliction and trauma the divine word can chart a course through the wilderness. Second, one could translate v. 111 as "I have claimed your testimonies as my eternal possession" and suggest that the language is similar to those passages in Deuteronomy and Joshua where the Israelites are enjoined to take possession of the land of Canaan as their inheritance. Just as each family is given land that represents a future for their descendants, so the testimonies of the law represent an eternal future (or portion) for the psalmist. As one group of scholars summarize, "In Psalm 119, then, the instruction of Yahweh is not presented as a strict set of rules and regulations, but a way of life or approach to being that brings one closer to God."[30] Psalms of wisdom are correspondingly designed to inspire confidence in the way of the Torah despite internal struggles or external arguments and enticements to the contrary.

Alongside instruction and reverence for divine revelation, wisdom psalms also provide an opportunity for philosophical reflection within

---

[30] DeClaissé-Walford, Jacobson, and Tanner, *The Book of Psalms*, 886. Interacting with the work of the German theologian Dietrich Bonhoeffer (1906–1945), Goldingay (*Psalms*, vol. 3: *Psalms 90–150*, 304) remarks, "The need to guard my way indicates that there are pressures not to walk this way. It is easy to stray. One pressure is the strange fact that not everyone enthuses over the wonders embodied in this teaching. Many people resist it. They like making up their own minds about how to live their lives. (They do not want to confine their worship to Yhwh alone, or to abjure worship by means of images, or to keep the Sabbath. . . .) That in its own right causes me to be overcome by strong feelings, both sadness and rage. And people attack and scorn and misrepresent those who press the importance of Yhwh's teaching. Thus whereas the psalm begins by declaring the good fortune of people of integrity, it goes on to complain about the oppression and sufferings of the righteous."

the Psalter, especially about the problems of evil and suffering. To be sure, searching questions about human life occupy a significant portion of the Writings: the first word of Ecclesiastes is *vanity* (*hebel*; the same term that occurs in Ps 144:4, "*adam* is like a *vapor*"), thus introducing a long reflection on the fleetingness of human achievement, while Lamentations is a sophisticated poetic elegy on the catastrophe of Jerusalem's invasion ("For your ruin is as vast as the sea, who can heal you?," 2:13). Among the most pressing existential questions revolves around apparent *injustice*: Why is it, numerous biblical texts ask, the righteous frequently suffer while the impious appear to be immune from any immediate consequences for their actions? This question is raised not only in the Wisdom literature of the Old Testament (e.g., Job 21:7, "Why do the wicked live on, reach old age, and grow mighty in power?") but also in the Prophets. For instance, Malachi 3:14–15 is worth considering: "You have said, 'It is vain to serve God. What is the profit of our keeping his charge or of walking as in mourning before the Lord of hosts? And now we call the arrogant blessed! Evildoers not only prosper but they put God to the test and they escape.'"[31]

The question of injustice and the *flourishing wicked* is approached in a different way in Psalm 73. Due to its location near the center of the Psalter, a number of commentators suggest that this lengthy composition presents a pivot point of some significance to the larger theology of the book of Psalms. Psalm 73 begins with a traditional affirmation of faith—*Truly God is good to Israel*—before the poet subjects that

---

[31] Discussed in Terrien, *The Psalms*, 530. A more extended and personal example can be found in Jeremiah 12, as the prophet experiences acute frustration when it is revealed that his own inner circle is treacherously plotting his demise. With brutal honesty and pained anguish, the prophet addresses his complaint squarely to God: "You are always righteous, Lord, when I bring a case before you. Yet I would speak with you about your justice: Why does the way of the wicked prosper? Why do all the faithless live at ease?" As Jer 12:1–4 unfolds, the prophet laments that criminals "produce fruit," whereas he languishes, and the reader straight away notes a contrasting isolation: Jeremiah feels utterly alone, whereas the faithless are a teeming multitude. Notably, God responds directly to the prophet's grievance with a long oracle beginning in v. 5, not so much a response to the compliant of injustice as a challenge to continue the "race" and not give up. Instead of an argument about theodicy, God provides further warnings about exile and the promises of restoration in the distant future, most certainly beyond the prophet's lifespan.

affirmation to the highest scrutiny in the first part of the psalm.[32] Consider the first half in the ESV rendering:

> [1] Truly God is good to Israel, to those who are pure in heart.
> [2] But as for me, my feet had almost stumbled, my steps had nearly slipped.
> [3] For I was envious of the arrogant when I saw the prosperity of the wicked.
> [4] For they have no pangs until death; their bodies are fat and sleek.
> [5] They are not in trouble as others are; they are not stricken like the rest of mankind.
> [6] Therefore pride is their necklace; violence covers them as a garment.
> [7] Their eyes swell out through fatness; their hearts overflow with follies.
> [8] They scoff and speak with malice; loftily they threaten oppression.
> [9] They set their mouths against the heavens, and their tongue struts through the earth.
> [10] Therefore his people turn back to them, and find no fault in them.
> [11] And they say, "How can God know? Is there knowledge in the Most High?"
> [12] Behold, these are the wicked; always at ease, they increase in riches.
> [13] All in vain have I kept my heart clean and washed my hands in innocence.
> [14] For all the day long I have been stricken and rebuked every morning.
> [15] If I had said, "I will speak thus," I would have betrayed the generation of your children.

---

[32] The NRSV has a different rendering of the opening clause, although there is no textual warrant: "Truly God is good *to the upright*." A major problem with this rendering, in my view, is that it obscures the corporate dimension of the psalm. To be sure, Psalm 73 is a personal journey of testing the tradition, but that very tradition is God's revelation to the people of Israel, and we imagine that the poet has heard this particular affirmation about God's *goodness to Israel* from infancy. Because the subject of Psalm 73 is whether or not such an affirmation stands up to reality, the NRSV risks losing this dimension, and hence the ESV translation is to be preferred.

Instead of detached philosophical thinking, in Psalm 73 there is a *story* about mounting frustration because of the success of the faithless. Not only is the psalmist angry and alienated by this injustice, but such observations caused a change in direction to the point that the poet's feet nearly slipped—nearly lost the plot, so to speak—while venturing on this new path. A complete derailing almost took place because the poet looked around at all the wicked who were apparently happy and carefree, and *jealousy* was aroused. In our contemporary world the temptations of envy are legion and no doubt range from Hollywood blockbusters to the trendiest social media of the moment. Evidently the ancient world carried its own set of allurements, and the inventory of the wicked behavior traits in Psalm 73 is telling. Habits of the evildoers' hearts include a laissez-faire attitude buoyed by healthy and well-fed bodies, a wardrobe that includes prestige as a necklace and garments of viciousness, along with scheming minds restlessly in search of their next target. Moreover, their speech patterns in vv. 9 and 11 carry a mocking assertiveness, and, what is most vexing for the poet, there is no immediate punishment meted out to them. The following summary captures several major points:

> The psalmist is thoroughly grounded in the Torah teaching that God's blessing comes to those who obey Torah. The life of Torah obedience, however, is restrictive and out of keeping with more attractive social options that focus on the satiation of the self. Verses 2–4 provide a rumination on the seductive alternative to Torah obedience that is so dramatically on exhibit in the lives of "the wicked, the arrogant" (v. 3). They know none of the restrictions of a life of Torah but live in their self-indulgent freedom. They are full of themselves, enjoy good health, and in general are cynical toward the old restrictions of Torah (v. 11). The speaker, moreover, having discerned the attractive power of the alternative, almost fell into that alternative (v. 2); he entertained the thought that the rigors of Torah obedience are "in vain" (v. 13). The psalmist is sorely tempted to give up Torah faith for this attractive alternative.[33]

---

[33] Brueggemann and Bellinger, *Psalms*, 318.

To further the last point, the poet's self-characterization in vv. 12–15 merits some attention, as there is a personal contrast with the faithless: they are basking in luxury and free of disease, whereas the poet has maintained purity and discipline *for nothing*, perceiving the effort as a complete waste of time. According to Psalm 1, the way of the wicked will perish, but the poet of Psalm 73 feels that he or she is the only one who is perishing. The poet keeps quiet about such thoughts, lest others among the family of the faithful be led astray (or perhaps out of an unwillingness to admit that envy has taken root). However, there is a decisive turning point, and the second half of Psalm 73 (vv. 16–28) has a radically different feel:

> [16] But when I thought how to understand this, it seemed to me a wearisome task,
> [17] until I went into the sanctuary of God; then I discerned their end.
> [18] Truly you set them in slippery places; you make them fall to ruin.
> [19] How they are destroyed in a moment, swept away utterly by terrors!
> [20] Like a dream when one awakes, O Lord, when you rouse yourself, you despise them as phantoms.
> [21] When my soul was embittered, when I was pricked in heart,
> [22] I was brutish and ignorant; I was like a beast toward you.
> [23] Nevertheless, I am continually with you, you hold my right hand.
> [24] You guide me with your counsel, and afterward you will receive me to glory.
> [25] Whom have I in heaven but you? And there is nothing on earth that I desire besides you.
> [26] My flesh and my heart may fail, but God is the strength of my heart and my portion forever.
> [27] For behold, those who are far from you shall perish; you put an end to everyone who is unfaithful to you.
> [28] But for me it is good to be near God; I have made the Lord God my refuge, that I may tell of all your works.

The poet was frustrated with the profitability of lawlessness in vv. 3–11 and frustrated with attempts to understand all this through natural reason in v. 16, and is wearied out by the process. Yet a transformation occurs through a comparatively uncomplicated action: the poet enters the holy places of God (*miqdeshê-ʾēl*) and there receives life-changing revelation. Scholars have varying views on the precise meaning of this phrase, the most common interpretation being the Jerusalem temple (and therefore the plural *places* would indicate the quality of the place, akin to Psalm 84). In this case, Psalm 73 would most likely be a preexilic composition. Alternatively, *the holy places of God* might refer to a number of sites where the people of God gather to worship and study the Torah, any number of avenues to come in contact with divine revelation. In this case, Psalm 73 would fit naturally in an exilic or postexilic setting.

Regardless of how the phrase is finally interpreted, it is in the spatial setting of the holy places of God that the poet is acquainted with the final end of the evildoers, a revelatory insight that becomes the theological fulcrum of the psalm. Despite appearances to the contrary, the poet discovers that the path of the lawless is precipitous, and certain doom awaits. After receiving the revelatory insight, there is a lengthy confession from the poet, who in v. 22 admits to acting like a beast toward God.[34] Later in our study we will analyze the larger organization of the Psalter and evaluate the thesis that there is a movement in the 150 psalms that transitions from *petition* to *praise*. Located at the halfway point of the book, Psalm 73 itself illustrates how the transition from complaint to wholehearted worship might take place in the memorable story of an individual's journey from resentment to revelation.[35]

In this chapter a sample of the variety of genres in the book of Psalms has been canvassed, and several other categories can be encountered as

---

[34] McCann, "Book of Psalms," 970 has some cogent reflections on the larger implications of this psalm for the life of faith: "Given the psalmist's initial dilemma (vv. 2–3) and the elaboration of it in vv. 13–14, we must reflect on the concept of reward and punishment. The psalmist almost lost faith, because he or she thought that good behavior should be materially rewarded; but it was not (vv. 13–14). What the psalmist came to realize is that true goodness, happiness, and peace consist of a different kind of reward—the experience of God's presence (vv. 23–28)." McCann concludes, "In a sense, faithful behavior (vv. 1, 13) is its own reward; it is rewarding, not because it earns God's favor, but because it derives from and expresses the power and presence of God in our lives, individually (vv. 25–26, 28) and corporately (v. 15)."

[35] On the strategic placement, see further Walter Brueggemann and Patrick D. Miller, "Psalm 73 as a Canonical Marker," *JSOT* 72 (1996): 45–56.

readers work through the Psalter. For example, Psalm 15 could be classified as a *temple* psalm ("O Lord, who can sojourn in your tent? Who can abide on your holy hill?"), and some might argue that it represents an ancient entrance liturgy to be prayed by people preparing for worship in the vicinity of the tabernacle or the Jerusalem temple. A *song of praise* is another genre, and a good example is Psalm 146 ("I will praise the Lord as long as I live, I will sing praises to my God while I have my being"), located near the end. Probably the most controversial category is the *psalm of imprecation* (e.g., Ps 58:6, "O God, break the teeth in their mouths, tear out the fangs of the young lions") that will be discussed later in our study. Similarly, in the next chapter *historical psalms* are our subject, a special genre that merits its own sustained treatment.

The five popular genres of *royal, creation, lament, trust*, and *wisdom* psalms do cover a sizable percentage of the Psalter, and I would suggest that the various genres of psalms are intentionally arrayed throughout the book. Much like a popular Broadway musical such as *Hamilton* combines and fuses a number of different musical genres in service of the overarching narrative, so it is with the Psalms: all sorts of genres are employed in the service of a larger story. Or, akin to a movie soundtrack, the Psalms provide an orchestral score that accompanies the story of Israel's experiment with monarchy; even though that experiment is a climactic failure, the music of divine grace can be heard in the background and gradually assumes center stage as the Psalter reaches its crescendo. Consequently, we can further explore how the book of Psalms is a soundtrack about grace that overcomes adversity in the long sojourn of Israel's descendants, a story that is further illuminated as we consider *historical* psalms in the next chapter.

# 4
# Israel's Story in the Psalms

Whether reading the "Funeral Oration of Pericles" in the history of Thucydides or *The Wasteland* by T. S. Eliot in the previous century, it is frequently the case that ancient and modern literary works were composed for specific occasions or as a response to a prevailing cultural situation or worldview.[1] It could be maintained that similar premises motivate the poetry in much of the book of Psalms, and that Israelite songwriters produced various compositions in order to invite the community to *re*imagine important events and to highlight the experience of a particular occasion or perhaps as an imaginative option to a prevailing ideology or belief system. Furthermore, as discussed in the preceding chapter, scholars tend to identify various *genres* of psalms based on shared characteristics and recognizable traits. Although there is certainly not a consensus by any means and any urge to be excessively taxonomic is best avoided, it is nonetheless helpful to appreciate the form taken by any group of psalms.

Another genre for us to consider is usually called the *historical psalms*. Throughout the book of Psalms there are occasions when core elements—or a sequence of episodes—from Israel's national history are poetically represented. Four different kinds of examples are surveyed in this chapter: Psalms 114, 78, 105, and 137. As we proceed, there are several kinds of interconnected elements that are of interest: some of the literary techniques (such as parallelism, irony, or wordplay) that are used in the historical psalms, the overall message of a given psalm when its entirety is considered, and ideas about *why* a particular historical psalm may have been composed and preserved and how it might have been used in ancient Israel's social setting. Also

---

[1] See William Empson, *Seven Types of Ambiguity* (London: Chatto and Windus, 1949), xiii: "Good poetry is usually written from a background of conflict, though no doubt more so in some periods than in others."

included will be a few reflections about the contribution of historical poetry to the drama of the Psalter.

## Seismic Shift

Placed near the beginning of Book V, Psalm 114 is framed by the defining event of Israel's departure from Egypt and subsequent journey through the wilderness toward the land of Canaan: "In a single verse, an entire historical narrative is encapsulated; the psalmist marks the beginning and the end of the exodus and the wilderness wandering, the single most formative period in the life of ancient Israel."[2] The poetic compression in Psalm 114 is notable: with only a handful of words and utilizing repetition and semantic range, the poet creates some striking effects on a relatively limited canvas. Owing to the use of this psalm as part of a Passover liturgy in emerging Judaism, scholars often posit an early date for the psalm and closely identify it with the celebration of deliverance from Egypt.[3] Alternatively, it could be argued that the psalm is probably written after the exile of 586 BCE and that the poet has in view a return from Babylonian captivity while using images from the exodus and wilderness wandering. Thus, key historical memories of the past become programmatic for a later generation.

> [1] When Israel came out from Egypt,
>   Jacob's house from a barbaric-tongued people,
> [2] Judah became its sacred place,
>   Israel its domain.
> [3] The Sea looked, and fled,
>   The Jordan turned around,

---

[2] DeClaissé-Walford, Jacobson, and Tanner, *The Book of Psalms*, 509. See also Alter, *The Book of Psalms*, 405: "It is unusual for a biblical poem to begin in this way with a subordinate clause (doubled, with the verb elided, in the second verse), given the strong predominance of parallel independent clauses (parataxis) in this body of literature. It is a strategy for sweeping us up from the beginning of the poem in a narrative momentum that invokes but also goes beyond the story of the exodus."

[3] Elizabeth Hayes, "The Unity of the Egyptian Hallel: Psalms 113–18," *BBR* 9 (1999): 145: "The 'Egyptian Hallel' (Psalms 113–18) has been a significant component of Jewish festival liturgy since the Tannaitic period, and it continues to hold a place of honor in contemporary Passover celebrations."

⁴ The mountains skipped like rams,
   The hills like sheep!
⁵ What is with you, O Sea, that you flee,
   O Jordan, that you turn around?
⁶ O mountains, that you skip like rams,
   O hills, like sheep?
⁷ Shake, O earth, before the Master,
   Before the God of Jacob,
⁸ The one who turns the rock into a water-pool,
   The hard stone into a fountain of water!

At the dramatic high point of the narrative of Israel's departure from Egyptian slavery in Exodus 14, there is considerable focus on Egypt's army. With the Israelites seemingly trapped by the waters in front of them, Pharaoh and his horde maniacally pursue the fugitives, intent on recovering their labor force. But just as their prey are firmly in sight, Pharaoh's army is on the wrong end of a divine intervention, finally drowned in a stunning twist of fate: earlier in Exodus 1 the Egyptians tried to destroy Israelite males by drowning, only to be drowned themselves in the waters of the Red Sea. Even though the same event is ostensibly in view in Psalm 114, there is no focus on the army of Pharaoh, which seems to be deliberately ignored. In fact, the enemy from whom Israel escapes has an interesting description in v. 1: instead of stressing liberation from slave masters, the psalmist emphasizes that Israel marches away from a people of strange speech.⁴ The noun for "strange speech" (*lōʿēz*) occurs only here in the Hebrew Bible, a situation that scholars refer to as a *hapax legomena*. In the Greek Septuagint tradition, the term is rendered *barbaros*, and I am following that with my translation of *barbaric-tongued*. We notice, then, a certain linguistic irony, as an obscure word is here used for a people of obscure language. Furthermore, there is a larger thematic field of reference when other texts are considered, as "comments about oppressors with a strange language usually come in connection with foreign invasion (e.g., Deut.

---

⁴ Hendrick Bosman, "Psalm 114 as Reinterpretation of the Exodus during and after the Exile," *OTE* 26 (2013): 559.

28:49; Isa. 28:11; Jer. 5:15). Perhaps the exodus is here portrayed in light of that experience, so that the reader makes a link between the Egyptians and its current overlords."[5] This is the first of several hints that we are dealing with a later rather than an earlier composition, and one that has a return from Babylonian deportation in view.

As discussed earlier in this book, a standard feature of Hebrew poetry is *parallelism*.[6] Instead of a rhyming of sound—as often found in English verse—biblical poetry features a rhyming of images or ideas. The most straightforward and common example in Hebrew poetry is *semantic* parallelism, as seen in the opening of Psalm 114: "When Israel came forth from Egypt//Jacob's house from a people of barbaric speech." Here *Israel* is functionally equivalent to *Jacob's house*, and there is a roughly synonymous relationship from one half-line to the next. But as scholars duly point out, Hebrew poetry is almost always more dynamic, and rather the synonymous repetition we often encounter a heightening or intensification from one line to the next. Indeed, the other elements in the opening of Psalm 114 illustrate the point: *Egypt* in the first half-line is enhanced with *barbaric-tongued people* in the next half-line. The notion of rhyming ideas should not be pressed too far, as it is only one basic part of a more complex literary operation. Indeed, the movement from Egypt to people of barbaric speech nicely illustrates that parallelism is far from static. Egypt is surely understood as a place of misery and oppression in Israel's history, but the poetic elaboration in Ps 114:1 highlights the linguistic dislocation during the period of slavery. In other words, the poet also

---

[5] Goldingay, *Psalms*, vol. 3: *Psalms 90–150*, 215.

[6] Cf. Tod Linafelt, "The Pentateuch," in *The Oxford Handbook of English Literature and Theology*, ed. Andrew Hass, David Jasper, and Elisabeth Jay (Oxford: Oxford University Press, 2009), 216; "[T]he most salient characteristic of ancient Hebrew poetry, what allows us in fact to call it poetry, is present, namely parallelism. That is, a line of Hebrew biblical poetry is composed of usually two, but sometimes three, short segments or cola placed in parallel relationship to each other. . . . In the most obvious form of this parallelism the second colon will correspond both semantically and syntactically to the previous. Thus, in the line from Moses' victory song in Exod. 15, 'Your right hand, O Lord, is mighty in power. | Your right hand, O Lord, smashes the enemy,' every element from the first half of the line is matched in the second half of the line. But clearly the ancient poets felt a good deal of freedom in articulating the parallelism of the line, as work in recent decades by Robert Alter, Adele Berlin, and James Kugel have made clear, and it is only rarely that one encounters the sort of strict phrase-by-phrase parallelism that we see above."

stresses that Israel experienced a kind of intellectual and social captivity that accompanied their physical servitude.

In Psalm 114 the varieties of parallelism are used by the poet to generate momentum from line to line, as the Israelites move out of Egypt and toward the land of promise. Usually more than mere synonyms, the interplay between the various lines in this psalm has a particular effect: for an audience aware of the lineaments of the story, there is a new significance attached to the familiar because the psalmist emphasizes that arrival into the land is just as momentous as departure from Egypt. Alongside parallelism, there are other poetic features in the psalm, such as *personification*. Addressing the Sea and the mountains as though they were animate beings, the poem dramatizes their reaction to the Israelites' journey toward the land where God established dominion and sanctuary. Not only have the Israelites been released from slavery, but their entrance into Canaan has implications for the entire created world. Moreover, *rhetorical questions* are posed in a serious tone, expecting the obvious answer that the Sea and the mountains are aware that the Israelites are no ordinary people group and the God who leads them has earth-quaking power. The rhetorical questions—perhaps in the manner of a victor addressing the vanquished—are enhanced with the final images of the poem about turning rocks into fountains of water. In contrast to translations such as the NASB or NKJV, the concluding participle should not be rendered as a past event ("Who turned the rock") but rather more actively, "The one who turns the rock into a water-pool." Psalm 114 ends on a note of possibility and affirms that, far from merely ancient history, such divine activity could well be a present-tense reality again.

The active participle in the last line of Psalm 114 provides a strong hint about the exilic origins and audience for this poem. Images of *water* and *rock* are familiar from the account of Israel in the wilderness, although it is most infamously associated with rebellion and striking in Numbers 20. As it turns out, there is a more specific intersection of language between Psalm 114 and other texts that speak about a return from exile to the land of Israel at the end of captivity. For instance, commentators point to Isa 41:18, a daring oracle with affinities to Psalm 114: "I will open rivers on the bare heights, and fountains in the midst of the valleys; I will make the wilderness a pool of water, and the dry land springs of water" (NRSV). Adele Berlin argues that the specific language in the psalm indicates that a return from exile is in view: "These terms are not used in the exodus/wilderness tradition in the Torah; they are, rather, among the terms describing how God can turn parched land into well-watered land (Isa 35:7, 41:18, Ps 74:13–15, 107:35), in poetry speaking about the return—another support for the idea that the unstated topic in our verse is traversing the wilderness for the return."[7] In this case, the poet is deploying well-known images from Israel's past to rekindle hope for a new generation in the future, for just as God dispensed water in the desert on the march out of Egypt, so God can transform hard rock into fountains on the long from Babylon back to the land of promise.[8]

Attempting to locate the time and circumstances of a psalm's composition is not meant to restrict or finalize its meaning. On the contrary, discussion about a psalm's origins can help the reader better appreciate its contribution to the larger book and its longer term significance.[9] Psalm 114 takes celebrated images from Israel's collective memory and poetically redeploys them—similar to the strategy in passages such as Isaiah 40–55 and elsewhere—for a new situation in the exile and beyond: "[T]he sequence serves to encourage the oppressed people of God in any age, as well as to give them words to articulate their faith in and praise for God's ongoing story with God's people."[10] Moreover, it could be noted that during the period of exile, those citizens of Judah

---

[7] Adele Berlin, "The Message of Psalm 114," in *Birkat Shalom: Studies in the Bible, Ancient Near Eastern Literature, and Postbiblical Judaism Presented to Shalom M. Paul on the Occasion of His Seventieth Birthday*, ed. Chaim Cohen, Victor Avigdor Hurowitz, Avi Hurvitz, Yochanan Muffs, Baruch J. Schwartz, and Jeffrey H. Tigay (Winona Lake, IN: Eisenbrauns, 2008), 355–356; cf. Goldingay, *Psalms*, vol. 3: *Psalms 90–150*, 216–217: "Yhwh did not merely produce water out of the rock but turned the rock into water, and not just into water but into a pool and a spring. Further, 'pool of water' and 'spring' suggest the transformation involved in the restoration from exile in Babylon (Isa. 41:18). And alongside the overt (though unusual) exhortation in v. 7, the line implies a covert exhortation, a challenge to the congregation to hope in this God."

[8] Bosman, "Psalm 114 as Reinterpretation of the Exodus during and after the Exile," 571: "The combination of elements of the exodus and creation traditions in both Isa 40 to 55 and Ps 114 enabled the emergence of new metaphors that rejuvenated the theological traditions in question and generated new expectations of the future."

[9] For those curious, see Jeffrey Einboden, "The Homeric Psalm: Milton's Translation of Psalm 114 and the Problems of 'Hellenistic Scripture,'" *Literature & Theology* 17 (2003): 314–323.

[10] McCann, "Book of Psalms," 1141.

who were left behind by the Babylonians were sorely tempted—and indeed many succumbed—to seek refuge in Egypt. The land of the Nile was notorious for offering Israelites the illusion of security, and so it is not a stretch to imagine that Psalm 114 may have been used as a kind of poetic warning to the community about seeking alternative sources of water and security in a land of foreign speech. Thus, as we will continue to discuss, historical psalms were not driven by purely antiquarian interests but have an immediate relevance and vitality.

## The Riddle

In some famous works of world literature, *riddles* occur at pivotal moments in the plot. For instance, Shakespeare's *The Merchant of Venice* features three caskets emblazoned with puzzling inscriptions placed before Portia's suitors to determine a worthy match for the heiress: the gold casket warns about judging matters solely on the basis of beauty or external appearance, the silver one invites reflection about self-worth and entitlement, while the lead casket ("Who chooseth me must give and hazard all he hath") hints at hard work and sacrifice. Portia's deceased father devised this series of riddles as a challenge, and so when Bassanio opts for the lead casket, he is rewarded with an intelligent and talented wife—although the drama is far from over.

Not only is Psalm 78 the second-longest poem in the book (after Psalm 119), but it is also presented as a *riddle*. In the opening verses the poet speaks directly to the people of Israel, inviting them to listen to a unique kind of history education: "I will open my mouth with a parable, I will belch out riddles from ancient times." But Psalm 78 is not just a boring list of moments from the distant past. Instead, the endgame of the psalm is to provide an immersive experience in the famous events of national tradition to influence one's view of the future. A poetic stream of images is organized into a meaningful pattern, and this rebooting of Israel's history encourages a later audience to learn from the past by internalizing earlier mistakes and missteps of their ancestors—along with God's consistent forgiveness—to forge hope for tomorrow. As we will see, the riddle of Psalm 78 does not have an answer; rather, *it asks a question*.

The psalm has a three-part structure, beginning with the prologue in vv. 1–11. The opening lines of the prologue emphasize the importance of knowing the past and the perils of forgetting. Hence the poet intends to belch forth—admittedly a graphic translation—riddles of the past in order to inspire later generations with the wonders and mysteries of God's actions. Even if Israel's history is littered with catastrophe, new chapters of the story can be written. A key theme of Psalm 78 is that divine miracles are too often followed by rebellions that have serious consequences, but God is always prepared to start again. So after every self-inflicted disaster in Israel's history, God extends a second chance. The national story needs to be passed down continually through the generations, and forgetting to do so itself constitutes rebellion. Included at the end of the prologue is a practical illustration in vv. 9–11 about how the Ephraimites (a label for northern Israel) failed miserably: "The Ephraimites, armed with the bow, turned back on the day of battle. They did not keep the covenant of God, and refused to walk according to his law. They forgot what he had done, and the miracles that he had shown them." The next sections of the psalm poetically recount a host of divine deeds that ought to be remembered.

After the prologue, the rest of this long psalm is structured in two "performances" of Israel's history. Because riddles and proverbs (v. 1) are often associated with wisdom traditions, the poet of Psalm 78 might be envisioned as a sage—that is, an acknowledged teacher of wisdom—who now performs this song about national events that cannot be forgotten if future disasters are to be averted. The first performance (vv. 12–39) is focused on the era of the wilderness wandering after the people were brought out of Egypt, a journey that begins with the defining miracle of crossing the Red Sea. In this section of Psalm 78, splitting the sea is presented as a victory over the dark forces of chaos as much as over Pharaoh and the hordes of Egypt: "He split the sea and brought them through, he piled up the waters like a heap." Like the creation story itself in Genesis 1, an unruly mess is transformed into something that makes life possible. After crossing through the waters, the people are guided (v. 14) by daytime clouds and nocturnal fires, and even rocks in the arid land are no obstacle; like the sea, they are split open and fresh water pours forth: "He split rocks in the wilderness, and gave them to drink like the abundant depths; he brought forth streams from the cliff, and made waters flow down like rivers." The same verb *split* stresses the continuity between the two miracles: just as God brought them through the waters of chaos, so God also sustains them with water in the wasteland. But instead of gratitude, vv. 18–20 unfurl a complaint:

> <sup>18</sup> In their heart, they tested God
>   By asking for the food they craved.
> <sup>19</sup> Then they spoke out against God. They said:
>   "Can God possibly spread a table in the wilderness?
> <sup>20</sup> Yes, he struck the rock, and waters gushed out
>   Rivers were overflowing.
>  But is he also able to provide food?
>   Can he really furnish meat for his people?"

Not only is there an absence of any kind of appreciation for the divine provision of water, but the people's unbelief is presented in their own voice. In the books of Exodus and Numbers, there are frequent complaints that typically involve a revision of culinary history (e.g., they claim to have eaten very well as slaves in Egypt, with pots of meat, melons, and garlic; Exod 16:3, Numb 11:5) and blaming Moses and Aaron for their plight. Their own words admit that the flow of water in the desert was impressive, but they scoff at the prospects of God providing a banquet in the wasteland. If the reader is taken aback by these words, then the poet's rhetorical point has been made. It is one thing to assert that the people are rebellious, but the effect is heightened when it is heard directly from their own mouths. It is no surprise that divine anger is kindled, but it *is* surprising that bread is provided in the wilderness ("he rained down on them manna to eat, and gave them the grain of heaven," v. 24). God also dispenses a supply of quail ("he rained meat upon them like dust, winged birds like the sand of the seas") yet exacts a harsh penalty ("But before they had satisfied their desire, while yet the food remained in their mouths, the anger of God arose against them. He killed some of their sturdiest, and choice men of Israel he subdued," vv. 30–31). Any repentance from the people was fleeting and soon took the form of mere flattery, according to v. 36. Despite the various divine measures that challenge them to return from their waywardness, there was obviously no lasting commitment to the covenant by the time we reach the end of the first performance in v. 39. To reiterate, an overarching pattern can be discerned: there are spectacular divine deeds on behalf of the Israelites, but they soon forget, although even after a string of rebellions God always extends them an olive branch.

The second performance, in vv. 40–72, begins with the people in the wilderness, but it is a place where God is grieved because of the ingratitude of those who have just been rescued from Egypt. In this second half of Psalm 78 the reader is transported from the desert back to Egypt for the plagues, then through the Sea and guided to settlement in the land of promise. By stressing the plagues—sounding like the steady rhythm of percussion instruments—the poet underscores how the Israelites were able to escape *to* the Red Sea in the first place. Instead of the ten plagues that are described in Exodus, only seven appear here, perhaps because the number seven is typically seen as the number of completion or perfection. There are several other unique contours, including some new characters: in Ex 12:23 the agent of destruction is cryptically referred to as "the destroyer," but in Ps 78:49–50 there is a band of powerful angels, a celestial team of agents dispatched to rescue the slaves from their ruthless oppressors: "He let loose on them his fierce anger, wrath, indignation, and distress, a company of destroying angels" (NRSV). Moreover, in the second performance the Red Sea is also prominent, but this time it is a force that is unleashed to engulf the Egyptian army ("the sea overwhelmed their enemies," v. 53) and consume the tyrannical abuser with the waters of chaos. There are some creative variations in the signs and wonders— perhaps a poetic effort to appeal to the imagination of younger listeners—but only dreary monotony in the people's rebellions despite the abundance of divine gifts. As illustrated in vv. 56–58, mutiny persists even once the Israelites leave the wilderness and are settled in the land:

> [56] But they tested and rebelled against God Most High,
>     and did not keep his testimonies.
> [57] They backed away, acted faithlessly like their ancestors,
>     Unsteady, like a deceitful bow.
> [58] They provoked him with their high places,
>     with their idols they incited his jealousy.

Skepticism and complaints in a barren wasteland are one category of rebellion, but once the people are dwelling securely in Canaan, their addictions to high places and idolatry result in a whole new level of treachery. The striking image used in v. 57 likens the people to a *deceitful bow*. As an effective weapon, a bow needs to be strong and reliable in order to shoot straight. The spiritual condition of the people, however, is that they are unreliable and veer off course, just like an arrow from a faulty bow. Earlier in v. 9, northern Ephraimites are well-equipped with bows, but they are unsuccessful due to their refusal to walk in the law. High places and idolatry point to the worship of other gods, and here it indicates that the people's dreams and desires have now been diverted toward such gods. Just as the wilderness generation tended to "crave and demand more than they were given," so the settled generation ventures to high places and seeks prosperity from sources other than God.[11] Such practices arouse God's jealous wrath in v. 58, much like the betrayal felt by a jilted lover. Consequently, vv. 59–68 describe the devastation that afflicts the land, with the destruction of Shiloh and capture of the ark of the covenant looming large (cf. 1 Sam 4). It is remarkable, though, that the journey of divine faithfulness continues. After the defeat of Shiloh and the rejection of that northern sanctuary ("He departed from the dwelling of Shiloh, a tent for dwelling with humanity," v. 60), there is yet another extension of grace. A new lineage of promise is established, a lineage that arguably contains the seeds of messianic hope as Psalm 78 reaches its climax:

> [67] He rejected the tent of Joseph,
>> The tribe of Ephraim he did not choose.
> [68] But the tribe of Judah he chose,
>> Mount Zion, which he loves.
> [69] His sanctuary he built to the highest heights,
>> Like the earth, he established it forever.
> [70] Also he chose his servant David,
>> Took him from the pens of the flocks.

---

[11] James L. Mays, *Psalms,* Interpretation (Louisville, KY: John Knox, 1994), 257.

> $^{71}$ From tending the ewes he brought him,
>     To shepherd Jacob his people,
>         Israel, his inheritance.
> $^{72}$ He shepherded them with integrity of heart,
>     With his skilled hands he guided them.

Throughout the long performance of Psalm 78, the reader is not merely told about history but is given an expansive tour that visualizes many significant moments in the national story. Such imaginative snapshots are designed to inspire the next generations to remember and flourish rather than forget and flounder. The second performance of Psalm 78 stresses that the people allowed themselves to be lured away by the seductive images and assurances of surrounding cultures. But in the final verses of the psalm there is once more a gracious divine initiative as God invests in a new place with a new leader. After the rejection and destruction of Shiloh, the sanctuary of Mt. Zion is built to last, with cosmic dimensions and secure foundations, difficult for any invading superpower to destroy. This is a place that God "loves," and more than a feeling or an emotional state, *love* in this context suggests lasting commitment. And, much like the fantastic description of the Mt. Zion sanctuary, the ideal picture of young David recruited from the sheepfold is deployed for a purpose. David's own life and reign, as the reader knows, had ample failure and rebellion, similar to the national story itself. Yet that same David was given an astonishing divine promise in 2 Sam 7:8–16: "I took you from the pasture, from following the sheep, to be ruler over my people Israel. . . . your house and your kingdom will endure before me forever." We recall that a key theme in Psalm 78 is God's willingness to start again after the nation's self-inflicted disaster, and this theme is highlighted in the final verses. The last words of the psalm are not about the people's rebellion but rather about a fresh divine initiative and the promise granted to a new leader, inviting the community to wonder how such a promise might be fulfilled in the future.

Mention of David at the end—for the first time in Book III of the Psalter—brings us back to the *riddle* of Psalm 78. If most riddles have an answer, it is notable that the riddle of this psalm is ultimately presented as a kind of question. The poet asks future generations, "Are you willing to remember the great deeds of the past and have confidence in God's provisions for the future?" It is now apparent that Psalm 78 is strategically placed. If Book III of the Psalter (Psalms 73–89) reflects the period of the exile, then during this dark era the people of Israel are invited to reevaluate their lives. This reevaluation includes learning how to cultivate real hope, not based on their circumstances but based on God's commitment and promise. At this critical juncture, it is vital that they keep their story alive, because it is a story of God's faithfulness despite their many relapses. An important purpose of the historical psalms, then, is to encourage the people to reimagine those famous moments in their past that can help guide them to a better life after the exile.[12] With the creative casting of Psalm 78 as a riddle (or a parable), history is presented in a manner that is hard to forget.

## Visual Effects

Popular feature films often include dazzling special effects, impressive visual sequences that in the best of movies are used in the service of storytelling. Similarly, historical psalms frequently use their own kind of special effects. But rather than computer-generated images, these "effects" take the form of fresh details or striking plot twists in famous events from the nation's past. A major purpose of this attention-grabbing technique is to heighten the audience's connection to their story through new and expansive details. By further absorbing the audience in the drama at hand, the historical psalm thus encourages an enhanced appraisal of where they might fit in in the still-unfolding national epic.

Psalm 105 is categorized as a historical psalm, and is the first in a threefold sequence at the end of Book IV and the start of Book V. Together, these three longer compositions recount the story from

---

[12] Cf. McCann, "Book of Psalms," 992: "[T]he primary purpose of the historical recitals seems to be the creation of a community that, despite its own failures and faithlessness, will live in hope (v. 7) as a result of the faithfulness and forgiveness of God (v. 38). In fact, this may be the solution to the psalmist's riddle (v. 2), which by inference can be stated as follows: 'How can the recollection of a history of failure lead to a future of hope?'"

the meager beginnings of Israel's ancestors to the regathering of those scattered after the exile. In particular, Psalm 105 traces the period from Abraham's tenuous wanderings to the conquest of Canaan under Joshua, highlighting the theme of divine provision and faithfulness over vast stretches of time. Although this story would presumably have been well known, there are some intriguing special effects in the performance of Psalm 105. Of these various features, our analysis focuses on the middle stanzas that present some new images of Joseph's march into slavery (vv. 16–22) and a startling variation in the plagues of Egypt (vv. 23–36).

Like an opening guitar riff in a hit song, Psalm 105 energetically starts with a sequence of imperatives (rejoice, seek, remember, etc.) unleashed at the beginning in vv. 1–6. This chorus of verbs invites the people to actively engage with God and to recognize the privilege of their divine relationship over the centuries: "Give thanks to the Lord, call on his name; make known among the people his deeds! Sing to him, make music to him; think about all of his wonders!" Historical psalms, as mentioned, provide inspiration for the future by imagining in a fresh way the major events and movements of the past, and it was a strategy for awakening hope in the community during difficult circumstances. Even in desperate times the Israelites still need to praise God because, as v. 6 declares, they are the *chosen* seed of Abraham and therefore heirs of a divine covenant. Indeed, the next stanza (vv. 7–15) illustrates how God extended protection and provision to Abraham, Isaac, and Jacob as they endured the hostilities of Canaan.

The first two stanzas of Psalm 105 emphasize how God repeatedly intervened to defend Israel's ancestors from the mischievous designs of foreign potentates, an idea that would be particularly relevant to the group after the exile, buffeted as they are on all sides. On the basis of God's promise, the people of Israel have been divinely guarded at every turn, and that—according to the psalmist—has not changed from the moment of inception. In their darkest moments, God remains with them, and the experiences of Joseph in vv. 16–22 highlight this reality:

> 16 He called a famine against the land,
> Every staff of bread he broke.

> ¹⁷ He sent someone before them:
> Joseph, sold as a slave.
> ¹⁸ They afflicted his feet with the shackles,
> Iron came up to his throat.
> ¹⁹ Until the time his word came to pass,
> The word of the Lord tested him.
> ²⁰ The king sent and released him,
> The ruler of peoples let him out.
> ²¹ He placed him as lord of his house,
> The ruler of all his possessions.
> ²² To bind his officials to his will,
> And impart wisdom to his elders.

Claiming that God *sends* natural disasters and global calamity could sound controversial to modern ears. But the poet of Psalm 105 has no qualms about saying exactly that in v. 16, stating that God not only "calls" a famine but also cuts off the food supply (similar descriptions are found in Lev 26:25–28 and 2 Kgs 8:1.) While such clear divine agency is not stated in the Genesis narrative, the fact that Joseph precedes the rest of the family in Egypt is advantageous once the famine reaches a high point.[13] So, just as God calls the famine in v. 16, God also sends Joseph in v. 17 when he is sold as a slave by his brothers (although the order is reversed in Genesis 37–42); they designed it for evil, but God transformed that evil into something that resulted in the saving of many lives (Gen 50:20). Admittedly there is a mysterious view of divine providence articulated in the psalm, but the theme of *triumph after adversity* can also be discerned. The painful picture of Joseph's binding for the march into slavery ("they afflicted his feet with the fetter, iron came upon his throat") certainly describes the adversity. Poetically, the mention of feet and throat in v. 18 can be labeled a *merismus*, "whereby the poet represents totality by mentioning two

---

[13] Cf. DeClaissé-Walford, Jacobson, and Tanner, *The Book of Psalms*, 467: "The psalm does not discuss God's motivation for calling the famine; it is content to assert that the famine was the divine will (a notion that is not found in Genesis, per se) and to imply that the resulting migration of the ancestral family to Egypt was also the result of divine providence."

extremes."[14] Not only does the use of a merismus paint a brutal picture with the iron and shackles, but the reader might actually feel a bit suffocated while imagining this situation. Joseph's adversity here, however, forms a contrast with the vindication in vv. 19–22: after a time of refinement or testing, Joseph is released by the king and arises to a position of prominence, as Pharaoh "placed him as lord of his house, the ruler of all his possessions."

When this section (vv. 16–22) of Psalm 105 is considered as a unit, we can better appreciate the purpose of the special effects of the iron collar and fetters that immobilize Joseph. By analogy, Joseph's march into slavery is comparable to the last king to reign in Jerusalem, Zedekiah. In Jer 52:11, after the destruction of the city by the Babylonians, Zedekiah is arrested (after trying to flee) and dragged in chains to prison in Babylon. The travails of Joseph echo the experiences of those citizens of Jerusalem marched into captivity in the wake of the city's destruction. But just as God never abandons Joseph—even in the bleakness of imprisonment—so God continues to be with the community in exile and beyond: "In the bitter fortunes of Joseph, God was preparing the way for eventual blessing not only for him but for his kin (Gen 45:5, 7). Joseph's experience was that of Israel in miniature. The path to glory lay through suffering—and had not Israel suffered in the exile?"[15] But if Joseph can rise above the bitterness of captivity, perhaps Psalm 105 carries a message to people who have likewise experienced adversity. The special effects in this section of the psalm might therefore be intended to help a later audience visualize events in their history in fresh ways, with application to their present situation. As we will see, techniques for *revisualizing* their history continue in the next section.

> [23] Then came Israel to Egypt,
>> Jacob sojourned in the land of Ham.
> [24] He caused his people to be very fruitful,
>> He made them mightier than their foes.

---

[14] Anthony R. Ceresko, "A Poetic Analysis of Ps 105, with Attention to Its Use of Irony," *Biblica* 64 (1983): 32, citing Mitchell Dahood, *Psalms III: 101–150*, AB 17a (New York: Doubleday, 1970), 55. A famous use of merismus occurs in Gen 1:1, "In the beginning God created *the heavens and the earth*," indicating totality.

[15] Leslie Allen, *Psalms 101–150*, WBC 21 (Waco, TX: Word, 1983), 58.

> $^{25}$ He turned their minds to hate his people,
>> To deal deceitfully with his servants.
> $^{26}$ He sent Moses his servant,
>> Aaron, whom he had chosen.
> $^{27}$ They performed among them the words of his signs,
>> Wonders in the land of Ham.
> $^{28}$ He sent darkness, and caused it to be dark,
>> They could not rebel against his words.
> $^{29}$ He turned their waters into blood,
>> He caused their fish to die.
> $^{30}$ Their land swarmed with frogs,
>> In the bedchambers of their kings.

Among the most striking events in the biblical story is the plagues of Egypt in the book of Exodus, a series of ecodisasters that wreak havoc on Israel's slave masters. Starting with the waters of the Nile turned to blood, the ten plagues escalate, from frogs and boils to hail and locusts, climaxing with the frightening assault against the firstborn. We have already seen the plagues, as Psalm 78 features seven of the plagues in its recounting of the nation's ordeal in Egypt. The plague of darkness is not mentioned in Psalm 78, though not only does darkness occur in Psalm 105, but it is included as the very first in the list of plagues (rather than in the ninth position, as in Exod 10:21–22: "The Lord said to Moses, 'Stretch out your hand over the heavens so that darkness will be upon the land of Egypt, a darkness that can be felt.' Then Moses stretched out his hand over the heavens, and thick darkness covered all Egypt for three days"). Frontloading the darkness could be considered another *special effect* in Psalm 105, and at least two purposes can be suggested. First, canceling sunlight in the land of Egypt is a political statement against the local powers, as one scholar explains: "The supremacy of the sun god Re (or Atum) throughout much of Egyptian history is well known. For this reason, the obscuring of the sun in connection with the 9th plague has been regarded as the triumph of the Hebrew God over the head of the Egyptian pantheon."[16] Second, in a wider picture

---

[16] James K. Hoffmeier, "Plagues in Egypt," in *Anchor Bible Dictionary*, 6 vols., ed. David Noel Freedman (New York: Doubleday, 1992), 2:374–378.

there is a contrast that emerges between the experience of Egypt and the wilderness journey of the Israelites: "Why the change? Presumably, it was done to contrast the land of Egypt with the desert: God's first act for Israel in the wilderness is to light their darkness with fire (v. 39), whereas God's first act against Egypt is to turn their light into darkness."[17] Other reasons might be offered for the poet's changing the order of the plagues, but the emphasis on the darkness in Psalm 105 allows the audience to experience afresh their story and appreciate the richness of a history that can shape their future.[18]

## Don't Look Back in Anger?

Although Psalm 137 is usually classified as a *communal lament*, there are a number of details in this poem that interest historians: it provides a snippet about life in Babylonian captivity and a glimpse of the long-standing grudge with Judah's neighbor, the nation of Edom.[19] In terms of structure, there are three parts to the psalm. First, vv. 1–3 unfold a memory, as the poet recalls a scene in captivity that evokes the sound of old music. This opening section outlines the foreign setting of the psalm and the context of forced relocation to a foreign locale. Second, the lament and oath language of vv. 4–6 give the poem an inward turn, as the writer fears that Jerusalem will be forgotten and be replaced by some alternative. The third part of the poem is the most controversial,

---

[17] Richard J. Clifford, *Psalms 73–150* (Nashville, TN: Abingdon, 2003), 154–155.

[18] For example, it has been argued that the account of the plagues in Ps 105:28–36 has a structure with similarities to the Genesis 1 creation account, perhaps implying that the rescue from Egypt is a kind of creation story: "The same movement from heaven, to waters, to earth is clearly discerned and the focus of concern is also on the earth. Both the creation and the Plagues are demonstrations of the might and power of Yahweh in nature and on earth. In creation, the creative order comes into being at God's demand, and in the case of the Plagues the whole creation is under his order and control. While he creates the light in the beginning and sets the luminaries in heaven to rule day and night, he also has the power to send darkness in Egypt." Archie C. C. Lee, "Genesis I and the Plagues Tradition in Psalm cv," *VT* 40 (1990): 259–260.

[19] Scholars have debated an exact date for the composition of the psalm, but it must have been written after the exile of 586 BCE and the destruction of the Jerusalem temple, since those past events are firmly in the poet's view. Tensions with Edom are also evident in the postexilic period (e.g., Lam 4:21–22; Mal 1:3–4), and so the psalm may provide a perspective *after* the rebuilding of Jerusalem.

as vv. 7–9 delineate the poet's desire for vengeance against the Edomites and for a horrible fate to befall Babylonian infants. Many readers are drawn to the evocative opening lines of the poem, but the chilling desire for vengeance at the end has shocked those same readers.[20] Our analysis here will concentrate on those aspects of Israel's story that emerge in this poem, which begins as follows:

> [1] By the rivers of Babylon,
>     There we sat, yes, we wept,
>         As we remembered Zion.
> [2] On the willows in its midst,
>     We hung up our lyres.
> [3] For there our captors asked us for the words of a song,
>     Our tormenters for rejoicing,
>         "Sing for us one of the songs of Zion!"
> [4] How can we sing the Lord's song,
>     In a strange land?
> [5] If I forget you, O Jerusalem,
>     May my right hand forget.
> [6] Let my tongue cling to my palate,
>     If I do not remember you,
>     If I do not lift up Jerusalem above my highest joy.
> [7] Remember, O Lord, the sons of Edom,
>     On the day of Jerusalem, those who said,
>         "Rip it down, Rip it down to its foundation!"
> [8] O daughter of Babylon, soon to be destroyed,
>     Blessed is the one who repays the wage that you paid us.
> [9] Blessed is the one who seizes and shatters
>     Your little ones against the rock.

The opening line of any poem frequently serves to orient the reader to the subject matter and theme at work. Consider the first words

---

[20] Note the remarks of Terrien, *The Psalms,* 865: "This is one of the most beautiful poems of the Psalter, yet it ends with a monstrous imprecation"; Brueggemann and Bellinger, *Psalms,* 573: "This unusual but finely honed text is a psalm packed with emotional freight and is often familiar to contemporary readers both because of its stunning beginning and its troubling ending."

of Dante's *Inferno*, as rendered by John Ciardi: "Midway in our life's journey, I went astray from the straight road and woke to find myself alone in a dark wood." Alongside a pair of temporal references—halfway through the poet's life, at a time when he is lost—the spatial dimension of the *dark wood* is a probing metaphor for the tangled forest of sin and corruption that epitomizes the poet's plight. The beginning of Psalm 137 likewise orients the reader to the *time* and *place* of the poem's subject matter. Alongside other portions of the Hebrew Bible, such as Daniel and Ezekiel, Psalm 137 is situated outside of Israel, in the land of Babylon during the period of exile.

For some contemporary readers, the *rivers of Babylon* might conjure up pictures of exotic hanging gardens with the groovy rhythms of Boney M. thumping in the background. Far from romantic, however, the rivers of this psalm suggest the opposite and refer to a very identifiable Babylonian landmark: human-engineered canals and irrigation systems. More precisely, the plural *rivers* (*naharot*) has been explained as "referring to the canal-system within the City of Babylon," and thus the poet of Psalm 137 would be situated within the walls of Babylon rather than somewhere out in the fields between the Tigris and the Euphrates.[21] There is a comparable reference to the canals (*naharot*) of Egypt in Exod 7:19, with slave labor used for the construction and maintenance of irrigation tributaries along the Nile that were a mainstay of the economy. "Ditches" or "trenches" might be translation options as well. The *naharot* (rivers or canals) of Babylon, then, should be understood as symbolizing the power and dominance of the conquering nation, and the urban equivalent of a dark wood where the poet of Psalm 137 was counted as lost.

A poignant moment in the early movements of the psalm is *hanging up* the lyres on the willows (or poplar trees). Associated with David from the outset of his career (1 Sam 16:23) and connected with the music of divine acclamation throughout the book of Psalms, the lyre "was an instrument of joy (Isa. 24:8, Gen. 31:27), so setting it aside

---

[21] Bob Becking, "Does Exile Equal Suffering? A Fresh Look at Psalm 137," in *Exile and Suffering: A Selection of Papers Read at the 50th Anniversary Meeting of the Old Testament Society of South Africa OTWSA/OTSSA, Pretoria August 2007*, ed. Bob Becking and Dirk Human, Oudtestamentische Studiën 50 (Leiden: Brill, 2009), 197.

reinforces the image of deep sadness."[22] Moreover, the verb *hang* (*talah*) is particularly foreboding, since in other biblical narratives it occurs in contexts that are decidedly lethal: Joseph predicts that his fellow prisoner is about to be *impaled* in Gen 40:19, while Absalom is seen *hanging* from an oak tree in 2 Sam 18:10 shortly before he is bludgeoned to death by Joab and his retinue of soldiers.[23] Far from incidental, the testimony of hanging up the lyre is a serious gesture: previous psalms we have looked at involve praising God by reaccentuating images from surrounding nations (e.g., our discussion earlier of Psalm 29), but 137:2 is about abandoning the music of praise as a captive in a foreign land.

Why would skilled musicians hang up their instruments and *not* sing songs of praise? Within the story of Psalm 137, the Babylonian overlords are demanding that their captives give them, literally, "the words of a song, a Zion song." This is not a harmless request for diversion or musical entertainment, but quite the opposite: the tormenters mockingly ask for a joyful song to reinforce their victory and remind the captives of their present humiliation, thus adding insult to the injury of exile. "Not satisfied with physical destruction," says one commentator, "some Babylonians seek further to damage the Lord's glory by ridiculing the songs that declare Zion unconquerable."[24]

If we pause to consider the basic elements of a *Zion song*, the viciousness of the taunt in v. 3 is better understood. The original meaning of the name *Zion* may be uncertain, but after the capture of the stronghold of Zion within the city of Jerusalem by David in 2 Sam 5:7, Zion became one of the most potent symbols of God's choice of Jerusalem and God's special revelation to the people of Israel: "Zion, as the dwelling place of God (cf. Ps 76:3; Isa 8:18), was understood by Israel as the symbol of God's presence in their midst. Therefore, they believed that Zion would never fall and they would always experience prosperity, safety and security. Even if other nations should attack,

---

[22] Christopher B. Hays, "How Shall We Sing? Psalm 137 in Historical and Canonical Context," *HBT* 27 (2005): 43–44.

[23] Cf. George Savran, "How Can We Sing a Song of the Lord? The Strategy of Lament in Psalm 137," *ZAW* 112 (2000): 46. For further context of the verb, see Steve A. Wiggins, "Between Heaven and Earth: Absalom's Dilemma," *JNSL* 23 (1997): 73–81.

[24] Clifford, *Psalms 73–150*, 167.

they would prevail and Yahweh would repel all attacks against them (cf. Pss 46:5, 48:3–8)."[25] Because many scholars maintain that Psalm 48 constitutes a psalm of Zion, the concluding section of vv. 11–14 is worth quoting:

> [11] Let Mount Zion rejoice,
>> Let the daughters of Judah be glad,
>> On account of your judgments.
> [12] Walk around Zion and circle about,
>> Count up the towers.
> [13] Fix your mind on the ramparts,
>> Pass between the citadels,
>> So you can report it to later generations.
> [14] For such is God,
>> Our God forever and ever,
>> He will guide us to the very end.

It is not inconceivable that lyrics such as Ps 48:11–14, with its celebration of Jerusalem's defense fortifications and God's abiding commitment, are what the Babylonians are demanding from the captives. For the musician in Psalm 137, this surely would have been galling in the highest degree and a depressing situation, as the Babylonians insist on reminding them about the apparent theological failure of the "glad" songs of Zion. The response in vv. 5–6, however, is a commitment to *not* believe the Babylonian version of reality, sealed with an oath about a paralyzed hand and an inarticulate palate if the poet ever forgets or gives up on Jerusalem. In the book of Daniel it emerges that pressure to conform and efforts to erase the religious heritage of the Judeans were serious, with new names and tempting offers for advancement (Dan 1:4–7). Swearing the oath, then, is an act of defiance, and one interpreter reflects further on this kind of strategy: "Resistance to power can take subtle forms, and in the history of oppression, song has often

---

[25] Leonard P. Maré, "Psalm 137: Exile—Not the Time for Singing the Lord's Song," *OTE* 23 (2010): 120. See also Mays, *Psalms*, 421: "The songs of Zion are hymns full of joy and confidence. In them, Jerusalem is majestic and invincible, secure against the threats of hostile armies (read Psalms 46 and 48)."

been used to circumvent, shame and subvert unjust uses of power. Slaves in the American South famously publicized covert meetings and Underground Railroad happenings through spirituals."[26]

Psalm 137 does not end with the poet's oath to remember (zakar) Jerusalem. Instead, v. 7 is directed toward the neighboring Edomites, a national antagonist whom the poet implores God to "remember" because of their actions during the invasion (see 2 Kings 25). On the one hand, there was long-standing animosity between Israel and Edom, and the rivalry between the two founding ancestors—Jacob and Esau—in the book of Genesis foreshadows the later struggles. On the other hand, it may seem odd that Edom is invoked, but commentators point out that mentioning the Edomites makes sense within the larger story of Jerusalem's destruction. Drawing on texts such as Ezekiel 35 and the short prophetic book of Obadiah, it becomes apparent that Edomite collaboration with the Babylonians on the "day" of the temple's razing is a source of particular grief.[27] Edom's conduct also awakened a desire for vengeance, especially when considering Joel 3:19, a prophetic text that alludes to the Edomites shedding innocent blood in the land of Judah. Like the Babylonians in Ps 137:3, Edom too spoke mocking words of derision when they cheered the razing of Jerusalem's temple; presumably the Babylonian taunt reminds the poet of earlier brutalities by Edom, and hence the request that God remember (zakar) such verbal abuse and respond with justice. Since Psalm 137 is placed in the second half of Book V, it may indicate that the postexilic community still struggles with anger and resentment over past events. In this regard, Psalm 137 provides a glimpse of internal battles within the hearts of the people even some time after traumatic events of the past.

If the psalm concluded on this note to remember Edom, most readers would probably be fine. But the poet then turns to the Babylonians with a haunting imprecation about smashing infants to pieces. There is a tendency in modern scholarship to reject and condemn the last line of the psalm. One suspects that if the poet wished for the Babylonian

---

[26] Hays, "How Shall We Sing?," 51.
[27] For example, John Ahn, "Psalm 137: Complex Communal Laments," *JBL* 127 (2008): 285–286; Graham S. Ogden, "Prophetic Oracles against Foreign Nations and Psalms of Communal Lament: The Relationship of Psalm 137 to Jeremiah 49:7–22 and Obadiah," *JSOT* 24 (1982): 89–97.

warriors to be liquidated, affronted readers would be assuaged somewhat. Indeed, Othmar Keel opts for a figurative reading, where *infants* represents the future of the nation, just as *daughter of Babylon* figuratively represents the city; rather than to be taken literally, Keel renders the final line as "Happy is he who puts an end to your self-renewing domination."[28] I certainly hope Keel is correct, but I fear otherwise, and the problem is that destroying infants is not limited to the end of Psalm 137. For instance, there is an awkward conversation in 2 Kings 8:9–13 when the prophet Elisha weeps in the presence of the Aramean commander Hazael, soon to be king in Damascus after he murders his master, Ben-Hadad. When pressed for an explanation, Elisha tells Hazael why he is weeping: "Because I know what evil you will do to the Israelites: to their fortresses you will send fire, their choice young men you will kill with the sword, their infants you will dash in pieces, and their pregnant women you will rip open." The same description of killing the young is attested twice in Isaiah 13, along with Hosea 10:14 and Nahum 3:10, not to mention King Herod's slaughter of innocents in Matthew 2. Given that curses and other vehement imprecations are common enough in the Psalms and elsewhere, it is difficult to avoid or dilute the violence described in the text.

Apart from the complicated moral issues, a central question for this study is *why* the final sentence of Psalm 137 is included; in answer, two lines of thought might be raised. First, it is easy to miss the deep irony that is at work in the psalm: *the poet writes a song about refusing to sing*. The Babylonians mockingly want to hear a glad song of Zion by the irrigation canals of the conquering city, yet the Israelite musician composes a quite different tune for the occasion, with a deep-seated desire for retribution in kind. Music is used as a form of resistance to tyranny and as a token of confidence that God will judge the guilty rather than the psalmist seeking to take revenge. Second, analyzing Psalm

---

[28] Othmar Keel, *The Symbolism of the Biblical World: Ancient Near Eastern Iconography and the Book of Psalms* (New York: Seabury Press, 1978), 9, cited in Savran, "How Can We Sing a Song of the Lord?," 54. Also note the position held by Erhard S. Gerstenberger, *Psalms, Part 2, and Lamentations*, FOTL 15 (Grand Rapids, MI: Eerdmans, 2001), 393, who labels Ps 137:9 "one of the most cruel, vengeful ill-wishes in the Bible. No matter how bestial were the sackings of the Edomites, this wish for the annihilation of children is a deplorable example of deep-rooted ethnic hatred, as shocking as those massacres among antagonistic cultural and religious groups we have to witness in our days."

137 in its entirety, and eschewing the temptation to excise the last line, allows us to understand important facets of the exile and receive poetic insight into the trauma of deportation. Including these controversial lines suggests that room is given in the Psalter to voice even the most aggressive outpouring without censoring the words.[29] After all, the poet of Psalm 137 is reacting to the enemy's taunt, and if the reaction is deemed abhorrent, the preservation of these words at least permits the reader to experience the depths of bitterness among some of the exilic constituency. Ultimately, the psalmist crafts a plea for *poetic justice*, and it could be suggested that a similar dynamic is found in the book of Esther (a story that is likewise situated during the exilic period). In his rage against Mordecai the Jew, Haman the Agagite prompts the king to issue a decree for the destruction of the Jewish population, and also proceeds to erect a seventy-five-foot gallows for the impaling (*talah*) of Mordecai. However, there is an ironic overturning in the denouement of the story, as the decree is reversed and the gallows is instead used for the hanging of Haman and his sons. Hoist by his own petard, as it were, Haman suffers the kind of poetic justice that the psalmist cries out for by the rivers of Babylon.[30] Psalm 137 describes an intense response to the humiliation of exile—voicing a plea for divine intervention in the strongest terms—but also has echoes and resonances elsewhere in the Scriptures.

To conclude our study of Israel's story in the psalms, we might briefly consider the career of Gideon in Judges 6. This character is first introduced threshing wheat in a winepress to hide it from the marauding Midianites, who are oppressing Israel during the turbulent period in the book of Judges. In the midst of such upheaval, a messenger of God greets him ("The Lord is with you, mighty warrior!") as

---

[29] Cf. Erich Zenger, *A God of Vengeance? Understanding the Psalms of Divine Wrath* (Louisville, KY: Westminster John Knox, 1996), 48: "Psalm 137 is not the song of people who have the power to effect a violent change in their situation of suffering, nor is it the battle cry of terrorists. Instead, it is an attempt to cling to one's historical identity even when everything is against it. Still more, it is an attempt, in the face of the most profound humiliation and helplessness, to suppress the primitive human lust for violence in one's heart, by surrendering *everything* to God—a God whose word of judgment is presumed to be so universally just that even those who pray the psalm submit themselves to it."

[30] On the larger issue of retribution, see Gordon J. Wenham, *Psalms as Torah: Reading Biblical Song Ethically* (Grand Rapids, MI: Baker Academic, 2012), 112–115.

a preface to his call to rescue Israel from the grip of their oppressors. But Gideon's dismissive reaction is telling: "Excuse me, my lord? Sure, the Lord is with us! So why has all *this* found us? Where is all his wonderful stuff that our ancestors have recounted to us, saying, 'Didn't the Lord bring us up from Egypt?' So now, the Lord has abandoned us, and given us into the grip of Midian!" These words reveal a character who seems to have little confidence in his ancestral faith, and bad circumstances have brought a cynical edge to his speech. While there are various purposes for the historical psalms—or more broadly, those psalms that reimagine elements of Israel's story—it could be that such compositions have an audience like Gideon in view, members of the community who have been afflicted with adversity and question their tradition. To that end, these psalms immerse the reader in dramatic events from the past to awaken dormant hope, inviting the people of God to revisualize some of these great moments through the special effects of poetic performance. Rather than random, it would appear that there is a strategic placement of historical psalms in the Psalter, with the highest concentration in those periods where a sense of defeat may have been most prevalent. This intentional distribution of psalms that retell parts of Israel's story can be interpreted as signposts in the larger journey of the Psalter, and further attention to the final shaping of the collection will be given in the next two chapters of our study.

# 5
# Psalm Titles and Collections

Our attention so far in this study has predominantly been on individual psalms, with some modest forays into the placement of various pieces within the five-book structure. So far, we have explored the background and backstories of certain psalms, the diversity of genres, and episodes from Israel's story that are poetically reimagined in some of these compositions. In the final two chapters, attention turns to questions of how the final form of the Psalter is organized. To that end, a pair of related issues are discussed in this chapter. First, the title of the book (why is it called "Psalms" anyway?) and superscriptions at the beginning of most psalms are introduced briefly, with some thoughts on how both might be interpreted. Second, we will look at various groupings or collections of poems within the larger book of Psalms. For instance, the *Songs of Ascents* (Psalms 120–134) is a repertoire often thought to have originated as pilgrimage music, performed or recited every year by travelers on their way to worship in Jerusalem. Several strategies for interpreting the *Songs of Ascents* are discussed in this section, with short studies of Psalms 120, 127, and 134 as illustrations. After that, we explore a collection of thirteen psalms with superscriptions that relate to events in the life of David, although they are not grouped in sequential order. Within this collection, three of these psalms in particular are analyzed briefly: Psalm 3, associated with the threat posed to David by his son Absalom and his bitter rebellion; Psalm 51, associated with Nathan the prophet's confrontation after David's adultery with Bathsheba; and Psalm 63, connected with the mortal threats during David's wilderness sojourn.

## More Than a Feeling

A book's title is the door through which the reader enters, creating a sense of expectation as the threshold is crossed into the world of the text. For instance, titles such as *Emma*, *Crime and Punishment*, and *East of Eden* prepare the reader in various ways for the book's content, themes, or major characters. *The Hunger Games* is a catchy title—all of us have been hungry, and many of us like games—although whether or not that book becomes a classic is an open question. But matters of taste aside, the title of a literary work or movie often is the first introduction to the story about to unfold.

Biblical books are often approached the same way, as readers arrive at the book of Exodus expecting departure, or Numbers expecting the enumeration of census lists. The matter is rather more complicated, however, because these ancient works were not given titles by the writer(s), and in the vast majority of cases are anonymously composed. In the case of *East of Eden*, John Steinbeck conferred this title on his novel, and it carries a certain interpretive weight as a result. The titles of books such as Exodus and Numbers are labels that derive from later reading communities, and so the title is a name attached to a book rather than inherent to the work itself. Based on criteria such as subject matter, a major character, or an assumed author, the title becomes part of the tradition long after the period of composition.

The matter is also complicated by the fact that numerous biblical books have been referred to by different titles over the years. For instance, the titles of Exodus and Numbers in the Hebrew Bible are *Shemot* (Names) and *B$^e$Midbar* (In the Wilderness) respectively, and these names are prompted by the opening clauses. When the book of Exodus is considered under the title *Names*, a different impression is conveyed: instead of a primary focus on the event of departure, one immediately thinks of real people who are named (and therefore a key subject matter of the book) and of course the revelation of the ultimate name in Exodus 3, the name of the Lord. Similarly, *In the Wilderness* evokes a spatial setting fraught with scarce resources and uncertainty, bringing to the reader's mind the notions of dangerous travel and dependence on God in an arena of insecurity. A title, therefore, carries a degree of interpretive significance and merits some reflection as one enters a literary world of words.

Turning to the book of Psalms, there likewise are several titles that have been used in different traditions. The most familiar title, used in every standard English translation, is *Psalms*. Drawing on the Greek versions, *psalmos* is a rendering of the Hebrew term *mizmor*, a common word occurring nearly sixty times in the superscriptions (from Psalm 3 all the way to 143).[1] A technical term that refers to songs that are played with the accompaniment of stringed instruments, *mizmor* was eventually used as a title for the entire book and stresses the musical dimension of the Psalms in a public setting.[2]

The Hebrew title of the book is *Tehillim*, "Praises," again evoking the musical side of public performance, although arguably with a slightly broader scope.[3] Derived from the verb *hallel*, various configurations for *praise* occur throughout the book, but perhaps most famously near the end with "hallelujah" (an imperative meaning "Praise the Lord," first occurring in Psalm 104, and approximately two dozen times afterward, including four times in the concluding Psalm 150). It could be that *praises* is the label under which an assortment of psalms are subsumed. Laments, insofar as they are directed to God, could be interpreted as a kind of praise, as well as historical psalms that recount divine faithfulness to the nation. We have already remarked on the variety of genres and poetic utterances within the collection: there are declarations of joy and spiritual euphoria, but also struggles of anguish

---

[1] McCann, "Book of Psalms," 657.

[2] On the term *Psalter*, see Charles A. Briggs and Emilie G. Briggs, *A Critical and Exegetical Commentary on the Book of Psalms*, ICC (Edinburgh: T&T Clark, 1906), 1:20. Note also Tyler F. Williams, "Towards a Date for the Old Greek Psalter," in *The Old Greek Psalter: Studies in Honour of Albert Pietersma*, ed. Robert J. V. Hiebert, Claude E. Cox, and Peter J. Gentry, JSOTS 332 (Sheffield: Sheffield Academic Press, 2001), 248–276.

[3] Denise Dombkowski Hopkins, *Journey through the Psalms*, revised and expanded edition (St. Louis, MO: Chalice Press, 2002), 38. Cf. Goldingay, *Psalms*, vol. 1: *Psalms 1–41*, 218: "As far as we can tell, biblical books originally had no titles; like other ancient Middle Eastern works, books such as Genesis were referred to by their opening words. The collection of hymns, testimonies, prayers, prophecies, and other material that we call the Psalms eventually came to be known in Hebrew as *těhillîm*, 'Praises.' In LXX, Vaticanus calls it *psalmoi*, 'Songs Sung to a Stringed Instrument,' while Alexandrinus calls it *psaltērion*, apparently a term for the instrument itself; these two words generate the English titles 'Psalms' and 'Psalter.' None of these titles is very accurate, but there is no title that really does justice to the varied contents of the work."

that express gloom and deep sorrow, with poets variously battling against internal depression and raging adversaries.

Such diversity, in fact, might be one of the great purposes of the book of Psalms, suggesting that both the scathing invectives against enemies and the darkest places of inner anguish can be recalibrated into affirmations of praise (rather than violence or despair). It could be that the boundaries or definition of praise is being expanded here, as the book of Psalms is making the startling claim that raging anger and lonely sadness can be redeployed, with significant implications for the psychological effect on the poet's (and, by extension, the reader's) mental health.[4] Assuming this is the case, the book of Psalms aims to provide a fund of practical examples of how the reader might deal with resentment or tragedy, using words and images, metaphors and pictures that have been recited and performed by a great cloud of witnesses across the ages.

If a book's title creates a sense of expectation in the reader's mind, then anyone who enters the book of *Praises* should anticipate a journey of discovery. More than a feeling, *praise* is a vocally expressed worldview, and therefore an opportunity for people to think about and articulate their place in the divinely created order. The journey toward praise is gradually understood as a process of orientation and a recognition that all of life is lived under the reign of God and an acknowledgment of God's universal kingship. As one writer notes, "While the title does not adequately indicate the nature of all the compositions in the book, it does capture the effect of the theological arrangement of the psalms in the book, which in the final analysis does become a book of praise in full awareness of and in spite of the experience of lament and sorrow in life." Altogether, "the Hebrew title (*tehillim*) highlights the overall effect of the collection with its movement from lament to praise, establishing the confidence and hope that despite the suffering realized in life, Yahweh's final word is always deliverance and benefit worthy of our most extravagant praise."[5] By means of the title,

---

[4] For an example with discussion and bibliography, see Brent A. Strawn, "Poetic Attachment: Psychology, Psycholinguistics, and the Psalms," in *The Oxford Handbook of the Psalms*, ed. William P. Brown (New York: Oxford University Press, 2014), 404–423.
[5] Wilson, *Psalms Volume 1*, 25.

the reader should expect to find an array of praises that can be voiced in every season of life, in the course of a journey through a corrupted and complex world. But the Psalms reveal that though the journey may have many shadows and valleys, it also has a destination and the goal of a life that is fully conscious of the reality of God's promises, covenant, and abiding presence.[6]

## Entitlement Matters

We have already noticed that most of the individual psalms have some sort of title as well. Statistically, about 85 percent of the psalms have one heading or another, usually referred to as *superscriptions*. While the Psalms provide the widest array of superscriptions, examples can be found elsewhere in the Hebrew Bible. For instance, at the beginning of Jeremiah 47—part of the collection of oracles directed against the foreign nations near the end of the book—the following superscription is found in the opening verse: "The word of the Lord that came to Jeremiah the prophet concerning the Philistines, before Pharaoh struck down Gaza."[7] Not only is the reader given some guidance and context for how to read this section of Jeremiah, but the superscription sounds like it has been added *after the fact*, and thus provides a set of guidelines for how best to interpret and appreciate this particular prophetic utterance. The Jeremiah example offers a helpful parallel to the Psalms: commentators generally argue that the superscriptions are affixed later in the tradition, but they also contain some clues as to how a given psalm may have been used in a public setting.[8] When

---

[6] On the importance of *way* as a key term, see the longer study of William P. Brown, *Seeing the Psalms: A Theology of Metaphor* (Louisville, KY: Westminster John Knox, 2002); cf. Walter Brueggemann, "Bounded by Obedience and Praise: The Psalms as Canon," *JSOT* 50 (1991): 63–92.

[7] Other examples are Isaiah 38:9 ("A writing of Hezekiah king of Judah, after his illness and recovery"), which provides the setting for the royal prayer that follows, and Habakkuk 3:1 ("A prayer of the prophet Habakkuk according to Shigionoth"; cf. v. 19, "For the choir director, on my stringed instruments"), which relates to the performance of these prophetic words.

[8] See Patrick D. Miller, "Gregory of Nyssa: The Superscriptions of the Psalms," in *Genesis, Isaiah, and Psalms: A Festschrift to Honour Professor John Emerton for His Eightieth Birthday*, ed. Katharine Dell, Graham Davies, and Yee Von Koh, VTSup 135 (Leiden: Brill, 2010), 215: "Their significance for interpreting the psalms has been rather

a particular superscription might have been added is a valid question, but *how* it should be interpreted is equally important. So, for our purposes, three aspects of a superscription will be considered here: proper names, musical directions and instruments, and the occasion for a psalm's performance.

The superscriptions throughout the book of Psalms often contain the proper name of an individual or a group. By far the most popular is *David*, and nearly half of the psalms include this name. It is often assumed that authorship is the reason, and indeed, the typical heading "of David" (*l$^e$David*) in the NRSV conveys this impression. But there are other ways to translate the preposition *lamed* (*l$^e$*), including "dedicated to," "on behalf of," or "belonging to."[9] Consequently, scholars understand the name *David* in the superscription as designating a tradition rather an individual author. Building on our earlier discussion, I would add that when David's name is encountered in the superscription, the reader has a series of expectations for the psalm and should anticipate that certain "plot contours" are more likely to occur. Typically, these psalms are associated with the era of kingship in the nation, with all the internal and external stresses of that long period. A royal figure or leader may well be a leading character in the drama of the Davidic composition, with a host of enemies or opponents who are verbal or physical agitators. Conflict and crisis can be expected in these psalms, and if there is a rescue, God is presented as attentive to the cry for help from the beleaguered Israelite. The reader is therefore provided with a certain perspective: living under divine promise does *not* guarantee a carefree existence, but the psalms of David do emphasize the sovereignty of God over creation and the maze of human history. Much more could be added to this simple overview—ranging from the persona of the king and integrity of the human heart to the schemes of foreign nations and the fertility of the land—but in general any Davidic

---

minor in modern Psalms study, symbolized best by their omission from the translation of the Psalms in the modern New English Bible, a move corrected in the later Revised English Bible."

[9] Brueggemann and Bellinger, *Psalms*, 2. For recent references and appraisal, see David Willgren Davage, "Why Davidic Superscriptions Do Not Demarcate Earlier Collections of Psalms," *JBL* 139 (2020): 67–86.

superscription creates a mood and provides a sense of what might be anticipated in the poetry that follows.

After David, the most popular names in psalm superscriptions are two groups of Levite musicians, Asaph and Korah, who are associated with the Jerusalem temple. Appointed by David in 1 Chr. 16 as a chief worship leader, Asaph is the founder of a group of musicians (and later renowned for his prophetic insight in 2 Chr. 29:30). The Asaph collection (50, 73–83) is placed in the lead position of Book III, speaking to Jerusalem's destruction in the wake of invasion. Along with the crisis of exile, prominent themes in the Asaph psalms include the loss of the temple and the contours of divine justice, as well as encouraging the faithful to recall the great deeds of the past and boldly question how God is at work in the present.[10] Korah is a name that surely would be enshrined in Israel's Hall of Shame. In Numbers 16 Korah and a band of followers rebel against Moses, his cousin. But there is a gaping ironic reversal, for just as Korah and his cohorts open their mouth in rebellion, so the earth opens its mouth and they are swallowed "alive to Sheol, and the earth closed over them and they perished from the midst of the assembly" (v. 33). However, Num 26:11 is a reminder that the offspring of Korah were *not* destroyed, and from these survivors the musical group "sons of Korah" derive, with eleven psalms (42–49 early in Book II; and 84–85 and 87–88 late in Book III). It should be no surprise that the Korah psalms typically emphasize themes such as regret, loss, restoration, and redemption, and the highest frequency of the term *Sheol* occurs in these compositions.[11] When a proper name occurs in a superscription, then, the reader can be oriented to some of the psalm's basic content.

Musical directions and/or instruments are often mentioned in psalm superscriptions, and through these the reader is attuned to the acoustics of a given composition. From the outset it needs to be acknowledged that many of the terms are obscure, often relying on

---

[10] Christine Brown Jones, "The Message of the Asaphite Collection and its Role in the Psalter," in *The Shape and Shaping of the Book of Psalms: The Current State of Scholarship*, ed. Nancy L. DeClaissé-Walford (Atlanta, GA: Society of Biblical Literature, 2014), 71–85.

[11] David C. Mitchell, "'God Will Redeem My Soul from Sheol': The Psalms of the Sons of Korah," *JSOT* 30, no. 3 (2006): 243–262.

inference or traditional interpretations. More than one-third have "to the choirmaster" (NIV; NRSV *to the leader*), and thirty psalms have "song" (*shir*), perhaps indicating voice only, without accompaniment.[12] It can be assumed that such notations are meant as signals or guidance for a conductor or worship maestro on matters of style or tempo. Other instructions apparently specify the kind of musical equipment that is optimal for the psalm (e.g., on stringed instruments, for the flutes or wind instrument; "upon the eighth" may be a musical key), while additional notations seem to indicate a tune or melody ("on the hind of the dawn," "according to the lily of testimony," "set to the dove of the far-off terebinths"; it could be that *Jeduthun* in Psalm 39 refers to a unique kind of vocal inflection). In the end, we have to concede that there is less data than we would prefer—not to mention the absence of any kind of sheet music or the equivalent of an orchestral score—and not much information elsewhere in the Hebrew Bible. Nonetheless, the musical superscriptions invite the reader to imagine a performance when entering certain psalms, and such notations highlight our point elsewhere in this study about the book of Psalms as a *soundtrack* to the faith of Israel.

Some of the superscriptions include an occasion for a psalm's performance or some other temporal marker. Whether headings with terms such as *miktam* (often interpreted as a reflective or contemplative type of psalm) or *maskil* (maybe a reference to an instructional or teaching composition) were proclaimed at specific times in a temple service is unknown.[13] But other headings are less obscure—such as "a song for the Sabbath day" or "song at the dedication of the temple"—prompting the reader to envision a weekly or annual gathering of the community. Also, it could be that a superscription such as "for the thanksgiving [or memorial] offering" indicates the kind of song that is performed during a sacrifice or for gratitude after a divine intervention.[14] It is even

---

[12] Timothy E. Saleska, *Psalms 1–50* (St. Louis, MO: Concordia, 2020), 120. He further comments on the term *Selah* that occurs more than seventy times in the midst of many psalms: "Most scholars believe it was used to signal a pause, allowing for a change in musical accompaniment" (121).

[13] Susan Gillingham, *Psalms through the Centuries: A Reception History Commentary on Psalms 1–72, Volume Two* (Chichester: John Wiley & Sons, 2018), 302.

[14] Cf. Wilson, *Psalms Volume 1*, 28–29.

possible that a longer heading, such as found in Psalm 102 ("A prayer of one afflicted, when faint and pleading before the Lord") that longs for the restoration of Jerusalem might point to a solemn day or hour within the nation's sacred calendar.[15] Many questions remain, but at the very least it could be suggested that these kinds of superscriptions are a reminder that the psalms were composed for all seasons and unfold communal memories about the rhythms of the year replete with echoes of splendid worship gatherings. Consequently, we can appreciate that the superscriptions have a minor but interesting place in the interpretation of a given psalm, with a combination of famous names, musical notations, and celebrations in the life of Israel's people.

## On the Road Again

Based on the discussion above, superscriptions can be interpreted as signposts to guide the reader and indicate the developing and shaping of the Psalter over time. Furthermore, there is a group of fifteen psalms with the same *Song of Ascents* (*shir hama'aloth*) heading, and to this collection our attention now shifts. Numerous views on the origin, background, and codification of the fifteen *Songs of Ascents* have been proffered by scholars over the years. As mentioned, there are many ideas about the background of these songs. They could provide a pilgrimage function; that is, the songs may have been composed for annual trips to Jerusalem that would be performed by travelers on the way upward, that is, the journey of ascent, since Jerusalem is situated at a relatively higher altitude in the Israelite topography.[16] Or perhaps *ascents* refers to a more literal passage up a stairway (compare Isa 38:8), even to the steps of the Jerusalem temple itself. Alternatively, it has been suggested that *ascent* is a poetic device and a reference to

---

[15] See Andrew Witt, "Hearing Psalm 102 within the Context of the Hebrew Psalter," *VT* 62 (2012): 582–606.

[16] It is possible that some of these psalms were tied to various festivals—such as Passover, the feast of Booths, or the Day of Atonement—at various times of the year; see Deut. 16:16, "Three times a year all your males shall appear before the Lord our God at the place that he will choose: at the festival of unleavened bread, at the festival of weeks, and at the festival of booths"; cf. Leviticus 23.

staircase parallelism that is found among some of the poems (when there is a repetition that is gradually enhanced), although the same feature is attested elsewhere in the psalter (such as Ps 93:3, "The floods have lifted up, O Lord,/The floods have lifted up their voice,/The floods lift up their pounding waves").[17]

Even a brief glance at several examples of the fifteen songs allows the reader to get a flavor of the rhythms and tone of this collection. In the lead position, Psalm 120 begins the *Songs of Ascents* with an individual's cry for help: the poet needs to be rescued from the *lip of falsehood*. Like most of the others in the collection, Psalm 120 is a compact song, but it starts with a picture of isolation, alienation, provocation, injustice, and despair; the poet evidently experiences loneliness and a yearning for *shalom* (which can include fellowship, worship, and instruction). In spatial terms, the poet appears to be located far away from the temple, but the key images of the psalm revolve around weapons of words. An array of weapons is featured in the Hebrew Bible (spears, javelins, slings, and swords, not to mention those associated with siegeworks and charioteering), but here in Psalm 120 *deceitful speech* is the weapon that poses a clear and present danger for the poet. For anyone who has lived in an age overwhelmed by fake news—where rumor, innuendo, and (false) accusation can ruin lives and destroy careers—a reminder of the potential devastation of slanderous speech is hardly necessary. In my rendering of Psalm 120 that follows, there are strange geographic references and an overall yearning for movement in the midst of a war of *words*:

> *A Song of Ascents*
> [1] To the Lord I call in my distress,
>   And he will answer me.
> [2] Rescue me O Lord, from lips of falsehood,
>   From the tongue of treachery.
> [3] What can you be given, O tongue of treachery,
>   What more can you gain?

---

[17] For options and related discussion, see Allen P. Ross, *A Commentary on the Psalms*, vol. 1: 1–41 (Grand Rapids, MI: Kregel, 2011), 126–130. He notes that *songs of ascents* also "has been taken to mean 'song of the repatriated,' i.e., when they ascended to Jerusalem after the captivity (Ezra 2:1; 7:7)" (127).

⁴ Arrows of a warrior,
   Sharpened with burning coals of broom-wood!
⁵ Terrible that I am a stranger in Meshech,
   I have lived among the tents of Kedar.
⁶ For too long my soul has lived,
   With those who hate peace.
⁷ I am all about peace,
   But when I speak, they are all about war.

Throughout the Psalms there are various cries for help and numerous categories of disaster. In Ps 22:21 the poet needs to be rescued from the lion's mouth, in Ps 69:1 from the engulfing waters, from the hand of the wicked in Ps 71:4. Here in Ps 120:2–3 the poet needs to be delivered from people who subvert language in a double-crossing or duplicitous way. An ambiguity is apparent in v. 4, as the poet is either describing their words as "arrows" or asking God to visit them with retribution. Equally complicated are the geographical references in v. 5: Meshech is usually associated with a far northern location in the vicinity of the Caspian Sea in modern-day Turkey, while Kedar is in southern Arabia, and such polarities are used together as symbolic of distance from God. Since it is implausible that any Israelite could possibly have lived in *both* of these faraway places, a metaphorical reading—the poet feeling or actually far away from the temple—is the most natural: "One could say, 'Alas, I live in Meshech and dwell in the midst of Kedar' as a way of characterizing any residence beset with social strife."[18]

After reading Psalm 120 a tension can be felt: the psalmist complains about violence, yet wishes violence upon his or her opponents. As one commentator notes, "The psalmist's words hardly suggest a person who is for peace. But typically of the Psalms, hostility is channeled into prayer rather than expressed or acted out toward the people one feels hostile toward."[19] On the one hand, perhaps the psalmist at

---

[18] Mays, *Psalms*, 388. Cf. Frank Lothar Hossfeld and Erich Zenger, *Psalms 3: A Commentary on Psalms 101–150*, Hermeneia (Minneapolis, MN: Fortress, 2011), 309: "The biblically attested characteristics of Kedar and Meshech thus are the best fit for the war metaphors presented in Psalm 120. The petitioner lives in a world that is at war with him," and the north/south extremities are thus "combined as the topographical corners of horrible desolation."

[19] Goldingay, *Psalms*, vol. 3: *Psalms 90–150*, 308.

least is being honest in pleading for *poetic justice*, that is, for violent instruments to be turned against the violent. On the other hand, the concluding line in the psalm—"I am all peace"—plays on the name of Jerusalem (translated in standard Hebrew dictionaries as *foundation of peace*), the poet's spiritual home. The concluding line is a spatial reference oriented toward the city of peace, and we get the impression that Psalm 120 functions as an introduction to the fifteen *Songs of Ascents*.[20]

It might be suggested that there is an order and a symmetry to the *Songs of Ascents*, especially if they are a collection of pilgrimage songs related to visiting Jerusalem. In the lead position, Psalm 120 evokes the perspective of someone who is far from the worshiping community and longs for the chance to move closer to Jerusalem. As it turns out, the *journey* is prominent in Psalm 121 and *arrival* is celebrated in 122. Psalm 121, the second of the *Songs of Ascents*, begins with a first-person visual perspective: "I lift up my eyes to the mountains, from where does my help come?" It is often pointed out that *two voices* speak in Psalm 121; the first voice issues the pressing question about the *mountains* and *help*. Although some interpreters affectionately view the mountains as those hills that surround Zion (cf. 125:2), there seems to be nothing particularly reassuring about the hills, and the psalmist appears to be apprehensive. If there is fear, what is the poet of Psalm 121 afraid of?

Lawless roads are mentioned in Judges 5:6, a period of turmoil and fractiousness that is caused by external foes and internal compromise brought about by the half-heartedness of God's people. Therefore, it is possible that practical dangers for travelers lurk in the hills, with varying degrees of uncertainties or threats of robbery: "Already challenging in their natural terrain, the hills may harbor those who would prey on the unsuspecting and the exposed. Here, before the hills' expanse, the vulnerable traveler contemplates jeopardy and asks a genuine question: can the journey's ordeal be survived?"[21] Furthermore, Canaanite religion long asserted that mountaintops were the residence of gods such as Baal, and narratives like 1 Kings 20:23–25 illustrate such belief patterns. The sun and the moon were often deified in the

---

[20] W. Dennis Tucker Jr., *Constructing and Deconstructing Power in Psalms 107–150* (Atlanta, GA: Society of Biblical Literature, 2014), 96.
[21] Karl A. Plank, "Ascent to Darker Hills: Psalm 121 and Its Poetic Revision," *Literature & Theology* 11 (1997): 154.

ancient Near East and are in the foreground of exhortations such as Deut 4:19: "When you look to the heavens and see the sun, moon, and stars, all the array of heaven, do not be led astray to bow down and worship them." In this case, the poet is debating a serious theological question: Where is the ultimate source of help?

Whether the psalmist's fear is practical or theological (or even a combination of both), Psalm 121 has a response given in a staircase parallelism: help comes from the maker of heaven and earth. The response could be spoken by a priestly figure or could be an internal dialogue of the poet. But this response—tied with a sixfold repetition of the verb *shamar*, meaning "to keep, guard, or protect"—reveals much about the character of God in the poem. In the context of the *Songs of Ascents*, Psalm 121 declares that the creator of the universe is vigilant and invested in the poet's journey, and thus there is confidence that God will grant safe passage to worship in Jerusalem and allow for a return journey back to every family's tribal inheritance, and such a God does not slumber and is an ever-present hand of help. But one expert wisely cautions against turning such confidence into a mechanical formula:

> The promised blessings upon the traveler might seem simply optimistic, the kind of easy assurance one sometimes gives to anxious children. One should not, however, view the blessing as a guarantee that nothing bad will happen on the journey. It is a blessing, that is, a wish uttered in the hope that the Lord will go with the traveler. God remains sovereignly free. The traveler accepts the assurance as a prayer and an expression of trust. To understand this prayer, one might keep in mind a helpful distinction between true and false religion. False religion prays for protection against evil in the conviction that if one prays with sufficient fervor, no evil will come upon one. True religion prays with the same fervor, but allows for the possibility, even the probability, that evil may well befall one. Its faith is that when trouble comes, God will be there to help one through the pain. This psalm is certain of one thing: God will accompany the journey to its end.[22]

---

[22] Clifford, *Psalms 73–150*, 134.

If Psalm 121 is about the journey, then 122 focuses squarely on the destination. In the superscription of Psalm 122 there is the added notation of *David*, an anticipatory reference in light of the two major houses of Jerusalem—the temple and the royal palace complex—that are firmly in view in Psalm 122, and thus a reminder that worship and justice are not mutually exclusive. "Let us go to the house of the Lord" in v. 1 may suggest that the poet has arrived in the city and joins the multitude in observing one of the great festivals in the Israelite calendar. Furthermore, the architecture and infrastructure of Jerusalem as pictured in Psalm 122 become an expression of the unity of God's people. Commentators also note the call to prayer at the end of Psalm 122, implying that the city of Jerusalem is susceptible to fissures or weaknesses. Among the many needs are a legitimate ruler centered on *tôrāh* as a champion of justice and equity, along with a people centered on God and a community bound by worship. When these elements are working cohesively, the longing of Psalm 120 and the journey of 121 move toward realization: the declaration of peace at the end of Psalm 120 becomes a prayer for peace at the end of Psalm 122. Some poetic momentum is generated when the first three psalms of the collection are read together, further strengthening the idea that there is an intentional arrangement of the fifteen compositions.

Moving ahead to the halfway point of the collection, Psalm 127 likewise appears to be strategically placed. Immediately preceding is Psalm 126, which contains a key portion of figurative language: "Restore our fortunes O Lord, like the watercourses in the Negev." In this case, *watercourses in the Negev* is a double-duty image, as the poet longs for restoration like a stream in the desert, but also longs to be back in the land of promise, where the (usually) dry Negev region in southern Judah is located. As for Psalm 127, two issues arise. First, how is this a pilgrimage song when there is not much by way of obvious sojourning? In response, one could say that the psalm addresses the durability of the family and the quality of the city that is the destination of a family's pilgrimage. Some interpreters have argued that Psalm 127 is a postexilic composition, when the matter of *rebuilding* and proper construction were priorities. If Psalm 127 is about restoring the temple and the nation, then it is powerfully apposite in the *Songs of Ascents*: on the heels of a psalm of restoration (126), Psalm 127 undoubtedly makes a larger contribution with its long-term interest in the stability of Jerusalem.

A second issue in Psalm 127 is the name *Solomon* that appears in the superscription. In a psalm about *building* and *security of the city*, such an ascription may not be overly surprising, since Solomon is popularly associated with the greatest of architectural projects and the apex of Jerusalem's strength. But the mention of Solomon—again at the midway point of the *Songs of Ascents*—also carries a significant warning, for his reign had a dark side as well. For all the success, there was even more corruption (e.g., violations of Deuteronomy 17 with wealth, horses, and foreign wives, and deviant religious installations on the Mount of Olives directly across the valley from the Jerusalem temple; 1 Kings 11:7–8). At various points in Solomon's career there are direct divine admonitions in 1 Kings 6:11–13 and 9:3–9, with ominous warnings about the reality of exile for covenant transgressions. In terms of the larger storyline, it is telling that Solomon's reign occurs at approximately the midpoint in Israel's history—the halfway mark between the exodus from Egypt and the exile to Babylon—and thus God's personal warnings to Solomon in 1 Kings 6–9 are located at a pivotal moment. By analogy, at the halfway point of the *Songs of Ascents* there is a reference to Solomon that operates as a reminder and a cautionary tale for the (re)building efforts of the sacred city and its families. Like most of the fifteen songs, Psalm 127 is a compact piece:

> *A Song of Ascents. About Solomon*
> ¹ If the Lord does not build the house,
>    In futility the builders labor.
> If the Lord does not guard the city,
>    In futility the guard stays awake.
> ² It is futility for you:
>    You who are early to rise,
>       Then stay up late,
>          Eating the bread of anxious toil.
>    Indeed, *he* gives rest to his beloved one!
> ³ Behold, children are an inheritance of the Lord,
>    The fruit of the womb is a reward.
> ⁴ Like arrows in a warrior's hand,
>    Thus are children of one's youth.

> ⁵ How blessed is the warrior whose quiver has been filled,
>   They will never be put to shame,
>     When they confront their enemies at the gate.

Several other remarks about Psalm 127 should be made at this point. To begin, the repetition of the Hebrew term *shavay*—usually rendered as *useless, vain*, or *futile*—is a key word in the poem. The term elsewhere occurs in Exod 23:1 in a legal context: "You shall not spread a false [*shavay*] report. You shall not join hands with the wicked to act as a malicious witness." But there is a slightly different semantic range at work in Psalm 127, and the noun *shavay* in this context means "unsuccessful, without result, ineffective." One commentator explains, "The psalm does not say that all human action is meaningless, reprehensible, and in vain, so that it would be better not to do it. Rather, the emphasis is on the idea that this action, which is necessary, succeeds only when and if YHWH is at work in it and brings it to completion."[23] Similarly, the term *house* has a broad semantic range, and while it can mean a physical structure (such as a palace, temple, or regular domicile), it can also refer to a family or a dynasty. Of course, families and houses can be built while ignoring God and eschewing the *tôrāh*, but according to Psalm 127 such enterprises will not finally endure. This could be why the psalm concludes with an image of the *gate*, the ancient Near Eastern equivalent of the law court, and in texts such as Deut 25:7 the city gate is the place where traditionally matters of justice are resolved. Ruth 4 provides another picture of the city gate as a place where issues of inheritance are attended to. In Psalm 127, it is possible to understand the final line as a kind of declaration: families (and houses, temples, and cities) built on the foundation of *tôrāh* finally have long-term sustainability and will not be put to shame despite any miseries or misfortunes.

Returning to the Solomonic superscription in the title of the psalm, the legacy of David's immediate successor intersects at numerous points with the theology of Psalm 127, namely, the ultimate precariousness of human ventures that are not underwritten by

---

[23] Hossfeld and Zenger, *Psalms 3*, 386.

divine stability. The Solomonic structures—his massive physical house located beside the Jerusalem temple for worship—do not last, razed by the Babylonians, so the psalm cautions against any similar ventures that will end in the same cycle of futility. Solomon is an heir of great promise, and just like the rest of the nation has been bequeathed an incomparable heritage. But how will such gifts be used? It is worth repeating that Solomon reigns at the midpoint between entrance *to* the land and exit *from* the land, and God's warnings to Solomon function as a kind of midterm examination for the people of Israel as a whole. Midway through the *Songs of Ascents*, therefore, Psalm 127 represents a pivot point and a check on motives: in the midst of a reminder about solid versus shaky foundations, every Israelite pilgrim is challenged about their purpose for making the journey. Such thoughts might be clearer after a brief consideration of Psalm 134. So, before making a few comments by way of conclusion, consider Psalm 134 as the final composition in the collection:

*A Song of Ascents*
¹ Now: bless the Lord, all servants of the Lord,
    standing all night in the house of the Lord!
² Lift up your hands to the sanctuary,
    and bless the Lord!
³ May the Lord bless you from Zion,
    the maker of heaven and earth.

Toward the end of the *Songs of Ascents* there is a gradual shift in emphasis, as tensions and issues of oppression are replaced by celebrations of the community with joy and unity. The first three psalms of the collection (120–123) feature a journey toward and arrival in Jerusalem, while in the final three psalms (132–134) there is "an increasingly clear focus on worship in the temple."[24] The capstone of the collection is

---

[24] Philip E. Satterthwaite, "Zion in the Songs of Ascents," in *Zion, City of Our God*, ed. Richard S. Hess and Gordon J. Wenham (Grand Rapids, MI: Eerdmans, 1999), 118. Cf. Hossfeld and Zenger, *Psalms 3*, 296: "The whole composition of Psalm 120–34 establishes an important arc of tension: the search for a place of safety and protection in the midst of a hostile world beginning with the psalm pair 120–21 finds its fulfillment in the cultic house and life community on Zion (Psalms 133–134)."

Psalm 134, and as we can see, it is composed entirely of direct speech, with a spatial setting that is exclusively within the temple. It is notable that there is no movement or plot in this psalm: if 129 struggles with painful memories of past trauma, 134 has reached the finish line and is totally immersed in the present with an absence of enemies and obstacles. The concluding psalm is an expansive indication of how far the reader has traveled, and a striking contrast with the first composition: in Psalm 120 the poet is assailed by the shrill blast of deceitful noise, but in 134 the poet is absorbed into the faithful community and receives the music and full-bodied language of blessing. If the poet of Psalm 120 yearned to be in the sacred place, that exact destination has been reached in Psalm 134. With its words of blessing that echo the prayer of 121 ("maker of heaven and earth"), it is not an overstatement to call Psalm 134 the crown jewel of the collection. It marks the completion of the journey in the *Songs of Ascents*, and its placement at the pinnacle of the collection can be visualized in the following diagram:

> Psalm 134—Worship: "May the Lord bless you from Zion"
> Psalm 133—Unity: "Like the dew of Hermon"
> Psalm 132—Promise: "O Lord, for David's sake, remember"
> Psalm 131—Waiting: "My heart is not proud"
> Psalm 130—Hoping: "I look to the Lord"
> Psalm 129—Disgrace: "They have often assailed me"
> Psalm 128—Fruitfulness: "Blessed are those who fear the Lord"
> Psalm 127—Foundations: "Unless the Lord builds the house"
> Psalm 126—Restore: "When the Lord restores the fortunes"
> Psalm 125—Trust: "The scepter of the wicked"
> Psalm 124—Testimony: "Were it not for the Lord"
> Psalm 123—Petition: "Show us favor"
> Psalm 122—Arrival: "Our feet are standing in your gates, O Jerusalem"
> Psalm 121—Journey: "I lift up my eyes to the hills"
> Psalm 120—Separation: "Woe to me that I sojourn in Meshech"

Overall, the fifteen *Songs of Ascents* are arranged in the shape of a journey, with no shortage of challenges, setbacks, reflections and suffering, but also with hope and the prospects of blessing along the way and upon reaching the final destination. In geographic terms, the collection begins outside the land but concludes in the midst of the assembled congregation in the sanctuary. In thematic terms, over the course of Psalms 120–134 one notices a gradual displacement of adversaries and hostility and an increase in the language of blessing and community. Moving toward the pinnacle, there are fewer cries for help and more corporate praise. Positioned near the midpoint of Book V, the collection reflects the motif of exile and return, taking the reader on a sojourn that ascends the steps of the rebuilt temple to arrive at the place of worship.[25] As it stands, the fifteen psalms are organized as a movement toward the presence of God, a journey that begins in a distant and forlorn place and concludes at home within the community of God's people.

## Fellowship of the King

Alongside the *Songs of Ascents* are several other groups of psalms: the Asaph (50, 73–83) and Korah (42–49, 84–85, 87–88) collections, as well as a cluster that are referred to as the Egyptian Passover psalms (113–118) that celebrate the exodus tradition. Another major group is the thirteen psalms with superscriptions that directly relate to events in the life of David, mostly distributed throughout Books I and II of the Psalter.[26] There is no scarcity of books and related summaries that attempt to present the turbulent life and times of King David. The name *David* is related to the Hebrew root for *beloved*, and hence the story of David—from his anointing to kingship in Jerusalem to exile

---

[25] Cf. the Spanish-language work of Tirsa Ventura, admirably summarized in a recent essay by Edesio Sanchez, "Psalms in Latin America," in *The Oxford Handbook of the Psalms*, ed. William P. Brown (New York: Oxford University Press, 2014), 475–481.

[26] The list includes Psalms 3 (when he fled from his son Absalom), 7 (that he sang to the Lord concerning Cush, a Benjaminite), 18 (on the day that the Lord delivered him from the hand of all his enemies), 34 (when he feigned madness before Abimelech), 51 (when Nathan the prophet came to him, after David had gone in to Bathsheba), 52 (when Doeg the Edomite came and reported to Saul), 54 (when the Ziphites revealed, "Is not David hiding among us"), 56 (when the Philistines seized him in Gath), 57 (when he fled from Saul in the cave), 59 (when Saul ordered that the house be watched in order to kill him), 60 (when he battled with Aram-naharaim and with Aram-zobah), 63 (when he was in the wilderness of Judah), and 142 (when he was in the cave).

and chastened return—remarkably corresponds to the larger history of God's people, and hence in some ways the figure of David represents the people of Israel.

At the risk of simplification, a short overview of David's eventful career might be summarized in three phases. First, his early life features his anointing by the prophet Samuel, followed by the spectacular victory over Goliath the Philistine, eventually becoming a member of the royal family as Saul's son-in-law.[27] But this relationship with Saul soon turns sour, resulting in a long period as a fugitive in the wilderness. Second, after Saul's death David is ensconced as king over all Israel in Jerusalem, although there are hints of increasing family and political tensions. Among the most astonishing promises in biblical history is the assurance that David will always have a descendant on the throne of Jerusalem (2 Samuel 7), a promise that is sorely tested in the days ahead. Third, a vicious civil war in the aftermath of Absalom's rebellion leaves lasting scars on both king and country, a conflict that arguably is sparked by David's ill-advised liaison with Bathsheba; the king chose not to accompany his troops in battle at the beginning of 2 Samuel 11, but is soon besieged by another battle within his own person. David survives this conflict, but never completely recovers and is succeeded by his son Solomon at the outset of 1 Kings.

It should also be noted that music is associated with David's earliest moments in the narrative. As events unfold in 1 Sam 16, David ends up as a music therapist in Saul's court, where his melodious playing allays the spiritual darkness that envelops King Saul. It also creates one of the great ironies in world literature: the tormented incumbent king can be soothed only by the one who has been secretly designated to replace him. Furthermore, David crafts a soaring eulogy in the wake of Saul's death (along with his son Jonathan), and the closing sections of 2 Samuel feature a number of lyrics attributed to the king. (Indeed,

---

[27] Triumph over the giant not only propels David into the national spotlight; it is also referred to in a couple of psalms, albeit obliquely. In the Greek version of Psalm 144, the superscription includes the name of Goliath, while the Greek Psalm 151 (included in most Eastern Orthodox Bibles) is a poetic recounting of that famous confrontation, ending with "I drew his own sword, I beheaded him, and took away disgrace from the people of Israel."

2 Sam 23:1 labels David "the sweet psalmist of Israel" or "Israel's beloved singer of songs.") Overall, it is possible to argue that David's life is a mirror of the nation in so many ways and as the representative Israelite, with ample potential and yet falling short too often; perhaps this explains the frequency of Davidic references throughout the Psalter. The narrative of Samuel and Kings and the image of David in the book of Psalms is not the same, although many readers are tempted to conflate the two. But we can get a better grasp of the picture after some analysis of several psalms.

## The Shield

The first of the psalms with a Davidic superscription—in fact, the first composition with any superscription at all—is Psalm 3, connected with his son Absalom's revolt and David's flight from Jerusalem. In 2 Sam 15:14 David is first informed of Absalom's treachery and immediately orders, "Arise and let us flee." So begins his exile from Jerusalem, walking barefoot with head covered. On the journey David encounters some declarations of loyalty, but also the searing insults of Shimei, who vehemently declares that God has brought this misery upon David because of his own transgressions, a claim that David does not publicly deny. He is able to cross the Jordan River, however, a tactical move of considerable benefit to the king's retinue. Various topics in Psalm 3 (many foes, insults, salvation, sleep, and blessing on the community) intersect in varying degrees with David's crisis during his son's hostile takeover.

> *A David Psalm: as he fled from Absalom, his son*
> [1] O Lord, how my foes have multiplied,
>     many are rising up against me.
> [2] Many are saying about me,
>     "There won't be any rescue of him by God!" *Selah*
> [3] But you, O Lord, are a shield around me,
>     you are my glory, and you lift up my head.
> [4] With my voice I cried out to the Lord,
>     and he answered me from his holy mountain.

⁵ I can lay down, I can rest,
    I can awaken, because the Lord sustains me. *Selah*
⁶ I will not be afraid of thousands of soldiers,
    who are all around, set against me.
⁷ Arise, O Lord, rescue me, my God!
    For you strike all my enemies on the cheek,
        you break the teeth of the wicked.
⁸ To the Lord belongs the rescue,
    May your blessing be upon your people. *Selah*

Some readers like to imagine that David, in deep distress with few options, writes this prayer in the midst of fleeing from his son. Hence, the superscription becomes a type of historical annotation or signature of authorship, and it is often assumed that the psalm is a composition from David's hand. However, because there is textual evidence from the Greek Septuagint and the Qumran manuscripts that the superscriptions were more fluid and usually added later, many scholars dismiss the historical connections and in general do not subscribe to Davidic authorship. What is a productive way to understand the role of the superscription in Psalm 3? A useful option, in my view, is to view the superscription—that is, the connection of Absalom's rebellion with the content of Psalm 3—in a canonical and intertextual framework. In other words, we can imagine that when the community of faith gathers around to hear the narrative of 2 Samuel 15–17, the response is to corporately pray the words of Psalm 3. It is not hard to picture this kind of response in a second temple setting, synagogue, or any kind of faith community: "Connection to the Absalom rebellion portrays a speaker—any speaker—whose life is deeply in jeopardy and who lacks resources to cope on his own. The specificity of the superscription permits hearing the psalm in many specificities of extreme threat when subsequent speakers of the psalm are also in deep jeopardy and without resources. Like David, every person of faith may, in the midst of jeopardy, appeal through this psalm to the God of deliverance."[28]

A question that quickly surfaces in Psalm 3 is the identity of "the foes" who are oppressing the poet. Commentators often point out that

---

[28] Brueggemann and Bellinger, *Psalms*, 3.

there are several terms for enemies in the Hebrew Bible, and the particular nuance here involves constriction, or suffocation; it is as though the foes (who are many, and multiplying) are forcing the poet into a narrow and claustrophobic place of confinement even as they are taunting him or her with contempt.[29] A key metaphor that emerges early in Psalm 3 is a *shield*, used perhaps to emphasize that trust in the character of God can serve to deflect such verbal attacks; a handheld shield might not be an offensive weapon as such but part of the poet's individual fortification in this time of siege.

The motif of rest or sleep also occurs in the narrative of Absalom's rebellion. There is a rapid sequence in 2 Sam 15:30–32 where David—having been apprised of his trusted senior counselor Ahithophel's betrayal and defection to Absalom's cause—cries out to God for help as he approaches the holy Mount of Olives. Almost instantaneously God evidently responds to this prayer by sending Hushai the Archite; as the later narrative unfolds, Hushai's role is absolutely indispensable to David's success in the longer term, and in the shorter term allows David to sleep with a measure of security on the other side of the Jordan. Psalm 3 poetically reinforces a reminder that anyone—even a person under the umbrella of God's promise who has wandered astray—can suffer a terrible assault, and yet is encouraged in the midst of any adversity to cry out in faith to God, who is more than capable of rescue. In fact, David's refreshment in 2 Sam 16:14 occurs *prior* to any victory in battle, and so this psalm testifies to a certain peace that flows from trust in God despite anxiety and a multitude of adversaries.

## Damage Control

The poet of Psalm 3 can stand firm despite myriad forces arrayed on every side because of the prospects of divine salvation. In Psalm 51, by contrast, the poet's guilt is front and center: if the foes of Psalm 3 are

---

[29] For example, Wilson, *Psalms Volume 1*, 129. On the taunt, see Mays, *Psalms*, 52–53: " 'No salvation for him in God' is a mortally dangerous weapon against the soul. It has an ally in every crevice of doubt, anxiety, and guilt in the heart. No reasoning or counsel or procedure is a sure defense against it. One can either believe it or believe in God."

*external*, the struggle in Psalm 51 is deeply *internal*. For many reasons this particular composition has a rich history of interpretation and use; it is a favorite of presidents who have gotten caught in dubious activities; musically it has been used by Bach, as well as Mozart (in a Lenten concert in Vienna in 1785), and in Felix Mendelssohn's oratorio *St. Paul* you can hear parts of Psalm 51 in the lyrics of Paul's prayer for forgiveness after his conversion.[30] I will divide the psalm into two parts—making several comments on each—starting with the first half:

> *To the chief musician, a David psalm, when the prophet Nathan came to him after he had gone into Bathsheba*
> 1 Be gracious to me, O God,
>     according to your covenant love,
>     according to the breadth of your mercy,
>     erase my rebellions.
> 2 Completely wash me from my wrongdoing,
>     cleanse me from my sin.
> 3 For I know my rebellions,
>     my sin is always before me.
> 4 Against you, alone, I have sinned,
>     done what is evil in your eyes,
>     for you are right when you speak,
>     you are blameless when you judge.
> 5 Yes, in iniquity I was born,
>     in sin my mother conceived me.
> 6 Yes, you delight in truth in the inner being,
>     in my hidden person you teach me wisdom.
> 7 Un-sin me with hyssop that I might be clean,
>     wash me so I can be whiter than snow.
> 8 Allow me to hear happiness and joy,
>     may the bones that you have broken rejoice.
> 9 Hide your face from my sins,
>     erase all my guilt.

---

[30] Gillingham, *Psalms through the Centuries*, 213–314.

Psalm 51 begins with one of the longest and most dramatic superscriptions in the book, associating this composition with the royal debacle of 2 Samuel 11–12, when David's personal sins nearly destroy both himself and the nation (as the civil war in the days of Absalom can be traced directly to these catastrophic events.) There are two main ways that the superscription has been interpreted. First, it is popularly understood as the voice of the king in the aftermath of Nathan's confrontation seeking to mitigate the damage of his sin to himself (and others).[31] There is a deep intimacy in this psalm: even though all David says is "I have sinned against the Lord" in 2 Sam 12:13 *after* getting caught, there is a much more elaborate prayer of repentance here. Second, the superscription has been be interpreted as an intertextual notice; in other words, when the community hears the story of 2 Samuel 11–12 they use this psalm as a prayer of response. At the end of Psalm 51 there is reference to building the walls of Jerusalem—implying that the city has been invaded—and most naturally we think of the destruction of 2 Kings 25 here.[32] So perhaps this psalm has been composed to create an even more immersive experience when reading about David's actions in the Bathsheba affair. I would suggest that the reader keep all available options on the table while studying this psalm and imagine several different scenarios when analyzing the poetry.

Early in the psalm a theological tempo is established through balanced three-word combinations. The poet asks God to be *gracious*, show *compassion*, and act on the basis of *covenant faithfulness*. In turn, the poet offers confessions for three kinds of offense (rebellion, wrongdoing, failure) and acknowledgment of the need for three kinds of divine remedy for sin: erase, wash, cleanse. Perhaps the poet is drawing on famous texts of divine self-disclosure from the Torah that

---

[31] R. Christopher Heard, "Penitent to a Fault: The Characterization of David in Psalm 51," in *The Fate of King David: The Past and Present of a Biblical Icon*, ed. Tod Linafelt, Claudia V. Camp and Timothy Beal, LHBOTS 500 (London: T&T Clark, 2010), 173.

[32] Schaefer, *Psalms*, 351: "David's experience provides a pattern for understanding human life, and thus it enables later generations to see their own sentiments and uncertainties in a larger context." Cf. Mays on these superscriptions: "The other narrative headings in the psalms are like this one in kind and function. Mistaken as historical notices, they lead to puzzlement. Taken as permission and encouragement to heuristic reflection, they lead to discoveries that lend concreteness and use to the liturgical language of the psalm" (*Psalms*, 54).

emphasize God's capacity to pardon the guilty (e.g., "the Lord, a God merciful and gracious, slow to anger, and abounding in steadfast love and faithfulness," Exod. 34:6–7; cf. Num. 14:18). If so, the poet admits to a comprehensive botch and pleads with God, "Don't deal with me as I deserve!" Furthermore, the scope of the evil deed(s) requires a massive divine intervention and a housecleaning, hence the *hyssop* imagery in verse 7. First used to apply the blood of the sacrificial lamb on the doorposts during the Passover ritual in Exodus 12, here the poet uses hyssop to express a need for protection from the consequences of his failure.[33] The request is enhanced through the verb that is translated more literally as "un-sin," that is, a plea to be cleansed so that all traces are removed entirely.

[10] Create in me a clean heart, O God,
    a right spirit make new within me.
[11] Do not cast me from your presence,
    or take your holy spirit away from me.
[12] Return to me the joy of your salvation,
    and sustain me with a wholehearted spirit
[13] Let me teach rebels your ways
    may sinners return to you.
[14] Rescue me from the guilt of shedding blood, O God,
    the God of my salvation,
        let my tongue loudly sing of your righteousness.
[15] Open my lips, O Lord,
    let my mouth report your praise.
[16] Surely you would not delight in any sacrifice that I may bring,
    even a burnt-offering would not please you.
[17] The godliest of sacrifices is a broken spirit,
    a broken and humbled heart, O God, you will never despise.
[18] In your favor, do what is good for Zion,
    may you build up the walls of Jerusalem.

---

[33] See Exod. 12:22–23, "Take a bunch of hyssop, dip it in the blood that is in the basin, and touch the lintel and the two doorposts with the blood in the basin.... For the Lord will pass through to strike down the Egyptians; when he sees the blood on the lintel and on the two doorposts, the Lord will pass over that door and will not allow the destroyer to enter your houses to strike you down" (NRSV).

¹⁹ Then you will delight in righteous sacrifices,
    burnt offerings and whole burnt offerings,
        young bulls that then are offered on your altar.

Even moving beyond the need for a deep cleansing, the second half of Psalm 51 contains the poet's wish for a new creative act. The verb *bara'* occurs in Gen 1:1 ("In the beginning God *created* the heavens and the earth"), and in the Hebrew Bible only God is the subject of this particular verb. So the gift of a new heart is something exclusively in the divine realm, and the poet must therefore believe that a new heart will prevent a relapse into sin. In fact, the theme of *heart* continues, for in verse 17 the poet juxtaposes traditional Israelite sacrifices with the sacrifice of a broken and repentant *heart*. "The words 'broken' and 'contrite/crushed' are figurative (implied comparisons); they refer to the penitence and submission of the sinner—he has to be humble and contrite, broken of self-will and arrogance. True contrition, that is, a spirit broken by guilt and remorse, is what God looks for in a penitent."[34] A comparable theology might be found in the book of Micah, albeit with some extreme hyperbole: in response to the rhetorical question "Will the Lord be pleased with thousands of rams, with ten thousand rivers of olive oil?," the prophet declares, "He has shown you, O mortal, what is good. And what does the Lord require of you? To act justly and to love mercy and to walk humbly with your God." The concluding verses of Psalm 51 point to a corporate renewal, implying that through the benefit of divine favor the city can be rebuilt. Just as the poet seeks restoration, so the city needs remaking after a disaster. According to Leviticus 1, *young bulls* would be among the most expensive of whole burnt offerings, so this final image points to a renewal and recommitment within the enclosure of the rebuilt walls of the city.

---

[34] Ross, *A Commentary on the Psalms, Volume 2: 42–89*, 198.

## On the Run

We have just explored two psalms with superscriptions that connect to a pair of harrowing experiences for David: the Absalom uprising with the ignominious exile from Jerusalem, and Nathan's prophetic denunciation after the king's adultery and murder. In the 2 Samuel narrative these miserable events are largely self-inflicted, and those two headings are easy to correlate with David's life. Our third example, Psalm 63, begins with a superscription that apparently relates to a much earlier episode. The last twelve chapters of the long 1 Samuel narrative are devoted to David's period as a fugitive in the wilderness, as he was driven from Saul's court and eventually gathers a band of followers who are likewise disaffected with the increasingly manic king. As listed earlier, there are several psalms with superscriptions that relate to this precarious phase in the career of David.

For example, Psalm 59—*when Saul sent men to watch his house in order to kill him*—connects with the dark night of the soul in 1 Samuel 19, when David's wife Michal counters her father's ambush by lowering David down through the window and, with shades of the old Clint Eastwood movie *Escape from Alcatraz*, fills his bed with a mannequin decoy and so buys time for David to flee. One can argue that the words of Psalm 59 have a certain resonance with the tense situation of 1 Samuel 19. Opening phrases such as "Deliver me from my enemies, O my God, protect me from those who rise up against me" cohere with David's predicament, and the lengthy explanation about a conspiracy ("they lie in wait for my life, fierce men stir up strife against me, for no transgression or sin of mine, O Lord") dovetails with the occasion in 1 Samuel 19.[35]

---

[35] On the portrayal of these enemies as "prowling dogs," see Vivian L. Johnson, *David in Distress: His Portrait through the Historical Psalms*, LHBOTS 505 (London: T&T Clark International, 2009), 40–41: "A telling image of Ps 59 is the one in which the dogs prowl throughout the city at night (vv. 7–8, 15–16). The psalmist imagines his foes as these wild dogs that lurk about the streets in search of food until their appetites are sated (vv. 7, 15–16). This comparison of his enemies to wild dogs illustrates the baseness of the psalmist's attackers; they pursue him like hungry animals foaming at the mouth. They are 'bloodthirsty' and 'mighty' adversaries who pose problems too great for him to resolve alone. Unless God intervenes, the psalm suggests that the petitioner will fall victim to them (v. 5)."

Nevertheless, there are other parts of Psalm 59 that are not so evidently applied to the nocturnal ruse and David's resulting escape from Saul's ambush, and vv. 11–14 are examples: "Kill them not, lest my people forget; make them totter by your power and bring them down, O Lord, our shield! For the sin of their mouths, the words of their lips, let them be trapped in their pride. For the cursing and lies that they utter, consume them in wrath; consume them till they are no more, in order that they may know that God rules over Jacob to the ends of the earth." Are such imprecations consistent with David's characterization in the 1 Samuel 19–21 narrative?[36]

Our goal is not to resolve such questions but instead to be aware of how the Psalms are approached by interpreters today, because similar matters can be found in the other compositions with superscriptions that relate to David's fugitive era. Whether one is analyzing Psalm 54 (when the Ziphites reveal his location to Saul: "Is not David hiding among us") or Psalm 34 (when he pretends to be a lunatic in the presence of the Philistine king), there are some aspects that fit and other elements that seem awkward when strictly applied to David during the long stretch of text when he is on the run in 1 Samuel.

But even if some of these Psalmic connections are a bit tenuous—some parts fitting the context, while others are in tension—at least the superscriptions in Psalms 34, 54, and 59 can be identified with a well-known incident during David's fugitive phase. This should be

---

[36] It is true that David says to Abishai, "Don't destroy him, for who can send his hand against the Lord's anointed and be innocent? . . . As the Lord lives, the Lord himself will strike him, or his day will come and he'll die, or he'll go down into battle and be swept away. Far be it from me by the Lord that I should send my hand against the Lord's anointed" (1 Sam 26:9–10). Yet some scholars maintain that these verses in the psalm seem to target *foreign* opponents rather than *internal* foes within the Israelite community. Consequently, it might be suggested that there is a national dimension to Psalm 59 that transcends the immediate context of escaping from Saul's mania, and as Mays avers, there is a broader application of the psalm: "The prayer seems to express the anxieties and needs of the postexilic religious community seeking to maintain its trust in the face of surrounding nations whose cultures and religions are viewed as hostile to the community's faith. The prayer is the voice of the congregation that has no refuge in the midst of history other than the Lord of hosts. The scholarly scribe who completed the title found a clue to the psalm's setting in the story of David (I Sam. 19:11)" (*Psalms*, 213).

kept in mind as we now listen to Psalm 63; while it might seem like *the wilderness of Judah* is a clear enough reference to this same period of uncertainty—both in geographic terms, with its fraught terrain, and existential terms, with the tenseness and the constant vigilance required because of Saul's hostile intent—it is actually more complicated in interpretive history than may appear at first glance.

> *A psalm of David, when he is in the desert of Judah*
> [1] O God, you are my God, I earnestly seek you,
>> my soul thirsts for you, my flesh yearns for you,
>>> in a parched and weary land without water.
> [2] In the holy place I have gazed at you,
>> to see your strength and your glory.
> [3] Your faithfulness is better than life,
>> so my lips will praise you.
> [4] I will bless you all my life,
>> I will lift my hands in your name.
> [5] As with luxurious and rich food my soul is satisfied,
>> with lips of joy my mouth will praise.
> [6] When I remember you on my bed,
>> in the night watches I will meditate on you.
> [7] Because you have been my help,
>> in the shadow of your wings I can sing for joy.
> [8] My soul keeps close to you,
>> your right hold upholds me.
> [9] But those who seek my soul's destruction,
>> to the depths of the earth they will go.
> [10] They will be handed over to the power of the sword,
>> they will be the portion of jackals.
> [11] But the king will rejoice in God,
>> all who swear an oath by him will boast,
>>> for the mouths of those who speak corruptly will be shut.

It requires some care to deduce exactly how the superscription of Psalm 63 should be understood. One commentator suggests that "the heading attributes the psalm to David, when he hid from Saul" in the desert of Judah; in other words, during the fugitive period of the 1 Samuel story.[37] This is not an unreasonable point by any means. However, another commentator has a quite different position, and rather than locate the superscription in reference to the fugitive period, he opts for later events associated with Absalom's uprising: "The last phrase alludes to the narrative in 2 Sam. 15–17, where one can indeed imagine David in a dry and thirsty land recalling how he had seen Yhwh in the sanctuary and had celebrated Yhwh's acts there and looking for Yhwh to put down his enemies again."[38] So here we are faced with competent scholars of these ancient texts arriving at different views on the heading of Psalm 63. To further complicate matters, there is a third alternative, more of a hybrid position:

> The psalm has a superscription added by a later editor indicating this prayer might have been prayed in a situation such as David experienced in the wilderness when he was running from King Saul or when he escaped from his son Absalom. Yet since many of the psalms connected to David's life on the run are prayers for help, this prayer could also indicate the times David spent in the wilderness in happier circumstances, such as when he is portrayed as tending the sheep for his father.[39]

One could continue to go back and forth. A problem with locating Psalm 63 with the 1 Samuel narrative is that David is not yet king, nor is there a "holy place" as such (which is an important venue in the drama of the psalm). All the same, the specific location *Judah's wilderness* does not exactly fit with the Absalom phase of 2 Samuel 15–19, but does fit nicely with Saul's pursuit and the various locations that are frequently mentioned in 1 Samuel 21–31. The *dry and thirsty land* fits the fugitive

---

[37] James H. Waltner, *Psalms,* BCBC (Scottdale, PA: Herald Press, 2006), 307.
[38] John Goldingay, *Psalms,* vol. 2: *Psalms 42–89* (Grand Rapids, MI: Baker, 2007), 307. The Victorian preacher Charles Spurgeon—whose voluminous writings on the Psalms are still consulted today—views the superscription in the same way: "This was probably written while David was fleeing from Absalom; certainly at the time he wrote it he was king (Ps 63:11), and hard pressed by those who sought his life." C. H. Spurgeon, *The Treasury of David, Containing an Original Exposition of the Book of Psalms,* 7 vols. (London, 1860–67) 3:143..
[39] DeClaissé-Walford, Jacobson, and Tanner, *The Book of Psalms,* 301.

phase, whereas the memory of a specific experience in the sanctuary is closer to the kingship period. The content of Psalm 63 no doubt could be further combed, with evidence gathered to buttress arguments for all of these positions, including the hybrid approach.

At this point it might be wisest to keep every option open, even while appreciating that the superscription provides its own set of interpretive clues because it speaks to *any* period of life that is arid and isolated: physically, spiritually, or some combination of both. In such crises, the poet of this psalm *earnestly seeks* rather than accepts spiritual dehydration as a new normal. Consider the following summary: "Psalm 63 brings to words the desert experience of hungering and thirsting after God, an experience brought about by lying oppressors. The satisfying of hunger and quenching of thirst is found in the God who comes to deliver and is present to bless. The psalmist encounters that one in the sanctuary's worship and so confesses trust for life's journey. The faithful psalmist trusts that the God who delivers will embrace the pain of this wilderness time and bring hope."[40] Regardless of exactly what period the superscription might refer to, numerous elements of David's life intersect with the words of the psalm and have abiding relevance for the community of faith.

As we conclude our discussion of this section of our study—and indeed, this whole chapter—it should be noted that it was common in times past to read those psalms with Davidic superscriptions in an individualistic way. The compositions were directly correlated to the events of David's life mentioned in the heading, and even interpreted as signatures of authorship. More recent trends have pointed to the communal cries in these prayers and interpreted the sweeping portrait of David as a representative character who stands for all of Israel in both longing and as heirs of promise. As one scholar writes, "David is presented as an example and a figure with whom the individual reader as well as the praying congregation can identify in times of need and distress. In particular. David stands as an example because almost every lamentation psalm related to David's name ends with an

---

[40] Brueggemann and Bellinger, *Psalms*, 279.

expression of hope and confidence in God's help."[41] Rather than dismiss the superscriptions, they can provide interpretive clues about the function of the psalm. As in the psalms attributed to the "sons of Korah" or the *Songs of Ascents*, we can glimpse ways that these various compositions were used and how they might have been appreciated at initial stages. Altogether, the headings and superscriptions collectively point to an intentional shaping of the individual psalms into larger units and, ultimately, a collection, and it is to that issue that we now turn in our concluding chapter.

---

[41] Rolf Rendtorff, "The Psalms of David: David in the Psalms," in *The Book of Psalms: Composition and Reception*, ed. Peter W. Flint and Patrick D. Miller Jr., with the assistance of Aaron Brunell and Ryan Roberts (Leiden: Brill, 2005), 54, cited by Heard, "Penitent to a Fault," 173. See also the study of James L. Mays, "The David of the Psalms," *Interpretation* 40 (1986): 143–155.

# 6
# The Fivefold Symphony of the Psalter

Having analyzed a number of individual psalms and larger groupings or collections, this last chapter in our study provides a more sustained consideration of the final form of the Psalter and how it is organized as a book. We will begin with the positioning of Psalms 1 and 2 at the outset of the book, as these opening psalms are often referred to as *the gateway to the Psalter*. Psalm 1 is a vigorous reflection on the advantages of a life rooted in God's word, contrasted with the instability and turbulence of a life lived apart from God. Psalm 2 then poetically announces the arrival of a new kind of kingship with multinational implications. After discussing these two psalms that are strategically placed at the entrance to the Psalter, our attention turns to the five-book structure of the Psalms, where we further explore the larger metanarrative or overarching plotline that can be discerned in arrangement of the 150 psalms. For example, can it be maintained that the structure of the book of Psalms generally corresponds to the history of Israel, from the reigns of David and Solomon through the murkiness of the divided kingdom, followed by the travail of exile and subsequent restoration to the land? Moreover, in the architecture of the book of Psalms is there a general movement from dwelling on past mistakes to a more joyful set of expectations for the future? Is there a journey from *petition* (cries for help and lament for circumstances) to *praise*, where everything that breathes is enjoined to give thanks to God using a wide array of instruments in unhindered orchestral praise? These are some of the main questions addressed in these final pages of our study.

## The Gateway

In the previous chapter it was suggested that superscriptions can be viewed as signposts for reading particular psalms, and overall these headings provide a window into the development of the Psalter and its intentional shaping over time. Another such indicator of the growth of the Psalter, in the opinion of many scholars, is the placement of the opening psalms at the entrance to the book. So we start by turning our attention to Psalm 1, which does not have any kind of title. Why would the book of Psalms start with a reflection about two different pathways, and why would it be followed immediately by a psalm about the nations raging against the anointed king of Israel? Just as the first scenes in a famous movie set the tone for the story to come, so the first psalms are an overture for the book: "The Psalter comes to be seen as a magnificent dramatic struggle between the two ways—that of Yahweh, his anointed king, and the company of the just, and that of the wicked, the sinners, the evil-doers."[1] The struggle itself is presented initially through a series of images, as the righteous are compared to a luxurious tree as opposed to wind-driven chaff, and a cabal of plotting kings compared to the divinely appointed king.[2] Our reading begins with Psalm 1:

[1] How blessed is the one who:
  in the counsel of the wicked does not walk,
    along the path of failures does not linger,
      and in a chair with cynics does not sit.
[2] But whose delight is in the *tôrāh* of the Lord,
  and in his *tôrāh* ruminates day and night.
[3] This one will be like a tree, transplanted near streams of water,
  bringing forth its fruit in season,
    whose leaf does not fade,
      and everything that is done, succeeds.
[4] Not so are the wicked,
  for they are like chaff driven by the wind.
[5] Therefore the wicked won't stand in the judgment,
  nor failures in the assembly of the righteous.

---

[1] John C. Crutchfield, "The Redactional Agenda of the Book of Psalms," *HUCA* 74 (2003): 26, citing Joseph P. Brennan, "Psalms 1–8: Some Hidden Harmonies," *BTB* 10 (1980): 29.
[2] Clifford, *Psalms 1–72*, 23.

> ⁶ For the Lord knows the way of the righteous,
> but the way of the wicked vanishes.

The opening term *blessed* is derived from the verbal root *to go straight* or *advance*, as along a road or a pathway. Rather than some sort of bubbly sensation, *blessedness* in this context (or *happiness*, as it has been translated in recent times) can be associated with a life direction or path traveled. In Psalm 1:1 there is no request or petition; instead, the quality of blessedness is attributed to someone who has made a sequence of choices, first described negatively, then positively (as one who delights in God's revelation). The negative choices and roadways are populated by a crowd whose actions and words are unfaithful to the great traditions of Israelite theology.[3]

Where else do the various members of this unfaithful crowd appear in the Hebrew Bible, and how are they characterized elsewhere in the book of Psalms? First, the wicked (*reshā'îm*) make an appearance in Psalm 10:4: "In the pride of his face the wicked does not seek him; all his thoughts are, 'There is no God.'" Second, most translations opt for *sinners* in rendering Ps 1:1, but I am here following John Goldingay's suggestion that *failures* is a helpful choice based on the root meaning of sin as *missing the target*.[4] Psalm 25:8 declares, "Good and upright is the Lord; therefore he instructs sinners [or failures, *ḥaṭṭā'îm*] in the way." Third, I am translating the last group as the *cynics* (*scoffers* or *mockers* is most common among recent versions), people who are particularly adept at abusing language for their own malicious ends. It is not a common term in the psalms, but the verbal form appears in Psalm 119:51: "Arrogant people do nothing but *scoff* at me. Yet I do not turn aside from your law." We should allow that none of these different characters is necessarily a foreign enemy or oppressor but could be an insider, that is, a fellow Israelite who has rejected his or her faith heritage. Psalm 1 could be presenting a self-criticism as well as an

---

[3] Cf. Ellen Charry, *Psalms 1–50*, BTCB (Grand Rapids, MI: Brazos, 2015), 2: "The message of this psalm anticipates the trenchant observation of Ps. 12:1 that faithfulness has vanished from Israel. The faithful feel isolated and ridiculed.... As a frame for the Psalter, Ps. 1 is exquisitely ambiguous, offering comfort and encouragement with one hand and challenge and threat with the other. Psalm 1 is a warning label."

[4] Goldingay, *Psalms*, vol. 1: *Psalms 1–41*, 82–83.

introduction to the larger book and reminds the reader that wickedness can be found much closer to home.

Having reviewed the characteristics of the crowd of wrongdoers in v. 1, we are now in a better position to evaluate the key botanical images of the psalm. The wicked are referred to as (fruitless) chaff, or "harvest waste."[5] The wicked might believe themselves to be independent and self-directed, but in Psalm 1 they are characterized as cast about by the wind or, as described by one early interpreter, driven by every breeze of temptation from without and driven by inner conflict and warfare from within.[6] But *chaff* is derivative and forms a contrast to the central image in the psalm of a *tree*, perhaps with echoes to the tree of life in the garden of Genesis. Those who delight in the *tôrāh* are rooted and stable—strong enough to withstand the inevitable storms—constantly nourished by streams of water that ensure a long-term future. In pointed contrast is the path of the wicked, which quite literally leads to nowhere; according to this opening psalm, "[B]eing the author of one's own fate is to march down the path of self-destruction. The wicked are their own lords, and thus they 'autonomously' move toward their own judgment."[7]

Psalm 1 begins with the picture of dusty chaff frantically driven in every direction, along with a warning that the path of the wicked will finally disappear. Opposite images are used to characterize the person who delights in thinking about *tôrāh*, who has been transplanted alongside rivers of life-giving water. The same verb *transplanted* later occurs in Ps 92:12–13: "The righteous person will grow like a palm tree, rise high like a cedar of Lebanon, transplanted in the house of the Lord, in the courts of our God they will flourish."[8] This opening psalm

---

[5] John Eaton, *The Psalms: A Historical and Spiritual Commentary with an Introduction and New Translation* (London: T&T Clark, 2003), 63. A number of commentators also draw attention to a similar text in Jeremiah 17:7–8, part of a prophetic oracle that compares different kinds of trust: "Blessed are those who trust in the Lord, whose trust is the Lord. They shall be like a tree planted by water, sending out its roots by the stream. It shall not fear when heat comes, and its leaves shall stay green; in the year of drought it is not anxious, and it does not cease to bear fruit" (NRSV).

[6] John Chrysostom (347–407), cited in Craig A. Blaising and Carmen S. Hardin, eds., *Psalms 1–50*, ACCSOT (Downers Grove, IL: InterVarsity Press, 2008), 9–10.

[7] DeClaissé-Walford, Jacobson, and Tanner, *The Book of Psalms*, 63, drawing on J. P. Fokkelman, *Major Poems of the Hebrew Bible: At the Interface of Prosody and Structural Analysis*, vol. 2: *85 Psalms and Job 4–14*, SSN (Leiden: Brill, 2000), 53.

[8] Brown, *Seeing the Psalms*, 75–76.

is often interpreted as a wisdom composition, but the next one is a different genre, having *kingship* as an obvious theme. Psalm 2 is structured in four parts, and each part introduces perspectives that will be encountered elsewhere in the book of Psalms. First, vv. 1–3 open with a rhetorical question ("Why do nations rage, and the peoples murmur emptiness?") before plunging the reader into a theater of war when a group of kings are plotting rebellion against God and his appointed king. But despite all of the sound and fury, the reader is told that such rebellions will never ultimately succeed. However threatening these words of defiance may be, any conspiracies of this kind are doomed to fail.

The second section of Psalm 2 (vv. 4–6) illustrates why this noisy tumult will dwindle, as the reader is transported to another spatial setting: the divine throne room, a much more powerful location high above the fretting kings. It is not quite so easy as the conspiring monarchs imagine to dislodge the king whom God has chosen. In a striking image, God *laughs* at such foolish overconfidence. If the reader is shocked by this image, that is probably the intention of the text, as it provides a radical perspective on God's attitude toward human rebellion and its myriad forms. The people of Israel can be intimidated and distracted by the rage and volume of the surrounding nations, and therefore Psalm 2 provides an alternative filter through which to hear the words of defiance. Unlike the plotting rulers, God has a future for Zion, and even if the divine promises are tested and appear to have failed in the days ahead, the believing community nonetheless is invited to have confidence in the declaration of this psalm.

In the third section (vv. 7–9) there is a new voice and point of view: the direct speech of the "anointed one" (literally, the *messiah*) whom God has appointed. These words underscore the durability of God's promise and tacitly imply the responsibility of God's appointed one to uphold the standards of justice. Through this voice the reader is reminded that God has "birthed" this particular kind of kingship. The reign of God's king does not operate according to the typical power patterns of the raging nations—there is no hostile takeover, no revolution or scheming in backrooms—instead, it is a gift of God and comes with a vast inheritance.

The fourth and final section of Psalm 2 (vv. 10–12) directly addresses the rebellious leaders and advises that they be wise and show proper respect for the true king: "Fear implies that God is the center of all existence and power, and that human beings, even kings who are powerful on a human level, are not. Rather, they are dependent on God for everything."[9] Altogether, the two psalms that begin the book of Praises (*Tehillim*) jointly articulate a series of reasons for praising God even when circumstances are profoundly difficult, when cynics are ascendant and doubt is rampant, and when the kings of the earth hurl scorn on God and God's anointed. In other words, there is a *drama of belief* that is about to unfold in the Psalter, and the community is encouraged to keep the promises of these compositions in mind throughout the turbulent days and seasons of their lives.[10] Just as Psalm 1 opens with a blessing, so Psalm 2 closes with a blessing that further indicates how these two opening performances form the gateway to the book. Having crossed the threshold, the reader is now poised to appreciate the five discrete movements in the book of Psalms and its overarching structure and theological vision.

## Division into Five Books

Many readers perceive the Psalms as a string of stand-alone compositions, gathered together simply as an assorted compilation of "greatest hits" over the Israelite centuries. The notion that the Psalms are organized and structured as a five-book symphony is unfamiliar, even though most contemporary editions of the Bible present the Psalms in this way. Standard English versions of the Bible such as the NJPS and

---

[9] Tremper Longman III, *Psalms: An Introduction and Commentary*, TOTC (Downers Grove, IL: Intervarsity Press, 2014), 62. See also Derek E. Wittman, "Let Us Cast Off Their Ropes from Us: The Editorial Significance of the Portrayal of Foreign Nations in Psalms 2 and 149," in *The Shape and Shaping of the Book of Psalms: The Current State of Scholarship*, ed. Nancy L. DeClaissé-Walford (Atlanta, CA: Society of Biblical Literature, 2014), 53–69.

[10] Norman K. Gottwald, "Kingship in the Book of Psalms, in *The Oxford Handbook of the Psalms*, ed. William P. Brown (New York: Oxford University Press, 2014), 439 notes that there is a story of kingship in the Psalter, a trajectory that "posits the king as starting off with high status and great power but descending by stages to a loss of status and power, even to the point of establishing the king's irrelevance to Israelite society and religion."

the NRSV, for instance, have "Book II" as a major heading just before Psalm 42. But as mentioned earlier in this study, the headings are not found in the Hebrew Bible. Instead, at pivotal moments there are signals that mark the close of one unit (or "book") and the beginning of another. To reiterate, the groupings are Book I (Psalms 1–41), Book II (42–72), Book III (73–89), Book IV (90–106), and Book V (107–150). The main signal that indicates the transition from book to book is the word *amen*, as can be seen in the following:

> Blessed be the Lord, the God of Israel,
>     from everlasting to everlasting.
> Amen and amen. (41:13)

> Blessed be the Lord God, the God of Israel,
>     who alone does wondrous deeds.
> Blessed be his glorious name forever,
>     may his glory fill all the earth.
> Amen and amen. (72:18–19)

> Blessed be the Lord forever.
> Amen and amen. (89:52)

> Blessed be the Lord, the God of Israel,
>     from everlasting to everlasting.
> And let all the people say, "Amen."
> Praise the Lord. (106:48)[11]

At one time or another most of us have heard the word *amen*—usually as a closing exclamation at the end of a prayer—as a declaration of agreement and shared belief. The Hebrew term is derived from the root "to be stable, firm, trustworthy, or reliable" and is commonly used to indicate "personal or corporate alignment with the sentiments or commitments expressed."[12] In the Psalms, the only time *amen* occurs

---

[11] As Zenger, "The Composition and Theology of the Fifth Book of Psalms," 79–80 notes, the concluding "Praise the Lord" in 106:48 (after "Amen and amen") operates as a segue to Book V.
[12] Wilson, *Psalms Volume 1*, 692. Wilson further remarks on *amen* in later biblical writings: "The Hebrew term comes over into Christian usage through the Greek transliteration *amen* and reflects similar usage in the New Testament. Jesus used the term to

is in those verses cited above. Moreover, *amen* is found only at the end of the first four books, and such a statistical distribution is unlikely to be a coincidence. As a result, the *amens* function like a trumpet blast signaling the end of one book and the start of a new one. After the sound of these trumpets we encounter a change in the name attached to the superscription and/or a shift in the genre or tone of the next psalm. For example, the last composition of Book I, Psalm 41, is often identified as an individual song of thanksgiving, with the name *David* in the superscription.[13] By contrast, in Psalm 42 we find the name *Korah* in the superscription, and because of the despondent self-talk ("Why so downcast, O my soul?") and the apparent distance from the temple and the worshiping community, this composition is classified as a lament. Psalm 42 is strategically placed as an overture to the next book, and the more somber mood of this poem prepares the reader for the anticipations of exile that periodically reverberate throughout Book II.

Within the five books are distinctive emphases and several different kinds of movements. For example, a higher percentage of lament psalms are found in the first three books. Since Books I and II reflect the turbulent period of Israel's monarchy, with all of its crises and travails, there are ample cries for help offset by various celebrations of victory. Book II also contains the greatest use of the divine term *Elohim*, perhaps indicating a northern influence or to emphasize more universal aspects of God's character. Furthermore, the question *why* is asked more than two dozen times in the first three books (e.g., "Why do you hide yourself in times of trouble?," 10:1; "Why, Lord, do you reject me and hide your face from me?," 88:14), but only once in Book V, and that with a triumphant note: "Why should the nations say, 'Where is their God?'" (115:2). There is a high concentration of terms such as *dark* and *darkness* in Book III, in keeping with the gloom of exile that pervades this book: "With their temple destroyed (Pss 74; 79) and the throne of David tossed into the dirt (Ps 89:44), the people wonder how

---

affirm the truth of his teaching by introducing statements with 'Amen, Amen, I say to you...' ('Truly, truly...'). Jesus is also called 'the Amen' (Rev. 3:14), affirming the truth of the testimony of his life and ministry."

[13] Brueggemann and Bellinger, *Psalms*, 199–201.

they will endure the insults and taunts of the enemy nations (89:50–51). How will Israel endure the humiliation of exile and, worse yet, the dismantling of the nation's theological worldview? Israel's response to these questions follows in Books 4 and 5."[14] Remarkably, the term *hallelujah* (praise the Lord) occurs once at the very end of Book IV but throughout all of Book V, underscoring renewed commitment and resolve as the people are restored to the land of promise. These are the kinds of questions and interpretive issues that should be kept in mind as we now turn to survey the content—looking at a few highlights and tracing some broader movements—of each of the five books.

## Book I

After entering the gateway of the first two psalms—with Psalm 1 emphasizing rootedness in the Torah and resisting the voices of cynicism, and Psalm 2 unfolding images of a divine kingship that will not be overthrown by the leaders of raging nations—the reader is soon fully immersed in the drama of the first book. If Book I features a series of poetic snapshots that capture some of the experiences and prayers during the era of the early monarchy, then Psalm 3 begins by immediately parachuting the reader into a crisis. As noted earlier, the superscription of Psalm 3 connects this composition with David's flight from Jerusalem during Absalom's hostile takeover, describing the hordes of foes who have arisen with destructive words of slander along with the psalmist's cry for help. Virtually every composition in Book I includes the name *David* in the superscription.[15] Consequently, the reader is encouraged to view these psalms through the lens of the divine promise about a lasting Davidic house (cf. 2 Samuel 7; "Great triumphs he gives to his king, and shows steadfast love to his anointed, to David and his descendants forever," Ps 18:50; "in your strength the king rejoices," Ps 21:1). The books of Samuel and Kings illustrate that the house of David

---

[14] W. Dennis Tucker Jr. and Jamie A. Grant, *Psalms*, Vol 2, NIVAC (Grand Rapids, MI: Zondervan, 2018), 26.

[15] Gordon J. Wenham, *The Psalter Reclaimed: Praying and Praising with the Psalms* (Wheaton, IL: Crossway, 2013), 53–54.

is often besieged from the outside by hostile invaders and frequently racked by strife within its own borders. But owing to God's promise, the rebellion of Absalom cannot finally succeed, and even the raging Babylonians will not extinguish the promise of David's house. Even though Psalm 3 is a prayer from an empty palace, the implicit message is that the dynasty of David will endure.

Following Psalm 3, the next sequence of psalms likewise are individual laments, variously asking God for rescue from distress, to catch the crafty in their own devices, to relieve the poet whose eyes are wasted by vexation, or to rise up in vengeance and bring the evil schemes of the wicked to an end. Part of the interpretive challenge is that Book I does not proceed sequentially, as there are sharp turns and different issues threaded throughout these various compositions. In this respect, the final form of the Psalms has some affinities with the book of Jeremiah, a prophetic scroll that immerses the community in the approach of the Babylonian army and the dismantling of Jerusalem. The story of Jeremiah does not always unfold in a strictly linear fashion and, like the arrangement of the Psalter, is rich with symbolic possibilities.[16] Book I of the Psalms features diversity and an array of genres, but also a larger message:

> Following the elevated hopes for kingship expressed in Psalm 2, Book 1 shifts decisively into a block of pleas for deliverance at its opening (3–7) and concludes with an extended block of psalms focused on instruction concerning continuing evil in the world (35–37) and additional pleas for deliverance (38–41). Between these two extremes, psalms with an awareness of evil and trouble (thanksgiving, instruction, pleas) outnumber psalms of praise and reliance two to one. The effect of this arrangement is to focus the collection on the experience of pain and suffering rather than on praise of God for a well-ordered and firmly established world.[17]

---

[16] On the organization of Jeremiah, see Louis Stulman, *Order amid Chaos: Jeremiah as Symbolic Tapestry*, Biblical Seminar 57 (Sheffield: Sheffield Academic Press, 1998).

[17] Wilson, *Psalms Volume 1*, 90. He adds, "Of the compositions in the book, twenty-seven are clearly individual psalms, of which eighteen are pleas for deliverance. An additional seven psalms (9; 10; 18; 21; 30; 32; 34) offer thanksgiving for deliverance from trouble, and five more (14; 15; 35; 36; 37) provide instruction regarding the experience of evil in the world. By contrast, unambiguous praise of Yahweh is encountered in only five

To consider an example, Psalm 11 illustrates the kind of compositions that mark the tenor of Book I. In this psalm, the poet is under attack yet continues to trust in God and stands fast rather than withdraw from the confrontation. But the temptation to flee is evidently quite strong, with whispers of skepticism from a group of confidants who are close to the poet; *they* say that evildoers are on the verge of triumph and have destroyed the foundations of social order, and therefore the poet should *fly like a bird* and seek safety on a mountain in order to escape the arrows of the wicked. These counsellors do not invoke God or any obvious traditions in the faith of Israel, but instead are mesmerized by the plots of the evildoers and conclude that matters are therefore hopeless for the believer. The bulk of Psalm 11 is a response to this temptation to give up under stressful adversity:

> *For the music director, a David psalm*
> ¹ In the Lord is my refuge,
>    how can you say to my soul,
>       "Fly like a bird to your mountain!
> ² For behold, the wicked arch their bow,
>    make ready their arrow on the string,
>       to shoot from the shadows at the upright of heart.
> ³ For when the foundations are torn apart,
>    what can the righteous do?"
> ⁴ The Lord is in his holy palace,
>    the throne of the Lord is in the heavens.
>       his eyes are perceiving,
>       his eyelids examine the children of Adam.
> ⁵ The Lord examines the righteous and the wicked,
>    the one who loves violence, his soul detests.
> ⁶ Upon the wicked he will rain snares, fire and sulfur,
>    a scorching wind will be the portion of their cup.
> ⁷ For the Lord is righteous,
>    righteousness he loves,
>       the upright will perceive his face.

psalms (8; 16; 19; 29; 33), and confident reliance on Yahweh is expressed in only three (11; 23; 27). A single psalm (24) represents an entrance liturgy."

There are a few textual puzzles with Psalm 11, but the basic meaning is clear: rather than flee to an apparently safer place (as the group of advisors are arguing) the psalmist resolves to stand firm in the midst of chaos and declares that the character of God is actually a refuge in the midst of such trouble. The picture that emerges in this psalm is that the poet can resist the temptation to withdraw in the face of evil because of an inner confidence that God will deal with the perpetrators in due course. In v. 6 some translators opt to emend the text, preferring *coals* to *snares*, even though the major ancient textual witnesses uniformly have *snares* (e.g., the NIV's "On the wicked he will rain fiery coals" reflects such an emendation). But as one commentator explains, this emendation obscures an irony in the psalm that underscores the poet's theological understanding of how God ultimately deals with the wicked: "Perhaps the psalmist used this word to express the irony of it: he was tempted to flee like a bird, but God would soon send snares—bird traps—to catch them in their wickedness. When judgment falls, it is the wicked who will flee to the mountains for safety (see Matt. 24:16), but they will find no escape."[18] Along with most other psalms, it is very difficult to determine with certainty the exact historical circumstances behind Psalm 11, but as it stands, this poem contributes to Book I of the Psalter by presenting an acute crisis: a leader is stalked by a band of evildoers and advised by a circle of friends to jump ship and avoid being destroyed.

In Psalm 11 the leader is presented in ideal terms and as representative of the community as a whole. The main character in this psalm is relying on the guiding promises and universal reign of God even while acknowledging a very real and present danger. Overall, the compositions of Book I of the Psalter unfold images of the establishment, struggles, stresses, victories, and tragedies of the people of God during the period of the early monarchy. In Book I there is a greater frequency of laments, providing a window into the turbulence of this era, as well as instruction for dealing with various setbacks and encouragement for framing all of life within the wisdom of Israel's faith tradition. The prayers and instruction of the Psalms contain a remarkable

---

[18] Ross, *Psalms 1–41*, 344.

honesty and candor, focused on stating "as clearly as possible, the challenge that life in God's creation and life in God's community are not filled with unambiguous experiences of God's grace. Rather, there is more than a little suffering in God's world and among God's people."[19] It would seem that it is this candor and honest grappling with the usually harsh realities of life that have perennially attracted readers to this collection.

The concluding composition of Book I, Psalm 41, features a main character who can be imagined as a king or leader in the community. Like the first psalm in the collection, Psalm 41 begins with *blessed*, establishing a pair of bookends around the opening book of the Psalter. A key element of the psalm is the quoted speech of the various characters, the murmurs of the adversaries contrasted with the prayers of the poet. The backdrop of a physical ailment looms large in the fabric of the poem, with the main character at death's door and voices of opposition eagerly waiting for the end. This Davidic psalm captures experiences in the early monarchy, but the final sequence in Book I reflects later travails as well:

> The uncertainty reflected in these concluding psalms is also consonant with that experienced by the Diaspora community, who had known not just the death of a king but of the monarchy altogether. The grouping of Psalms 38–41 here provides counsel and hope that would have resonated deeply with the needs of those struggling to survive in exile. These psalms affirm that despite the suffering of attack, Yahweh is the only source of salvation; he is salvation! (38:22).[20]

The emphasis on social justice might also provide a subtle critique of Israel's monarchy and suggests that priorities have not always been with the Torah. Compared with Psalm 2, the king in Psalm 41 is not triumphing over the nations but surrounded by internal strife and opportunists hoping to profit from his demise.

---

[19] DeClaissé-Walford, Jacobson, and Tanner, *The Book of Psalms*, 33.
[20] Wilson, *Psalms Volume 1*, 107.

*To the leader. A David Psalm*
¹ Blessed is the one who is considerate to the poor,
  on the evil day, may the Lord rescue him.
² May the Lord guard and preserve his life,
  may he be blessed in the land—do not hand him over to the desire of his enemies.
³ May the Lord sustain him on the bed of sickness,
  may you turn him out of his bed in his illness.
⁴ I myself said to the Lord, "Be gracious to me,
  heal my soul, for I've sinned against you."
⁵ My enemies speak evil against me,
  "When will he die, and his name perish?"
⁶ If one comes to see me, he speaks falsehood,
  his mind gathers maliciousness, then he goes outside and speaks.
⁷ Together, against me they all whisper, all who despise me,
  against me they plot evil schemes:
⁸ "A hellish thing is poured out on him,
  when he lies down, he will not rise again!"
⁹ Even my friend in health, who I trusted,
  with whom I shared my meals, he too has turned his heel against me.
¹⁰ But you, O Lord, be gracious to me,
  raise me up, that I might repay them,
¹¹ In this I'll know that you delight in me:
  when my enemy does not shout triumphantly over me.
¹² For you will uphold me in my integrity,
  establish me in your presence forever.
¹³ Blessed is the Lord, the God of Israel,
  from everlasting to everlasting, amen and amen!

Two brief points can be made about Psalm 41 as the conclusion to Book I. First, the protagonist of this psalm underscores the image of the king as an advocate for justice and a leader with responsibilities to the poor. If the various kings in Jerusalem failed on this count, they could expect divine disfavor, not least because the portrait of God that emerges from this psalm is of a passionate champion of the marginalized and the defenseless. Second, even if a leader is appointed and anointed by God, there is no free pass from affliction. In fact, the psalm seems to be teaching that adversity and suffering are expected parts of leadership: in this case, there are dark conspiracies, physical illness, and cruelty from insiders, with no immunity from the travails of life, implying that great leaders need to cultivate reliance on God rather than human machinations. Book I ends with the monarch in peril but nonetheless ensconced on the throne in Jerusalem. However, that throne appears increasingly precarious in Book II, where our attention now turns.

## Book II

Just as Psalm 3 plunges the reader into the maelstrom of the king's crisis in the opening moments of Book I, Psalm 42 transports the reader into a key time period of Book II, which begins with a collection of psalms (42–49) from *the sons of Korah*. Earlier in this study we discussed the family of Korah, a group of Levitical musicians whose infamous story in the book of Numbers connects them with the revolt of Korah and his followers against Moses. Yet the sons of Korah were granted a reprieve (Num 26:11) and, despite their murky past, are associated with this group of temple songwriters (2 Chron 20:19). Commencing Book II with a Korah psalm creates an effect on the reader, since these compositions often have a theme of rebellion and are infused with an ambiance of regret. But Korah psalms also can feature a main character who has a certain resolve and determination that comes from receiving the gift of a second chance. At the end of Psalm 41 the king is imperiled yet hanging on, and so we wonder if any trace of a Davidic voice can be found or heard as we consider Psalm 42:

> *To the Chief Musician: a Maskil according to the Sons of Korah*
> [1] Like a deer longs for streams of water,
>     so my soul longs for you, O God.
> [2] My soul thirsts for God, for the living God,
>     when will I arrive and see God's face?
> [3] My tears, day and night, have been my food,
>     while all day long they are saying to me,
>         "Where is your God?"

⁴ These things I recall as I pour out my soul within me,
    for I was once passing along with the crowd,
        leading them to the house of God,
            with a ringing voice and thanksgiving,
                a multitude attending the festival.
⁵ Why so bent low, O my soul? Why in turmoil within me?
    Hope in God! For yet again I will give him thanks,
        the salvation of his presence.
⁶ My God, how my soul is bent low within me,
    therefore I remember you from the land of the Jordan,
        from the peaks of Hermon, from Mount Mizar.
⁷ Deep calls out to deep in the sound of your waterfalls,
    all your breakers and waves have billowed over me.
⁸ By day the Lord commands his steadfast love,
    by night his song is with me, a prayer to the God of my life.
⁹ I say to God, my rock: "Why have you forgotten me?
    Why do I go around mourning because of my enemy's oppression?"
¹⁰ As a shattering in my bones my enemy taunts me,
    while they say to me all day long, "Where is your God?"
¹¹ Why so bent low, o my soul? Why in turmoil within me?
    Hope in God! For yet again I will give him thanks,
        the salvation of his presence.

If Book II had opened with Psalm 45 ("My heart overflows with a pleasing theme, I address my verses to the king, my tongue is like the pen of a ready scribe. You are the most handsome of the sons of men, grace is poured upon your lips, therefore God has blessed you forever"), it would have provided a quite different feeling after the questions raised in Psalm 41 at the end of Book I. Many interpreters argue that Psalm 45 is a wedding hymn for royalty, with celebratory lyrics composed by the priestly clan of Korah for performance at the Jerusalem temple: "All glorious is the princess in her chamber, with robes interwoven with gold. In many-colored robes she is led to the king, with her virgin companions following behind her. With joy and gladness they are led along as they enter the palace of the king."

The tone of Psalm 42 is manifestly different, with a more melancholic mood and somber feeling. It is often thought that Psalms 42 and 43 form one continuous psalm, since 43 lacks a superscription and evidently continues the flow with similar language.[21] But here we will limit our remarks to 42 as the opening psalm of Book II. There are various theories of the identity of the main character, some suggesting that the speaker is actually a figurative cipher for the royal court, away from Jerusalem because of a military operation or paying tribute to a foreign potentate. The idea of submission before an overlord is worth pondering, because if that is the correct interpretation, then the opening message of Book II becomes a subtle critique of the monarchy.

More commonly, however, the speaker is thought to be an individual. Although Psalm 42 is tantalizingly vague on the precise details, it would seem that a leader or high-ranking citizen is stuck in the rugged northern terrain outside of the promised land. Overwhelmed by trouble and taunts, the poet thirsts for divine community in the sanctuary and respite from the insults of adversaries. The opening image of a (wounded) *deer* panting for water is poignant and resonates with Lamentations 1:6: "All the honor of the Daughter of Zion has departed, her captives are like deer who found no pasture, too exhausted to escape from the hunter." Perhaps the poet has been (or feels) attacked and removed from the land, as a prisoner taken captive and now in a foreign land.[22] Although the *peaks of Hermon* are far away in Syria, the exact location Mt. Mizar is unknown, adding to the poet's sense of geographic and spiritual isolation, and is quite literally in the middle of nowhere. We guess that the captors are taunting, and the rhetorical question "Where is your God?" aims to reinforce the sense of defeat. The poet's inner turmoil is caused by these hostile circumstances, and the fact that water is everywhere (i.e., waterfalls and rivers with rapids in rugged terrain) serves to remind the poet of spiritual dryness and an intense thirst for God. By means of inner dialogue, the poet seeks to hope in God as an antidote to despair. On this reading, Psalm 42 presents the image of a faithful Israelite who is cut off from Jerusalem

---

[21] For example, Weiser, *The Psalms*, 347–348.
[22] Paul R. Raabe, "Mizar," in *Anchor Bible Dictionary*, 6 vols., ed. David Noel Freedman (New York: Doubleday, 1992), 4:879.

and experiencing acute anxiety, foreshadowing the large-scale exile to come (or at least, perhaps, the division of the kingdom into northern Israel and southern Judah in 1 Kings 12). So at the start of Book II is a hint that monarchy is not the answer to the national difficulties, and that at some point the people of God will find themselves far away from the Jerusalem temple.[23]

It was discussed earlier that Book I does not unfold an exact chronology but is more like a kaleidoscope or a collage of images going back and forth in time to provide a vision of a period of time: an elliptical poetic immersion in an era rather than a strictly linear report. Book II is roughly similar. Like many modern screenplays or sophisticated TV series, there is time-splitting and movement back and forth in Book II, with snapshots of the turbulence so often associated with the later monarchy—and yet cries for relief during such difficulties—themes that will be continued and expanded as the larger book of Psalms develops.

As the first two parts in a five-act drama, Books I and II provide perspectives on the earlier and later days of the Israelite monarchy, with poetic angles and theological reflections on the inauguration of kingship and the various crises that came along in its aftermath, including threats, enemies, slander, military attacks, corruption, bitterness, individual lament, idolatries, despair, and confusion, juxtaposed with moments of celebration, trust, and corporate rescue. Being under the aegis of divine promise guarantees no immunity from the darker powers of this fallen world, and the first two books of the Psalter unfold a chorus of voices ranging from reorienting praise to nuanced critique.

Book II of the Psalter basically shifts slightly to an overarching point of view that has Jerusalem as the primary *spatial* field of reference, with the temple, monarchic symbols, and urban accouterments occurring prominently. Along with flashbacks to David's career and Solomon's reign, later monarchic periods also seem to be represented, and the

---

[23] See Wilson, *Psalms Volume 1*, 433: "Book 2 of the Psalter begins much as Book 1 ends, with lamenting and pleas for deliverance. Book 1 concluded with a sense of human weakness facing extinction, and yet a contrasting hope for restoration by God, who would yet set the psalmist in his presence forever. Book 2 begins in the combined Psalms 42–43 with a longing for restoration by God, in which the psalmist's disquieted soul is balanced by confident trust in God, the Savior (42:5, 11; 43:5)."

compositions of Book II usually tend to presuppose a more established monarchy. As noted, Book II begins with a Levitical collection (42–49) from the sons of Korah, and then Psalm 50 is an Asaph composition (in 2 Chr 29:30 Asaph is referred to as a *seer*.) The heart of Book II is a Davidic collection (51–65) that variously includes some famous superscriptions relating to harrowing and sordid experiences in the king's career (underscoring that many of the nation's problems were internal; e.g., 55:12–13: "It is not enemies who taunt me—I could bear that . . . but it is you, my equal, my companion, my familiar friend") and other psalms that combine to provide a more conflicted view of kingship, in which often the malevolent or more problematic sides come to the fore. If Israel is intent on putting its hope in princes, such hopes are bound to be disappointed.

In a similar vein, Psalm 62 carries a warning about the fleetingness of human life and the danger of excess confidence in falsehood: "Humans are but a vapor, mortals are but a delusion: in the scales they go up, together they are lighter than breath. Trust not in extortion, do not count on robbery; if wealth increases, do not set your heart upon it" (vv. 9–10). The difficult and sometimes obscure Psalm 68 recites old traditions about divine victories over superior foes when the nation was helpless and the people had no chance of success on their own merits: "The chariots of God beyond number, multiple thousands, the Lord was among them at Sinai in the holy place. You ascended on high, capturing captives; you received gifts from mortals, even from the stubborn, that the Lord God may abide" (vv. 17–18). During the long and nerve-wracking advances of the Assyrian and Babylonian armies, we might visualize these psalms performed in the temple and providing a faith option amid the mayhem of approaching hoofbeats.

The final composition of Book II is Psalm 72, a prayer for succession that should probably be understood as *for* Solomon or later Solomonic sons and successors: "O God, bestow your judgments to the king, your righteousness to the king's son. May he judge your people in righteousness, your afflicted ones with justice!" Indeed, if the kings of Israel and Judah had maintained such a posture—concerned with Torah and mindful of justice—many of the woes described in the book of Kings might have been mitigated. Psalm 72 thus provides a glimpse of what might have been: if we imagine that these words were proclaimed at the coronation of new monarchs, the positioning of this psalm becomes an indictment for a train of leaders who did not live up to their calling. As it stands, the last words of Book II are "The prayers of David son of Jesse are ended." A natural way of interpreting this final sentence is that the temple—the *place* of prayer—has been destroyed and the Davidic king has been taken into captivity. The early harbingers of Psalm 42 and the poet's lament because of separation from Jerusalem have now been experienced on a national scale. The next installment of the story takes the reader to that undesirable place of exile, with all of its searching, confusion, and confession.

## Book III

The third book in the Psalter's grand ensemble is the most somber. A collection of Asaph psalms forms the initial core, followed by a cluster of Korah compositions (with the name *David* occurring in the superscription of Psalm 86). It was suggested that Book II generally evokes the spatial atmosphere of Jerusalem, often in a temple setting. Taken as a whole, the psalms of Book III provide voices of response to the destruction and looting of the temple and the disruptive reality of exile. These seventeen psalms variously grapple with the collapse of the royal house of cards, and instead of the voice of an incumbent king, the reader hears a chastened chorus of Levitical singers who themselves have been displaced from the temple. Throughout Book III the reader is immersed in an experience where the familiar is shattered, giving voice to a deep-seated anxiety that results from the disaster of invasion and the destruction of Jerusalem. In the aftermath of such devastation there is an appalling sense of divine abandonment as the nation enters into the valley of death's shadow. In Book III we are confronted with certain modes of expression and poetic anguish that have not yet been heard in the Psalter.

A gripping story of regret and sober reflection is presented in the first composition of Book III.[24] Earlier in our study we briefly explored Psalm 73, a poignant and agonized look at a disordered world where

---

[24] On the placement of psalms in Book III, see further Robert L. Cole, *The Shape and Message of Book III (Psalms 73–89)*, JSOTSup 307 (Sheffield: Sheffield Academic Press, 2000).

unfairness seems to reign supreme and the wicked prosper. Caught in the claws of envy, the only way out for the embattled poet is by entering the *holy places* of God (*miqdešê-ʾēl*), where a radically new perspective is granted to the poet. Making sense of reality in the midst of chaos is admittedly a more difficult task when the temple is destroyed, and so perhaps Psalm 73 invites new possible meanings for entering into the presence of a sovereign God who is not subject to any geographic restrictions. The "individual" voice can also be heard as a representative of the citizens: collectively, the people of God fell prey to envying foreign nations, with their glamorous kings and powerful warriors. After an initial confession, the poet of Psalm 73 provides an autopsy of the problem, followed by charting a way forward that points to a solution: "[T]he psalmist realizes that the greatest good is to be found not in who has external prosperity but rather in the presence of God."[25] With this solution we can perceive the strategic placement of Psalm 73 and a larger message that is stressed at the outset of Book III: *even in the nation's darkest moment, God's promises have not been annulled or negated*. The poet's testimony in Psalm 73 will one day become the testimony of the nation (which lost its grip and yet came back from the other side).

Approaching the halfway point of Book III, Psalm 79 is a lament that has several interpretive difficulties. A sequence of Asaph psalms opens Book III, and we mentioned that Asaph compositions often tend to evince a strong interest in the theology of the covenant, operation of the temple, divine election of Zion, along with sustained meditation on various historical crises and national events leading up to the exile and beyond. It is not insignificant that the bands of Asaph musicians are portrayed in Chronicles as being active throughout the entire period of the monarchy, from the very inception of the temple. A painful and forlorn tone is palpable in Psalm 79, as this chorus is lamenting the temple's demise. There are a number of comparisons with Psalm 74, a poem that likewise evokes the loss of exile ("O God, why do you cast us off forever? Why does your anger smoke against the sheep of your

---

[25] David G. Firth, "Asaph and Sons of Korah," in *Dictionary of the Old Testament: Wisdom, Poetry and Writings*, ed. Tremper Longman III and Peter Enns (Downers Grove, IL: InterVarsity Press, 2008), 25.

pasture?," v. 1) and the barbarians at the gate who were responsible for the sanctuary going up in flames ("all of its carved wood with axes and hammers they hacked, they cast fire into your holy place, to the ground they defiled the dwelling place of your name," vv. 6–7). Such damage and the resulting heartache continue as central themes in Psalm 79:

*An Asaph Psalm*
[1] O God, the nations have entered your inheritance,
    defiled your holy temple,
        turned Jerusalem into a heap of ruins.
[2] They have given the corpses of your servants,
    as food for the birds of the air,
The flesh of your faithful ones,
    to the beasts of the field.
[3] They have poured out their blood
    like water, all around Jerusalem,
        with none to bury them.
[4] We have become a joke to our neighbors,
    mocked and insulted by those around us.
[5] How long, O Lord? Will you be angry forever,
    will your jealousy burn like fire?
[6] Pour out your wrath on the nations who do not know you,
    upon kingdoms who do not call on your name.
[7] For they have devoured Jacob,
    his dwelling place they have made desolate.
[8] Do not remember against us the iniquities of our ancestors,
    may your compassion hurry to meet us,
        for we have been knocked down.
[9] Help us, O God of our salvation:
    rescue us for the glory of your name,
        cover up our sins for the sake of your reputation.
[10] Why should the nations say, "Where's their god?!"
    Let it be known among the nations—right in front of our eyes—
        revenge for the blood of your servants that they have
        poured out.
[11] May the cries of the prisoner come before you,
    according to your great power, preserve those under a
    death sentence.

> ¹² Repay our neighbors seven times, right in their gut,
>   with the same insults that they have insulted you, O Lord!
> ¹³ In order that we—your people and the sheep of your pasture—
>   might give you thanks forever,
>     generation after generation might recount your praise.

When turning to 1 Kings 6–7, the reader is welcomed with an ornate account of the temple's construction in Jerusalem during the reign of Solomon. There is lavish specificity that ranges from the massive bronze sea that symbolizes the subjugation of chaos, to the carvings on the wooden walls of pomegranates whose many seeds symbolically represent the fulfillment of God's promise of many offspring to Abraham. An opposite style is found in the short narrative of the temple's destruction in 2 Kings 25: with grim understatement, only a few sentences are used to describe the ruination, and more attention is given to various articles of value the Babylonians carted away than to the awfulness of the desecration. Psalms in Book III have no such reticence, and instead of sidestepping, confront the nightmare directly. Psalm 74, we noted, relentlessly plunges the reader into the very precincts of the temple as it is being defiled with sledgehammers and hacksaws, even quoting the very thoughts of their foes: "They said in their minds, 'Let us oppress them completely!'" (74:8). Continuing the story, Psalm 79 refracts other angles of the trauma and focuses on the human cost of the invasion. The graphic poetry about the carnage (unburied bodies ravaged by wild beasts) and brutality meted out to Jerusalem's citizens (blood running through the emptied streets) exposes the reader to the searing loss of the poet's community, if not a circle of friends and relatives as well.

Critics often distinguish between *telling* and *showing* when analyzing a literary work. Without pressing too hard, in general terms it can be helpful to appreciate when a work is describing a particular event ("telling") and when a scene is dramatized ("showing") in more or less elaborate ways.[26] Depending on the purpose of the literary

---

[26] For example, David Herman, "Introduction," in *The Cambridge Companion to Narrative*, ed. David Herman (Cambridge: Cambridge University Press, 2007), 15.

work, different styles can be used. One approach is not better than the other; rather the style depends on the rhetorical purpose. In 2 Kings 25 there is an intentional minimalism because for centuries the people of God had a minimal response to the prophetic word and now face the consequences. In Book III of the Psalter the reader is plunged into the painful experience of invasion and devastation. The visual perspective of the massacre in Psalm 79 not only has a haunting immediacy, but it also sets the stage for the cry of vengeance that follows: "Repay our neighbors seven times, right in their gut."[27] Fellow citizens have been killed by marauders, the temple ripped to pieces by cruel machinery, and God has been mocked. But Psalm 79 unfolds another side of the coin because now the exiles are captives in a foreign land. The call for help near the end of the psalm ("May the cries of the prisoner come before you") has echoes of the Exodus story. The placement of Psalm 79 near the halfway point of Book III underscores a situation of captivity and the need for a new kind of divine intervention and rescue akin to the days of slavery in Egypt.

Book III is significantly shorter than the previous two books, but nonetheless there is an intensity that can be perceived at every turn. Part of this intensity can be ascribed to the various voices that are heard in these psalms, and not to be overlooked is the divine voice and point of view that are especially concentrated in the middle portion of Book III. Psalm 79, for example, expresses a longing for God to arise in vengeance, but alongside such cries for retribution the reader can also hear "God's frustration with the people, first as a narrative in Psalm 78 and then in God's own words in Psalm 81. Then Psalm 82 offers a unique look at God's work that is outside of the human realm. This psalm affirms that God has duties other than tending to the humans. The collection reminds us that God, too, has a story to tell about the people."[28] A soaring instance of divine speech occurs in Psalm 87, a Korah composition that celebrates God's commitment to Zion. Riffing on the previous psalm ("All the nations that you have made will come

---

[27] For a theoretical framework on understanding such impassioned pleas, see Gary A. Anderson, "King David and the Psalms of Imprecation," in *The Harp of Prophecy: Early Christian Interpretation of the Psalms*, ed. Brian E. Daley and Paul R. Kolbet (Notre Dame, IN: University of Notre Dame Press, 2015), 29–45.

[28] DeClaissé-Walford, Jacobson, and Tanner, *The Book of Psalms*, 582.

and bow down before you, O Lord, and they will glorify your name," 86:9), the divine words in Psalm 87 foreshadow a day when all nations can be grafted onto the community of God's people and can be considered Zion's residents. Included in this new group of citizens is an international crowd of perennial foes (including Rahab, an ancient chaos monster that is a nickname for Egypt): "I will make mention of Rahab and Babylon among those who know me, look, even Philistia, Tyre and Cush: this is one who was born there" (87:4). That day will occur at an unknown time after the rebuilding of Jerusalem by those who return from exile and have been released from captivity.

The hopes of Psalm 87, however, seem a long way off, and from the dizzying heights of Zion's mountaintop, with singers and dancers, suddenly the reader is dropped into the abyss of Psalm 88. In many respects the despair of exile reaches its nadir in the two closing compositions of Book III, as the divine voice gives way to laments. The doleful poet of Psalm 88 begins by describing a troubled life of valleys and shadows, rivaling Tolkien's landscape of Mordor in *Lord of the Rings*. Like a tractor beam, this psalm pulls in several threads from Book III and lays these before the reader. There is no "answer," nor is there an illuminating change of perspective. The superscription includes the term *illness*, which may point to a physical or indeed a spiritual malady that has beset the poet.[29] Yet we should note from the outset that the poet is calling out to God—implying the possibility of belief amid suffering—and asking that God attend to this nocturnal cry for help before outlining a grim situation and sprawling geography of the grave:

> ³ For my soul is full of miseries, my life is touching Sheol.
> ⁴ I am counted among those who descend to the Pit,
>     I have become like a warrior whose strength is lost.

---

[29] See Marco Pavan, *"He Remembered That They Were but Flesh, a Breath That Passes and Does Not Return (Ps 78-39)": The Theme of Memory and Forgetting in the Third Book of the Psalter (Pss 73-89)* (Frankfurt am Main: Peter Lang, 2014), 163. Goldingay, *Psalms*, vol. 2, 659 writes, "Beth LaNeel Tanner [*The Book of Psalms through the Lens of Intertextuality* (New York: Lang, 2001)] puts it alongside Judg. 19 and suggests that it resonates with the experience of abused women, for whom 'sometimes the story does not end happily ever after.'"

⁵ Among the dead I drift, like those slain, lying in the grave,
   those you remember no more, cut off from your hand.
⁶ In the lowest of Pits you've put me,
   in the darkest places, in the deepest of waters.

Feeling submerged in the deepest of waters, the poet never makes it to the surface in this psalm. If any psalm was to end abruptly—or even remain unfinished, running out of gas, psychologically exhausted without strength to finish—it would be Psalm 88. The sense of alienation is complete in the final verse of the poem, which I would render, "Friends and lovers you have removed from me, my only companion: darkness," at best implying that the psalmist's only acquaintances are other inhabitants of murky Sheol. Piling up all these images of deathly hallows seems to take a psychological toll on the poet, and the picture emerges of a writer who hardly has the energy to continue. In the context of Book III, the message that emerges is that even in the darkest night, cut off from the land and its familiarities, in a dismal place where faith is rejected and Israel's traditions are marginalized, there remains a place for the prayers and anguished cries of the people. In fact, the opening invocation ("God of my salvation/rescue") is instructive, for the only hope in exile is a work of God, and the shape of the Psalter should lead the reader to believe that such a work is in fact underway whether one realizes it or not.[30] The threefold structure of the psalm is marked by three references to persistent prayer (in the beginning, vv. 1–2; at the middle, v. 9b; and near the end, v. 13), strongly implying that the poet believes there is something in the character of God that is responsive to such prayers.[31] While it is true that the poet believes that God is responsible for this hardship, it is also clear that God is the only option for escape in the long term.

---

[30] Kathleen Norris, *The Cloister Walk* (New York: Riverhead Books, 1996), 96 remarks, "The psalms make us uncomfortable because they don't allow us to deny either the depth of our pain or the possibility of its transformation into praise."
[31] See Craig C. Broyles, *Psalms,* NIBC (Peabody, MA: Hendrickson, 1995), 352. Cf. Brueggemann and Bellinger, *Psalms,* 382: "William Styron, *Sophie's Choice* (Toronto: Bantam Books, 1979), 614–615, utilizes Psalm 88 as a 'prescription for my torment' by the lead character, Stingo. Styron and the woman on the bus understand that voiced pain to God matters in unbearable situations, even when there is no response."

The closing *amen* of Book III is positioned at the end of Psalm 89. A movement can be discerned in this last psalm that starts with opening stanzas that highlight the divine covenant with the house of David, and the dimensions of this covenant are emphasized in the clearest possible language. Various facets of the divine rule are likewise celebrated in the first half of Psalm 89. God reigns over the assembly of the gods with unrivaled faithfulness and unchallenged dominion. The God of Israel has undertaken magnificent feats in the past, such as the crushing of Rahab (as mentioned above, the chaos monster akin to Leviathan, and spelled slightly differently in Hebrew than the Jericho prostitute with a similar name). It is *this* God—who presides over the assembly and who has destroyed horrible monsters—who has chosen the people of Israel and the house of David, and hence vv. 28–29 form the centerpiece of Psalm 89: "Forever will I keep my steadfast love for him, my covenant with him will stand firm. I will establish his line for ever, his throne as long as the heavens endure."

But there is a pointed shift in the second half of the psalm, as the poet pours out a complaint: "But you have cast off and rejected, you are full of anger against your anointed one; you have spurned the covenant of your servant, you have defiled his crown in the ground" (vv. 38–39). In the last sections of Psalm 89 the poet variously protests the scorning, rejecting, and defiling, followed quickly by asking "how long" and pleading with God to "remember" the taunts and insults directed toward the humiliated exiles. On the one hand, the complaint at the end of Psalm 89 voices the frustration of so many of God's people who have known darkness and rejection, lonely nights and days cut short. And so this fervent complaint about God not keeping a promise is raw and surely strikes a chord with many in the community. On the other hand, there is a certain dramatic edge to the conclusion of Psalm 89 and Book III that creates a measure of suspense: God has made a promise, but *how*, *when*, and in *what form* will that promise reach fulfillment? For that, one is compelled to keeping reading the Psalter and transition to the next installment of the story.

## Book IV

Starting with the reflections on suffering in Psalm 73 at the outset of Book III, there is a descent into darkness that arguably reaches the low point of the Psalter itself with Psalm 88 and the apparent rejection of the Davidic covenant proclaimed by the poet of Psalm 89. Altogether, a chorus of *voices from exile* can be heard throughout the complaints, laments, and prophetic visions of Book III, variously responding to the national crisis of Jerusalem's destruction and the formal loss of the institutional monarchy. But there is a noticeable shift in Book IV, and while chastisement and humility are at the forefront, the reader gradually emerges from the valley of the shadow of death and is invited to begin rebuilding a shattered world with new actions and daring leaps of imagination. Book III chronicles the plight of the community in a situation of exile dealing with taunting overlords and loss of the temple, and it is followed by a counterpoint: "Book Four will admonish the Israelites to look back and remember the time in their past when, not an earthly king, but the Lord their God was sovereign over them—and was their sole means of survival."[32]

A pivot point in the Psalter, one could maintain, is Psalm 90. The psalm contains archaic language—for example, "sons of Adam" and *enosh* (humanity)—that provides an ancient feel to the lyrics, but the stress on the fleetingness of human life and the absence of overt references to royalty or temple would have a compelling relevance in the postexilic period. Reference to Moses in the superscription—the first of seven references to Moses in Book IV—evokes a time when the people of God had just been released from captivity and a superpower was humbled in the process. So the mention of Moses in this psalm is striking at the outset of Book IV:

> If there was any star on Israel's horizon larger than David, then surely it was Moses. The beginning of Book Four remembers that there was a time before land, kings, and palaces. It hints that before Mt. Zion there had been another sacred mountain. Before the wilderness of

---

[32] Nancy DeClaissé-Walford, *Introduction to the Psalms: A Song from Ancient Israel* (St. Louis, MO: Chalice, 2004), 98.

Babylonian Exile, there had been another wilderness through which Israel had been guided without king by pillars of fire, clouds, and the Ark to reunite with an earlier promise made to Abraham.[33]

As we consider the first lines of Psalm 90, in many ways this is a signature psalm of Book IV. It evokes the ambiance of the wilderness, serving to remind the community that they may have lost the monarchy, but they have always had a divine king:

> *A prayer of Moses, the man of God*
> [1] Lord, *you* have been our dwelling place,
>    from generation to generation.
> [2] Before the mountains were born,
>    or you gave birth to the earth and the world,
>    from everlasting to everlasting you are God.
> [3] You turn humanity back to the dust, saying,
>    "Turn back, O children of Adam."
> [4] For in your eyes, a thousand years are like yesterday gone by,
>    like a watch in the night.
> [5] You sweep them away, they are in sleep,
>    in the morning they are as grass that sprouts again.

The key spatial locale for Psalm 90 is the *dwelling place* or *safe house*. Thus, the psalm opens with the confession that God's character, promises, and commitments are the only reliable mainstays in a world of confusion. Since Book IV commences with the acknowledgment that many decisions made by Israel's leadership have proven to be bankrupt, the long process of recalibration and falling back on the covenant starts with recognizing that God has always been the true place of dwelling securely. Why return to language of the wilderness? Again, the reference to Moses in the superscription reminds the reader of how God works outside the land of Israel. In Exodus 2 the name *Moses* means "to draw out (of the waters)," and this reminder of the first exodus is subtly pointing to the hopes for a new kind of rescue.

---

[33] Steven Parrish, *A Story of the Psalms: Conversation, Canon, and Congregation* (Collegeville, MN: Liturgical Press, 2003), 5.

Moses was never a king and spent all of his days outside the land, but near the end of his life he was given the title *man of God*.[34] The next sections of Psalm 90 implore the people to live wisely in light of the national experiences and ask God to send joy that corresponds to their days of affliction in Babylonian exile. There also is a concluding double call that God "establish" (a common verb for temple construction) the "work of our hands." This final call, it can be interpreted, implores God in a double request to *prosper* the reconstructive efforts of the community's return to the land, where their identity is rooted in the one who has been their dwelling place (an idea that is further developed in Psalm 91).

The core of Book IV is composed of two major groupings: Psalms 93–99 and 100–106. The first grouping is usually referred to as *enthronement* psalms, and it is notable that both Psalm 93 and 99 include the refrain *the Lord reigns*:

> Although each psalm in this group is unique, they all share a set of metaphors associated with God's kingship: God is king; God is supreme over all the other gods; God is the Creator of all peoples; the earth is created and maintained by God; God protects the righteous and the lowly; God will judge the earth; all the gods and all the peoples of the earth are to give God praise; all the creation—land, sea, and heavens—are to give praise. Each psalm uniquely combines several of these themes.[35]

Indeed, several of these themes can be observed in Psalm 97, a composition that begins with a call to the distant shores—the farthest outposts of the earth—to rejoice in God's kingship. This might be perceived as a strange call to rejoice, but because God's throne is

---

[34] Susan Gillingham, "Psalms 90–106: Book Four and the Covenant with David," *European Judaism* 48 (2015): 87 argues that there are a number of other biblical texts that move in a similar direction: "There is no doubt that the emphasis here on Moses and the Exodus traditions corresponds with other biblical texts which were written during the time of the exile. The best example is Isaiah 40–55, a prophetic book which also addresses the trauma of the people in Babylon."

[35] DeClaissé-Walford, Jacobson, and Tanner, *The Book of Psalms*, 687. Note also the study of Robert E. Wallace, *The Narrative Effect of Book IV of the Hebrew Psalter* (New York: Peter Lang, 2007).

founded on justice, there is cause for celebration among all who acknowledge such reality. The first section of Psalm 97 presents a resplendent vision of God, before whom a personified creation reacts with quaking:

> ¹ The Lord reigns, let the earth be glad,
>     the faraway islands rejoice!
> ² Cloud and thick surround him,
>     righteousness and justice are his throne's foundation.
> ³ Fire strides before him,
>     burning up his adversaries all around.
> ⁴ His lightning bolts illuminate the world,
>     the earth sees, and trembles!

The poet of Psalm 89 protested that God has brought the splendor of the Davidic crown to an end and has "hurled his throne to the ground" (v. 45). As a counterpoint, Psalm 97 and the enthronement hymns present a vision of God's kingship that eclipses any earthly equivalent.[36] The central images of Psalm 97 carry echoes of God's appearance on Mt. Sinai in the days of the exodus and are reminiscent of other experiences, such as the call of the prophet in Isaiah 6 in the divine council chamber.[37] Other thrones—from Egypt to Babylon and beyond—are secured through varying degrees of military might and coercion. Not only is God's throne infinitely more powerful, but it is founded on justice and thus towers high above corruption. Consequently, in Psalm 97:7 the other gods bow down in submission, and the people of Zion are commanded to turn aside from evil and acclaim God's incomparable name (v. 12). In the context of

---

[36] Wenham, *The Psalter Reclaimed*, 67 suggests that Psalm 89 and the failure of the Davidic monarchy "[prepare] the way for book 4 of the Psalter, which celebrates the reign of Yahweh substituting for the rule" of the Davidic dynasty. Citing the work of Gerald Wilson, *The Editing of the Hebrew Psalter*, 215, D. M. Howard, "Recent Trends in Psalms Study," in *The Faces of Old Testament Studies: A Survey of Contemporary Approaches*, ed. D. W. Baker and B. T. Arnold (Grand Rapids, MI: Baker, 1999), 336 provides a summary of features of these psalms (and what they declare): "(1) YHWH is king; (2) He has been our 'refuge' in the past, long before the monarchy existed (i.e., in the Mosaic period); (3) He will continue to be our refuge now that the monarchy is gone; (4) Blessed are they that trust in him!"

[37] See also Terrien, *The Psalms*, 680.

Book IV, those Israelites in exile (who are dominated by a superpower advocating other gods and their claims) are summoned to change their way of thinking as they hear these hymns that reboot dormant memories with a present-tense vitality. Reflecting on Psalm 93 at the outset of the collection, one commentator writes, "The lines of the hymn evoke for the imagination a word picture of the One who cannot be represented by images. This king is clothed, not with garments, but with majesty and power (v. 1); his attributes are for him what splendid royal robes are for an earthly king. His reign is not measured in years but spans all of time."[38] The enthronement hymns in Book IV combine to unpack the meaning of *the Lord reigns*, and this affirmation will be a key to the people's restoration in the land of promise after the exile.

The second grouping, Psalms 100–106, begins with a call to *all the earth*, a broad invitation to worship issued to the restored community: "enter through his gates with thanksgiving, his courts with praise" (100:4). The reader also hears a sober poetic reflection on leadership, pointing to a fresh resolve to establish a firm foundation when rebuilding the broken city out of the ruins of exile. A chastened Davidic voice speaks in Psalm 101 with a commitment to inward integrity ("I will not set anything vile in front of my eyes," v. 3), teamwork ("the one who walks blamelessly will serve with me," v. 6), and social justice ("morning after morning I will eliminate all the wicked in the land," v. 8). Furthermore, in the closing compositions of Book IV there are recitals and creative allusions to Israel's story, stressing the consistent faithfulness of God despite the persistent waywardness of the community. Psalms 104–106 further underscore prominent themes of Book IV, such as God's sovereignty over creation and within the vortex of world events. In the center of the closing collection is Psalm 103, where forgiveness and restoration are especially prominent, as can be seen early in the poem:

> *About David*
> [1] Bless the Lord, my soul,
>     everything in me, his holy name!

---

[38] Mays, *Psalms*, 300.

> ² Bless the Lord, my soul,
>> do not forget all of his undeserved gifts.
> ³ Who pardons each of your guilty deeds,
>> heals all of your sickness.
> ⁴ Who redeems your life from the Abyss,
>> crowns you with faithful love and compassion.

Earlier in Psalm 88, at perhaps the darkest point in Book III, the poet was on the edge of the grave ("my life inches towards Sheol," v. 6), the murky netherworld and abode of the dead where nothing productive happens. But here in Book IV, the poet of Psalm 103 describes being redeemed from the Abyss (*šaḥat*); this could be interpreted as a picture of Israel being drawn out of the quagmire of exile and on the road to return to the promised land. The prospect of restoration flows from the covenant commitment of God, punctuated with a reference to Exodus 34:6 in 103:8: "The Lord is merciful and gracious, slow to anger and abounding in faithful love." Since the community has fallen woefully short of their own covenant obligations, at the heart of Psalm 103 is a lengthy testimony of forgiveness and the experience of divine grace that has not been earned: "He does not deal with as our sins deserve. . . . as far as the east is from the west, so far does he remove our transgressions from us" (vv. 10–12). Book IV thus unfurls a revolutionary kind of thinking: God is not fair and does not treat us as our sins warrant: "sometimes he shows mercy when we deserve punishment."[39] The response to such unmerited favor in Psalm 103 is worship, and the performance of this psalm begins with a call to "bless" God (implying a physical kind of gesture akin to bowing the knee) in gratitude for such beneficent royalty. However, formal restoration has yet to take place as Book IV draws to a close, and in fact there is a plea for God to mobilize and bring back the scattered people in the long historical reflection of Psalm 106: "Rescue us, O Lord our God, and gather us from among the nations" (v. 47). Just as the cries of despair in Book III receive a response in Book IV, so the reader now anticipates

---

[39] Barry C. Davis, "Psalms," in *The Baker Illustrated Bible Commentary*, ed. Gary M. Burge and Andrew E. Hill (Grand Rapids, MI: Baker, 2012), 525.

a regathering of the exiled community in the final installment of this five-book drama.

## Book V

The edict of Cyrus in 538 BCE formally sets in motion the era of restoration, allowing those displaced citizens of Jerusalem to begin a long journey: just as Abraham set out from Ur of the Chaldeans because of a divine word, so now the descendants of Abraham likewise start their return to the same land. In their case, however, the word is proclaimed by a foreign ruler, although interpreted to be a divine initiative, and in the final chapter of 2 Chronicles (the last words, as it turns out, of the canonical Hebrew Bible), the decree is cited:

> Now in the first year of Cyrus king of Persia, in order to fulfill the word of the Lord by the mouth of Jeremiah, the Lord roused the spirit of Cyrus king of Persia, so that he sent a speaker throughout all his kingdom, and also put it in writing:
> "Thus says Cyrus, king of Persia: all the kingdoms of the earth the Lord God of the heavens has given, and he has appointed me to build a house for him in Jerusalem, in Judah. Whoever is among you—from all his people—may the Lord his God be with him, and let him go up!!" (2 Chron 36:22–23)

A series of political events remarkably coincided for Cyrus to issue this edict, though in a wider biblical theology it is viewed as a movement that is orchestrated under the aegis of God's global dominion, to the point that Isaiah 45:1 refers to Cyrus as God's *anointed*, and 44:28 with probing language extols, "He is my shepherd and will accomplish all that I please; he will say of Jerusalem, 'Let it be rebuilt,' and of the temple, 'Let its foundations be laid.'" This decree of Cyrus is poetically celebrated with immense geographic reach in Psalm 107, the composition that begins Book V with a story of regathering. The psalm begins with a call to give thanks for God's enduring faithfulness, and is addressed to all who have been rescued and gathered from "the east and west, the north and from the sea" (vv. 1–3). The four compass

THE FIVEFOLD SYMPHONY OF THE PSALTER   167

points are followed with four mini-narratives in the heart of Psalm 107. These stories variously describe different kinds of rescue from perilous circumstances, such as healing from terrible diseases (vv. 17–22) or pulled out of a shipwreck in a tempest (vv. 23–32). The first group wanders in a desert wasteland but safely arrives in a better place after crying out to God (vv. 4–9). The second group is incarcerated in prison but is set free from chains of darkness in vv. 10–16:

> [10] Some were dwelling in darkness and the shadow of death,
>     prisoners in misery and iron chains.
> [11] For they had rebelled against God's words,
>     the counsel of the Most High they rejected.
> [12] He humbled their heart with hard labor,
>     they stumbled, but there was no one to help.
> [13] Then they cried out to the Lord in their distress,
>     from their dire straits he rescued them.
> [14] Out of darkness and death's shadow he brought them,
>     tore off their shackles.
> [15] Let them give thanks to the Lord for his faithful love,
>     for his wonders on behalf of the offspring of Adam.
> [16] For he has shattered the gates of bronze,
>     ripped apart bars of iron!

Scanning the reminder of Psalm 107, an argument can be made that it is strategically placed at the outset of Book V. As we have noted, the psalm presents a story of people who are regathered from a host of places and distresses: wandering and lost in the desert, prisoners in gloomy darkness, afflicted because of unwise conduct, or even on storm-tossed waters in a world of chaos. Each of these groups has been "redeemed from the grip of the oppressor" (v. 1), which sets the stage for Book V by portraying the community's return from exile as a new exodus experience. So, for instance, the emphasis on the wilderness in the first part of Psalm 107 points to the need for relying on God when comparatively powerless, akin to Israel's need for divine provision after emancipation from Egypt in days of old. Despite the challenges that lay ahead, the community is characterized as those who have been given a second chance. The reader might therefore picture the next cycle of songs as performed by the people of God who should be defined by gratitude and with the resolve to live wisely.

A trilogy of David psalms (108–110) follow, the first of these compositions remixing material from earlier in Book II (Pss 57 and 60), forming a reflection on God's sovereignty in and around the promised land. Psalm 109 features a shocking invective—perhaps a throwback to the bitterness of factionalism and betrayal in the worst days of the monarchy—reminding the reader that the restoration community faces struggle from within as well as external difficulties. Psalm 110 is a complement to Psalm 2, glancing back to the days of Abraham with the mention of the priest Melchizedek and underscoring God's victory and universal dominion. The most quoted psalm in the New Testament, the vision of kingship and the priesthood in Psalm 110 has long been understood as a messianic anticipation by Christian interpreters.[40]

Early in Book V there is a combination of new images and rebooted pictures of the past. In particular, the term *hallelujah* (praise the Lord) is frequently encountered, having been introduced for the first time in the Psalter near the end of Book IV. A pair of acrostic compositions both begin with hallelujah, as Psalm 111 uses the Hebrew alphabet in a hymn of praise, while Psalm 112 meditates on the qualities of the person who has an all-encompassing faith in God. Increasingly the reader will encounter the hallelujah imperative as the Psalter moves toward a climactic conclusion. Meanwhile, the hallelujah acrostics of 111–112 form a preface to the grand Egyptian Passover collection of 113–118, a group of psalms that commemorate the rescue from slavery and divine faithfulness to the community of Israel. Surely it is not an accident that a crown jewel of Book V, Psalm 119, is then placed immediately after the Egyptian Hallel (praise) collection, a majestic celebration of the Law given on Mt. Sinai as the culmination of the journey out of Egypt and crystallization of the covenant community.

---

[40] For several recent studies with copious reference to secondary literature, see Jared Compton, *Psalm 110 and the Logic of Hebrews*, LNST 537 (London: T&T Clark, 2015); Ian J. Vaillancourt, *The Multifaceted Saviour of Psalms 110 and 118: A Canonical Exegesis* (Sheffield: Sheffield Phoenix Press, 2019); Richard Anthony Purcell, "The King as Priest? Royal Imagery in Psalm 110 and Ancient Near Eastern Iconography," *JBL* 139 (2020): 275–300.

Just as the Hallel collection of 113–118 uses historic images and provides insight into the ideals of worship in the restoration era, so the *Songs of Ascents* (120–134) in Book V take the ancient genre of a pilgrimage composition and reapply these tunes after the rebuilding of Jerusalem and the (second) temple, where the community can gather for a response to the Torah. The *Ascents* collection is followed by another pair of hallelujah psalms in 135 and 136 that emphasize divine control over nature and provision for the people of Israel during the exodus and period of wilderness wandering. We have already discussed the contours of Psalm 137, but it is worth reiterating that dealing with past trauma is part of the rebuilding process as much as physically restoring the city and temple.[41] The penultimate collection of Psalms 138–145 includes the name *David* in each superscription. In particular, Psalm 145 is an acrostic composition that closes this grouping with a focus on God's reign ("a kingdom that endures in all ages," v. 13) and accessibility ("The Lord is near to all who call on him, to each one who calls on him in truth," v. 18). Although this "last Davidic psalm in the Psalter opens with a confession of YHWH as king and does not demand restoration or long for an earthly reign," the reader is nonetheless reminded that a descendant of David may yet arise to be seated on the throne of Israel.[42]

All the psalms in the final group, 146–150, begin with *hallelujah* and bring the Psalter to a climax with a call to praise. At the head of this last collection, Psalm 145 encourages the community to realign their priorities. In the past they have sought security from a monarchy patterned on the nations around them. But now they are enjoined to turn their trust away from earthly rulers and toward God, the one who "opens the eyes of the blind" (v. 7) and has a heart for the

---

[41] On the placement of Psalm 137 after the *Songs of Ascents* and before the end of the royal compositions, see Erich Zenger, "The Composition and Theology of the Fifth Book of Psalms, Psalms 107–145," *JSOT* 80 (1998): 96.

[42] Robert E. Wallace, "Gerald Wilson and the Characterization of David in Book 5 of the Psalter," in *The Shape and Shaping of the Book of Psalms: The Current State of Scholarship*, ed. Nancy L. DeClaissé-Walford (Atlanta, GA: Society of Biblical Literature, 2014), 198. I would be prepared to argue that Book V features the highest percentage of quotations in the New Testament. As one example of the creative use of the Psalter, see Peter Doble, "The Psalms in Luke-Acts," in *The Psalms in the New Testament*, ed. Steve Moyise and Maarten J. J. Menken (London: T&T Clark, 2004), 83–117.

marginalized: "The fatherless and the widow he will make firm, but the way of the wicked he will make crooked" (v. 9). Even though the world is a complex place, they are summoned to praise the Lord, who "will reign for all time," in contrast to the temporary power of the empires. Psalm 150 concludes both Book V and the Psalter by rolling out a cascade of imperatives that erupt in a concert of praise featuring the highest concentration of musical instruments in the entire book. Echoes of Israel's story can be heard in the list of these wood, string, and percussion instruments: the blasting of the ram's horn (*shofar*) is a centerpiece in the episode of Jericho's destruction (Joshua 6), while tambourines and dancing are used to celebrate the rescue from Egyptian slavery (Exod 15:20). Regardless of status or location, every breathing thing in the sprawling "cathedral" of creation is invited to this concert, underscoring "the limitless range of those called to acknowledge God's beneficence. Musical instruments, the products of human ingenuity, support and extend the human voice in its God-given task."[43] There is no closing *amen* in Psalm 150, but instead a final *hallelujah* that suggests an open-ended and enduring invitation to praise.

## Conclusion

What happens when the Psalms are studied as a book with a five-part drama? As a conclusion to this chapter—and our study as a whole—I would suggest three points. First, the reader is invited to consider a life that is lived with an awareness of God in the midst of trials, suffering, and the vicissitudes of existence, and also with an honest view of the inherent deceit of the human heart, capacity for error, and inclination toward trouble. But alongside this striking exploration of the human heart, the *character of God* is also subject to a powerful and complex portrayal over the drama of the five books. Through the highs and lows of Israel's story, the reader is privy to a God who is tenacious, refuses to give up, keeps promises, reprimands when necessary, and

---

[43] Clifford, *Psalms 73–150*, 320.

whose apparent absence elicits deep lament. From start to finish, these ancient poets and lyricists responsible for this soundtrack of the faith of Israel variously proclaim that God is ultimately reliable even in the worst of circumstances. One scholar writes that the five-book drama of the Psalter does not shy away from the most unsettling but desperately important matters:

> In light of the psalms that follow, especially in Book 1 of the Psalter (Pss. 1–41), the issue driving the division is theodicy, the goodness and power of God in light of human suffering and Israel's public defeats. If God does not answer when we are in trouble, is he really "there"? Are we foolish to remain faithful? This penetrating question hangs over the Psalter, bubbling over in the laments and supplications. One of the psalmists' hopes in writing these poems is to strengthen faithful Israelites that they might cling to God's power and goodness, come what may.[44]

Second, over the course of the 150 psalms that are arranged as a symphony, the reader can observe a general *dwindling of evil* as the Psalter moves toward the finish line. Statistically, one commentator observes, "[t]he antithesis between righteous and wicked is more frequent in Book 1 than in Books 2–5. Nearly half the Psalter's references to 'the wicked' after Pss 1 and 2 occur in the next thirty-nine psalms."[45] Over the course of the drama, then, deep-rooted concern with enemies and oppression is gradually displaced by a movement toward unfettered praise. The movement in these lyrics captures something important: instead of giving up or despairing in the face of evil, there is a belief that such darkness will be vanquished by the God who is consistently characterized as one who triumphs over evil and overcomes the darkness. By the end of Book V a vision is slowly emerging that transcends the interests of Israel alone. An inclusivity can be glimpsed as the symphony moves toward the climax, and the volume increases as everything that breathes is summoned to join the concert of praise throughout the vast arena of creation. The drift

---

[44] Charry, *Psalms 1–50*, 1.
[45] Clifford, *Psalms 1–72*, 34.

from crisis to celebration, it should be stressed, is not a replacement of sadness with happiness. Rather, it is a heightened confidence in God's reign in broken and disordered circumstances. It is not as if the situation that gives rise to *lament* changes; rather, there is a recognition that the God who makes promises (e.g., about the eventual fulfillment of the promise to David that a descendant will always be on the throne of Israel) is worthy of praise in every season. Perhaps the book is finally titled *Praises* (*Tehillim*) in Hebrew because praise is the endgame for the believing life.

Third, the journey of the Psalter leads the people of God away from misplaced confidence in human machinery and closer to the divine throne. Such a development can be seen faintly in Book III but is particularly acute in Books IV and V: "The intention of the last two books of the Psalter—to point postexilic Israel away from reliance on human kings toward trust in Yahweh, who alone rules eternally—is already discernible in book three."[46] Perhaps Psalm 73, at the midpoint of the book, provides an illustration. The poet was assailed by envy and nearly slipped up when observing the prosperity of the wicked. But when the poet enters the holy places of God, there is a shift in perspective, eliciting the confession "I have always been with you, you took hold of my right hand" (v. 23). Similarly, the poet of Psalm 23 declares that even in the darkest valley of the shadow of death, "I do not fear evil, because you are with me; your scepter and your staff, *they* give me courage" (v. 4). In our present age, surely faith communities can agree that these are beautiful and compelling images, testifying that the plot and poetry of the book of Psalms can nurture hope and possibility within a fractured world.

---

[46] Gerald H. Wilson, "The Shape of the Book of Psalms," *Int* 46 (1992): 136. As Wilson further notes, there is "a significant concentration of lament psalms in the first half of the book, whereas one can observe that the last half is increasingly dominated by forms of praise. This trend reaches its climax in the concluding *hallel* in Psalms 146–150, which in a sense do not end the psalter but rather catapult the reader onward into an open and unending paean of praise for Yahweh."

# Bibliography

Ahn, John. "Psalm 137: Complex Communal Laments." *JBL* 127 (2008): 267-289.
Allen, Leslie. *Psalms 101-150*. Waco, TX: Word Books, 1983.
Alter, Robert. *The Art of Biblical Poetry*. Revised and updated edition. New York: Basic Books, 2011.
Alter, Robert. *The Book of Psalms: A Translation with Commentary*. New York: W. W. Norton, 2009.
Anderson, Gary A. "King David and the Psalms of Imprecation." In *The Harp of Prophecy: Early Christian Interpretation of the Psalms*, edited by Brian E. Daley and Paul R. Kolbet, 29-45. Notre Dame, IN: University of Notre Dame Press, 2015.
Ballentine, Debra Scoggins. *The Conflict Myth and the Biblical Tradition*. New York: Oxford University Press, 2015.
Barbiero, Gianni. "The Two Structures of Psalm 29." *VT* 66 (2016): 378-392.
Barré Michael L., and John S. Kselman. "New Exodus, Covenant, and Restoration in Psalm 23." In *The Word of the Lord Shall Go Forth: D. N. Freedman Festschrift*, edited by Carol L. Meyers and M. O'Connor, 97-127. Winona Lake, IN: Eisenbrauns, 1983.
Becking, Bob. "Does Exile Equal Suffering? A Fresh Look at Psalm 137." In *Exile and Suffering: A Selection of Papers Read at the 50th Anniversary Meeting of the Old Testament Society of South Africa OTWSA/OTSSA, Pretoria August 2007*, edited by Bob Becking and Dirk Human, 183-202. Leiden: Brill, 2009.
Berlin, Adele. "The Message of Psalm 114." In *Birkat Shalom: Studies in the Bible, Ancient Near Eastern Literature, and Postbiblical Judaism Presented to Shalom M. Paul on the Occasion of His Seventieth Birthday*, edited by Chaim Cohen, Victor Avigdor Hurowitz, Avi Hurvitz, Yochanan Muffs, Baruch J. Schwartz, and Jeffrey H. Tigay, 345-361. Winona Lake, IN: Eisenbrauns, 2008.
Berlin, Adele. "The Wisdom of Creation in Psalm 104." In *Seeking Out the Wisdom of the Ancients: Essays Offered to Honor Michael V. Fox on the Occasion of his Sixty-Fifth Birthday*, edited by Ronald L. Troxel, Kelvin G. Friebel, and Dennis R. Magery, 71-83. Winona Lake, IN: Eisenbrauns, 2005.
Blaising, Craig A., and Carmen S. Hardin, eds. *Psalms 1-50*. Downers Grove, IL: InterVarsity Press, 2008.

Bosman, Hendrick. "Psalm 114 as Reinterpretation of the Exodus during and after the Exile." *OTE* 26 (2013): 559–582.
Brennan, Joseph P. "Psalms 1–8: Some Hidden Harmonies." *BTB* 10 (1980): 25–29.
Brettler, Mark Zvi. "Jewish Theology of the Psalms." In *The Oxford Handbook of the Psalms*, edited by William P. Brown, 485–498. New York: Oxford University Press, 2014.
Briggs, Charles A., and Emilie G. Briggs. *A Critical and Exegetical Commentary on the Book of Psalms*. Vol. 1. Edinburgh: T&T Clark, 1906.
Brooks, Peter. *Reading for the Plot: Design and Intention in Narrative*. Cambridge, MA: Harvard University Press, 1984.
Brown, William P. *Seeing the Psalms: A Theology of Metaphor*. Louisville, KY: Westminster John Knox Press, 2002.
Broyles, Craig C. *Psalms*. Peabody, MA: Hendrickson, 1995.
Brueggemann, Walter. "Bounded by Obedience and Praise: The Psalms as Canon." *JSOT* 50 (1991): 63–92.
Brueggemann, Walter. *Isaiah 1–39*. Louisville, KY: Westminster John Knox Press, 1998.
Brueggemann, Walter, and William H. Bellinger Jr. *Psalms*. New York: Cambridge University Press, 2014.
Brueggemann, Walter, and Patrick D. Miller. "Psalm 73 as a Canonical Marker." *JSOT* 72 (1996): 45–56.
Bullock, C. Hassell. *Encountering the Book of Psalms: A Literary and Theological Introduction*. 2nd edition. Grand Rapids, MI: Baker, 2018.
Ceresko, Anthony R. "A Poetic Analysis of Ps 105, with Attention to Its Use of Irony." *Biblica* 64 (1983): 20–46.
Charlesworth, James H. *The Good and Evil Serpent: How a Universal Symbol Became Christianized*. New Haven, CT: Yale University Press, 2010.
Charry, Ellen. *Psalms 1–50*. Grand Rapids, MI: Brazos, 2015.
Clifford, Richard J. *Psalms 1–72*. Abingdon Old Testament Commentaries. Nashville, TN: Abingdon, 2002.
Clifford, Richard J. *Psalms 73–150*. Abingdon Old Testament Commentaries. Nashville, TN: Abingdon, 2003.
Cole, Robert L. *The Shape and Message of Book III (Psalms 73–89)*. Sheffield: Sheffield Academic Press, 2000.
Compton, Jared. *Psalm 110 and the Logic of Hebrews*. London: T&T Clark, 2015.
Coogan, Michael D. *A Reader of Ancient Near Eastern Texts: Sources for the Study of the Old Testament*. Oxford: Oxford University Press, 2013.
Coogan, Michael D., and Mark S. Smith, eds. and trans. *Stories from Ancient Canaan*. 2nd edition. Louisville, KY: Westminster John Knox Press, 2012.
Cross, F. M., Jr., and D. N. Freedman. "A Royal Song of Thanksgiving: II Samuel 22 = Psalm 18." *JBL* 72 (1953): 15–34.

Crutchfield, John C. "The Redactional Agenda of the Book of Psalms." *HUCA* 74 (2003): 21–47.

Dahood, Mitchell. *Psalms III: 101–150*. New York: Doubleday, 1970.

Davage, David Willgren. "Why Davidic Superscriptions Do Not Demarcate Earlier Collections of Psalms." *JBL* 139 (2020): 67–86.

Davis, Barry C. "Psalms." In *The Baker Illustrated Bible Commentary*, edited by Gary M. Burge and Andrew E. Hill, 494–535. Grand Rapids, MI: Baker, 2012.

Day, John. *God's Conflict with the Dragon and the Sea: Echoes of a Canaanite Myth in the Old Testament*. Cambridge: Cambridge University Press, 1985.

Day, John. *Psalms*. Sheffield: JSOT Press, 1990.

DeClaissé-Walford, Nancy. *Introduction to the Psalms: A Song from Ancient Israel*. St. Louis, MO: Chalice, 2004.

DeClaissé-Walford, Nancy J., Rolf A. Jacobson, and Beth LaNeel Tanner. *The Book of Psalms*. Grand Rapids, MI: Eerdmans, 2014.

Dobbs-Allsopp, F. W. *On Biblical Poetry*. New York: Oxford University Press, 2015.

Doble, Peter. "The Psalms in Luke–Acts." In *The Psalms in the New Testament*, edited by Steve Moyise and Maarten J. J. Menken, 83–117. London: T&T Clark, 2004.

Eaton, John. *The Psalms: A Historical and Spiritual Commentary with an Introduction and New Translation*. London: T&T Clark, 2003.

Einboden, Jeffrey. "The Homeric Psalm: Milton's Translation of Psalm 114 and the Problems of 'Hellenistic Scripture.'" *Literature & Theology* 17 (2003): 314–323.

Empson, William. *Seven Types of Ambiguity*. London: Chatto and Windus, 1949.

Firth, David G. "Asaph and Sons of Korah." In *Dictionary of the Old Testament: Wisdom, Poetry and Writings*, edited by Tremper Longman III and Peter Enns, 24–27. Downers Grove, IL: InterVarsity Press, 2008.

Fokkelman, Jan P. *Major Poems of the Hebrew Bible: At the Interface of Prosody and Structural Analysis*. Vol. 2: *85 Psalms and Job 4–14*. Leiden: Brill, 2000.

Geller, Stephen A. "Myth and Syntax in Psalm 93." In *Mishneh Todah: Studies in Deuteronomy and Its Cultural Environment in Honor of Jeffrey H. Tigay*, edited by Nili Sacher Fox, David A. Glatt-Gilad, and Michael J. Williams, 321–331. Winona Lake, IN: Eisenbrauns, 2009.

Gerstenberger, Erhard S. *Psalms, Part 2, and Lamentations*. Grand Rapids, MI: Eerdmans, 2001.

Gillingham, Susan. "Psalms 90–106: Book Four and the Covenant with David." *EJ* 48 (2015): 83–101.

Gillingham, Susan. *Psalms through the Centuries: A Reception History Commentary on Psalms 1–72*. Vol. 2. Chichester: John Wiley & Sons, 2018.

Goldingay, John. *Psalms*. Vol. 1: *Psalms 1–41*. Grand Rapids, MI: Baker, 2006.

Goldingay, John. *Psalms*. Vol. 2: *Psalms 42–89*. Grand Rapids, MI: Baker, 2007.

Goldingay, John. *Psalms*. Vol. 3: *Psalms 90–150*. Grand Rapids, MI: Baker, 2008.

Goldingay, John. "The Theology of the Hebrew Bible/Old Testament." In *The Cambridge Companion to the Hebrew Bible/Old Testament*, edited by Stephen B. Chapman and Marvin A. Sweeney, 466–482. New York: Cambridge University Press, 2016.

Gottwald, Norman K. "Kingship in the Book of Psalms." In *The Oxford Handbook of the Psalms*, edited by William P. Brown, 437–444. New York: Oxford University Press, 2014.

Grant, Jamie A. "The Psalms and the King." In *Interpreting the Psalms: Issues and Approaches*, edited by David G. Firth and Philip S. Johnston, 101–118. Downers Grove, IL: InterVarsity Press, 2013.

Hallo, William W., and K. Lawson Younger Jr., eds. *The Context of Scripture*, 3 vols. Leiden: Brill, 1997–2003.

Hayes, Elizabeth. "The Unity of the Egyptian Hallel: Psalms 113–18." *BBR* 9 (1999): 145–156.

Hays, Christopher B. "How Shall We Sing? Psalm 137 in Historical and Canonical Context." *HBT* 27 (2005): 35–55.

Heard, R. Christopher. "Penitent to a Fault: The Characterization of David in Psalm 51." In *The Fate of King David: The Past and Present of a Biblical Icon*, edited by Tod Linafelt, Claudia V. Camp, and Timothy Beal, 163–174. London: T&T Clark, 2010.

Herman, David. "Introduction." In *The Cambridge Companion to Narrative*, edited by David Herman, 3–21. Cambridge: Cambridge University Press, 2007.

Hoffmeier, James K. "Plagues in Egypt." In *Anchor Bible Dictionary*, 6 vols., edited by David Noel Freedman, 2:374–378. New York: Doubleday, 1992.

Holladay, William. *The Psalms through Three Thousand Years: Prayerbook of a Cloud of Witnesses*. Minneapolis, MN: Fortress, 1993.

Hopkins, Denise Dombkowski. *Journey through the Psalms*. Revised and expanded edition. St. Louis, MO: Chalice Press, 2002.

Hossfeld, Frank Lothar, and Erich Zenger. *Psalms 3: A Commentary on Psalms 101–150*. Hermeneia. Minneapolis, MN: Fortress, 2011.

Howard, David M. "Recent Trends in Psalms Study." In *The Faces of Old Testament Studies: A Survey of Contemporary Approaches*, edited by D. W. Baker and B. T. Arnold, 329–368. Grand Rapids, MI: Baker, 1999.

Howard, David M., Jr. "The Psalms and Current Study." In *Interpreting the Psalms: Issues and. Approaches,* edited by David Firth and Philip S. Johnston, 23–40. Downers Grove, IL: InterVarsity Press, 2005.

Howard, Thomas. *Dove Descending: A Journey into T. S. Eliot's Four Quartets*. San Francisco, CA: Ignatius Press, 2006.

Hutton, Jeremy M. "Isaiah 51:9–11 and the Rhetorical Appropriation and Subversion of Hostile Theologies." *JBL* 126 (2007): 271–303.

Johnson, Vivian L. *David in Distress: His Portrait through the Historical Psalms*. London: T&T Clark International, 2009.

Johnstone, William. *Exodus*. Old Testament Guides. Sheffield: Sheffield Academic Press, 1990.

Jones, Christine Brown. "The Message of the Asaphite Collection and Its Role in the Psalter." In *The Shape and Shaping of the Book of Psalms: The Current State of Scholarship*, edited by Nancy L. deClaissé-Walford, 71–85. Atlanta, GA: Society of Biblical Literature, 2014.

Keel, Othmar. *The Symbolism of the Biblical World: Ancient Near Eastern Iconography and the Book of Psalms*. New York: Seabury Press, 1978.

Kraus, Hans-Joachim. *Theology of the Psalms*. Minneapolis, MN: Augsburg, 1986.

Lee, Archie C. C. "Genesis I and the Plagues Tradition in Psalm cv." *VT* 40 (1990): 259–260.

Lewis, C. S. *Reflections on the Psalms*. New York: Harcourt, Brace, 1958.

Linafelt, Tod. "The Pentateuch." In *The Oxford Handbook of English Literature and Theology*, edited by Andrew Hass, David Jasper, and Elisabeth Jay, 214–226. Oxford: Oxford University Press, 2009.

Longman, Tremper, III. *Psalms: An Introduction and Commentary*. Downers Grove, IL: Intervarsity Press, 2014.

Machinist, Peter. "How Gods Die, Biblically and Otherwise: A Problem of Cosmic Restructuring." In *Reconsidering the Concept of Revolutionary Monotheism*, edited by Beate Pongratz-Leisten, 189–240. Winona Lake, IN: Eisenbrauns, 2014.

Mandolfo, Carleen. "Language of Lament in the Psalms." In *The Oxford Handbook of The Psalms*, edited by William P. Brown, 114–130. New York: Oxford University Press, 2014.

Maré, Leonard P. "Psalm 137: Exile—Not the Time for Singing the Lord's Song." *OTE* 23 (2010): 116–128.

Mays, James L. "The David of the Psalms." *Int* 40 (1986): 143–155.

Mays, James L. *Psalms*. Interpretation. Louisville, KY: John Knox, 1994.

McCann, J. Clinton, Jr. "The Book of Psalms: Introduction, Commentary, and Reflections." In *The New Interpreter's Bible*, vol. 4, edited by Leander E. Keck, 641–1280. Nashville, TN: Abingdon, 1996.

Miller, J. Maxwell, and John H. Hayes. *A History of Ancient Israel and Judah*. 2nd edition. Louisville, KY: Westminster John Knox, 2006.

Miller, Patrick D. "Gregory of Nyssa: The Superscriptions of the Psalms." In *Genesis, Isaiah, and Psalms: A Festschrift to Honour Professor John Emerton for His Eightieth Birthday*, edited by Katharine Dell, Graham Davies, and Yee Von Koh, 215–229. Leiden: Brill, 2010.

Mitchell, David C. *The Message of the Psalter: An Eschatological Programme in the Book of Psalms*. Sheffield: Sheffield Academic Press, 1997.

Mitchell, David C. "'God Will Redeem My Soul from Sheol': The Psalms of the Sons of Korah." *JSOT* 30, no. 3 (2006): 243–262.

Norris, Kathleen. *The Cloister Walk*. New York: Riverhead Books, 1996.

Ogden, Graham S. "Prophetic Oracles against Foreign Nations and Psalms of Communal Lament: The Relationship of Psalm 137 to Jeremiah 49:7–22 and Obadiah." *JSOT* 24 (1982): 89–97.

Pardee, Dennis. "On Psalm 29: Structure and Meaning." In *The Book of Psalms: Composition and Reception*, edited by Peter W. Flint and Patrick D. Miller, with the assistance of Aaron Brunell and Ryan Roberts, 153–183. Leiden: Brill, 2005.

Parrish, Steven. *A Story of the Psalms: Conversation, Canon, and Congregation*. Collegeville, MN: Liturgical Press, 2003.

Pavan, Marco. *"He Remembered That They Were but Flesh, a Breath That Passes and Does Not Return (Ps 78–39)": The Theme of Memory and Forgetting in the Third Book of the Psalter (Pss 73–89)*. Frankfurt am Main: Peter Lang, 2014.

Plank, Karl A. "Ascent to Darker Hills: Psalm 121 and Its Poetic Revision." *Literature & Theology* 11 (1997): 152–167.

Pritchard, James B., ed. *Ancient Near Eastern Texts Relating to the Old Testament*. 3rd edition. Princeton, NJ: Princeton University Press, 1969.

Purcell, Richard Anthony. "The King as Priest? Royal Imagery in Psalm 110 and Ancient Near Eastern Iconography." *JBL* 139 (2020): 275–300.

Raabe, Paul R. "Mizar." In *Anchor Bible Dictionary*, 6 vols., edited by David Noel Freedman, 4:879. New York: Doubleday, 1992.

Rendtorff, Rolf. "The Psalms of David: David in the Psalms." In *The Book of Psalms: Composition and Reception*, edited by Peter W. Flint and Patrick D. Miller Jr., with the assistance of Aaron Brunell and Ryan Roberts, 53–64. Leiden: Brill, 2005.

Ross, Allen P. *A Commentary on the Psalms, Volume 1: 1–41*. Grand Rapids, MI: Kregel, 2011.

Ross, Allen P. *A Commentary on the Psalms, Volume 2: 42–89*. Grand Rapids, MI: Kregel, 2013.

Ross, Allen P. *A Commentary on the Psalms, Volume 3: 90–150*. Grand Rapids, MI: Kregel, 2016.

Saleska, Timothy E. *Psalms 1–50*. St. Louis, MO: Concordia Publishing House, 2020.

Sanchez, Edesio. "Psalms in Latin America." In *The Oxford Handbook of the Psalms*, edited by William P. Brown, 475–481. New York: Oxford University Press, 2014.

Satterthwaite, Philip E. "Zion in the Songs of Ascents." In *Zion, City of Our God*, edited by Richard S. Hess and Gordon J. Wenham, 105–128. Grand Rapids, MI: Eerdmans, 1999.

Savran, George. "How Can We Sing a Song of the Lord? The Strategy of Lament in Psalm 137." *ZAW* 112 (2000): 43–58.

Schaefer, Konrad. *Psalms*. Berit Olam. Collegeville, MN: Michael Glazier, 2001.

Schipper, Bernd U. "Egyptian Backgrounds to the Psalms." In *The Oxford Handbook of the Psalms*, edited by William P. Brown, 57–75. New York: Oxford University Press, 2014.

Sommer, Benjamin D. "A Little Higher Than Angels: Psalm 29 and the Genre of Heavenly Praise." In *Built by Wisdom, Established by Understanding: Essays on Biblical and Near Eastern Literature in Honor of Adele Berlin*, edited by Maxine L. Grossman, 129–153. Bethesda: University Press of Maryland, 2013.

Soskice, Janet Martin. *Metaphor and Religious Language*. New York: Oxford University Press, 1985.

Spurgeon, Charles H. *The Treasury of David, Containing an Original Exposition of the Book of Psalms*. 7 vols. London, 1860–1867.

Strawn, Brent A. "Poetic Attachment: Psychology, Psycholinguistics, and the Psalms." In *The Oxford Handbook of the Psalms*, edited by William P. Brown, 404–423. New York: Oxford University Press, 2014

Stulman, Louis. *Order amid Chaos: Jeremiah as Symbolic Tapestry*. Biblical Seminar 57. Sheffield: Sheffield Academic Press, 1998.

Styron, William. *Sophie's Choice*. Toronto: Bantam Books, 1979.

Tanner, Beth LaNeel. *The Book of Psalms through the Lens of Intertextuality*. New York: Lang, 2001.

Terrien, Samuel L. *The Psalms: Strophic Structure and Theological Commentary*. Grand Rapids, MI: Eerdmans, 2003.

Tigay, Jeffrey H. "'The Voice of Yhwh Causes Hinds to Calve' (Psalm 29:9)." In *Birkat Shalom: Studies in the Bible, Ancient Near Eastern Literature, and Postbiblical Judaism Presented to Shalom M. Paul on the Occasion of His Seventieth Birthday*, edited by Chaim Cohen, Victor Avigdor Hurowitz, Avi Hurvitz, Yochanan Muffs, Baruch J. Schwartz, and Jeffrey H. Tigay, 399–411. Winona Lake, IN: Eisenbrauns, 2008.

Tucker, W. Dennis, Jr. *Constructing and Deconstructing Power in Psalms 107–150*. Atlanta, GA: Society of Biblical Literature, 2014.

Tucker, W. Dennis, Jr., and Jamie A. Grant. *Psalms*. Vol. 2. Grand Rapids, MI: Zondervan, 2018.

Tull, Patricia K. "1 and 2 Samuel." In *Theological Bible Commentary*, edited by Gail R. O'Day and David L. Petersen, 101–117. Louisville, KY: Westminster John Knox Press, 2009.

Vaillancourt, Ian J. "Formed in the Crucible of Messianic Angst: The Eschatological Shape of the Hebrew Psalter's Final Form." *SBET* 31 (2013): 127.

Vaillancourt, Ian J. *The Multifaceted Saviour of Psalms 110 and 118: A Canonical Exegesis*. Sheffield: Sheffield Phoenix Press, 2019.

Vanderhooft, David S. "Marduk." In *Eerdmans Dictionary of the Bible*, edited by D. N. Freedman, 856. Grand Rapids, MI: Eerdmans, 2000.

Venter, Pieter M. "Spatiality in Psalm 29." In *Psalms and Liturgy*, edited by Dirk J. Human and Cas J. A. Vos, 235–250. London: T&T Clark, 2004.

Wallace, Robert E. "Gerald Wilson and the Characterization of David in Book 5 of the Psalter." In *The Shape and Shaping of the Book of Psalms: The Current*

State of Scholarship, edited by Nancy L. deClaissé-Walford, 193–207. Atlanta, GA: Society of Biblical Literature, 2014.

Wallace, Robert E. *The Narrative Effect of Book IV of the Hebrew Psalter*. New York: Peter Lang, 2007.

Waltke, Bruce K., and James M. Houston, with Erika Moore. *The Psalms as Christian Worship: A Historical Commentary*. Grand Rapids, MI: Eerdmans, 2010.

Waltner, James H. *Psalms*. Scottdale, PA: Herald Press, 2006.

Wenham, Gordon J. *Psalms as Torah: Reading Biblical Song Ethically*. Grand Rapids, MI: Baker Academic, 2012.

Wenham, Gordon J. *The Psalter Reclaimed: Praying and Praising with the Psalms*. Wheaton, IL: Crossway, 2013.

Whybray, Norman. *Reading the Psalms as a Book*. Sheffield: Sheffield Academic Press, 1996.

Wiggins, Steve A. "Between Heaven and Earth: Absalom's Dilemma." *JNSL* 23 (1997): 73–81.

Wiggins, Steve A. *Weathering the Psalms: A Meteorotheological Survey*. Eugene, OR: Cascade Books, 2014.

Williams, Tyler F. "Towards a Date for the Old Greek Psalter." In *The Old Greek Psalter: Studies in Honour of Albert Pietersma*, edited by Robert J. V. Hiebert, Claude E. Cox, and Peter J. Gentry, 248–276. Sheffield: Sheffield Academic Press, 2001.

Willis, John T. "Yahweh Regenerates His Vineyard: Isaiah 27." In *Formation and Intertextuality in Isaiah 24–27*, edited by J. Todd Hibbard and Hyun Chul Paul Kim, 201–207. Ancient Israel and Its Literature 17. Atlanta, GA: Society of Biblical Literature, 2013.

Wilson, Gerald H. *The Editing of the Hebrew Psalter*. Chico, CA: Scholars Press, 1985.

Wilson, Gerald H. *Psalms Volume 1*. NIVAC; Grand Rapids: Zondervan, 2002.

Wilson, Gerald H. "The Shape of the Book of Psalms." *Int* 46 (1992): 129–142.

Wilson, Gerald H. "The Structure of the Psalter." In *Interpreting the Psalms: Issues and Approaches*, edited by David G. Firth and Philip S. Johnston, 229–246. Downers Grove, IL: InterVarsity Press, 2013.

Witt, Andrew. "Hearing Psalm 102 within the Context of the Hebrew Psalter." *VT* 62 (2012): 582–606.

Wittman, Derek E. "Let Us Cast Off Their Ropes from Us: The Editorial Significance of the Portrayal of Foreign Nations in Psalms 2 and 149." In *The Shape and Shaping of the Book of Psalms: The Current State of Scholarship*, edited by Nancy L. deClaissé-Walford, 53–69. Atlanta, GA: Society of Biblical Literature, 2014.

Zenger, Erich. "The Composition and Theology of the Fifth Book of Psalms, Psalms 107–145." *JSOT* 80 (1998): 77–102.

Zenger, Erich. *A God of Vengeance? Understanding the Psalms of Divine Wrath*. Louisville, KY: Westminster John Knox, 1996.

Zernecke, Anna Elise. "Mesopotamian Parallels to the Psalms." In *The Oxford Handbook of the Psalms*, edited by William P. Brown, 27–42. New York: Oxford University Press, 2014.

# Index

*For the benefit of digital users, indexed terms that span two pages (e.g., 52–53) may, on occasion, appear on only one of those pages.*

Aaron, 34, 82, 90
Abimelech, 118
Abishai, 128
Abraham, 3, 4, 5, 16, 18, 53, 87, 155, 161, 166, 168
Absalom, 94, 100, 118, 119, 120, 121, 122, 127, 130, 141, 142
Adam, 53, 143, 160, 167
Adonijah, 29
Ahithophel, 122
Ahn, John, 96
Akhenaten, 25
Allen, Leslie, 59, 89
Alter, Robert, 9, 12, 23, 43, 63, 77
Anderson, Gary A., 156
Arnold, Bill T., 163
Asaph, 14, 49, 106, 118, 151, 152, 153, 154
Assyria, 5, 20, 40, 41, 151
Aten, 25, 35
Augustine, 18, 23

Baal, 13, 14, 25, 27, 28, 31, 32, 36, 37, 38, 41, 111
Babylon, 1, 5, 6, 20, 33, 35, 37, 40, 41, 61, 63, 75, 77, 79, 80, 89, 91, 92, 93, 94, 95, 96, 97, 98, 114, 116, 142, 151, 155, 157, 162, 163
Bach, J, S., 123
Baker, David W., 163
Ballentine, Debra Scoggins, 32
Barbiero, Gianni, 27
Barré Michael L., 64
Bathsheba, 100, 118, 119, 124, 125
Beal, Timothy, 124
Becking, Bob, 93

Bellinger, William H., Jr., 29, 49, 58, 65, 70, 92, 105, 131, 140, 157
Ben-Hadad, 97
Berlin, Adele, 28, 52, 77, 79
Blaising, Craig A., 136
Bonhoeffer, Dietrich, 67
Bosman, Hendrick, 76, 79
Brennan, Joseph P., 134
Brettler, Mark Zvi, 6, 61, 66
Briggs, Charles A., 102
Briggs, Emilie G., 102
Brooks, Peter, 18
Brown, William P., 6, 10, 25, 50, 58, 103, 104, 118, 136, 138
Broyles, Craig C., 157
Brueggemann, Walter, 21, 29, 32, 49, 58, 65, 70, 72, 92, 104, 105, 131, 140, 157
Brunell, Aaron, 31, 132
Bullock, C, Hassell, 55
Burge, Gary M., 165

Camp, Claudia V., 124
Canaan, 4, 25, 26, 27, 28, 31, 34, 36, 37, 40, 67, 75, 78, 84, 87, 111
Celan, Paul, 23
Ceresko, Anthony R., 89
Chapman, Stephen B., 13
Charlesworth, James H., 8
Charry, Ellen, 135, 171
Chrysostom, John, 136
Ciardi, John, 93
Clifford, Richard J., 28, 91, 94, 112, 134, 170, 171
*Cloister Walk, The*, 157
Cohen, Chaim, 30, 79

Cole, Robert L., 152
Compton, Jared, 168
Coogan, Michael D., 25, 27, 32, 37, 41
Cox, Claude E., 102
*Crime and Punishment*, 101
Cross, Frank Moore, Jr., 45
Crutchfield, John C., 134
Cush of Benjamin, 118
Cyrus, 5, 6, 166

Dahood, Mitchell, 89
Daley, Brian E., S.J., 156
Damascus, 59, 97
Dante, 93
Davage, David Willgren, 105
David, 2, 4, 5, 17, 18, 19, 20, 21, 26, 29, 41, 44, 46, 48, 49, 50, 61, 62, 84, 85, 93, 94, 100, 105, 106, 113, 115, 118, 119, 120, 121, 122, 123, 124, 127, 128, 129, 130, 131, 133, 140, 141, 143, 145, 147, 150, 151, 152, 156, 160, 163, 164, 168, 169, 172
Davies, Graham, 104
Davis, Barry C., 165
Day, John, 28, 32, 48, 54
DeClaissé-Walford, Nancy J., 20, 39, 45, 53, 62, 67, 75, 88, 130, 136, 138, 145, 156, 160, 162, 169
Dell, Katharine, 104
Dickinson, Emily, 23
Dobbs-Allsopp, F, W., 8
Doble, Peter, 169
Doeg the Edomite, 118

*East of Eden*, 101
Eastwood, Clint, 127
Eaton, John, 136
Edom, 91, 92, 96
Egypt, 4, 5, 14, 26, 28, 32, 33, 34, 35, 40, 41, 48, 64, 75, 76, 77, 78, 79, 81, 82, 83, 88, 89, 90, 91, 93, 99, 114, 118, 156, 157, 163, 167, 168, 170
Einboden, Jeffrey, 79
Eliot, T, S., 7, 74
Elisha, 59, 97
Emerton, John, 104
Empson, William, 74

*Emma*, 101
Enns, Peter, 153
*Enuma Elish*, 37, 39
Esau, 96
*Escape from Alcatraz*, 127
Esther, 6
Euphrates River, 40, 93

Firth, David G., 21, 49, 50, 153
Flint, Peter W., 31, 132
Fokkelman, Jan P., 136
Fox, Michael V., 52
Fox, Nili Sacher, 37
Freedman, David Noel, 37, 45, 90, 149
Friebel, Kelvin G., 52
Funeral Oration of Pericles, 74

Gath, 118
Gaza, 104
Geller, Stephen A., 37
Gentry, Peter J., 102
Gerstenberger, Erhard S., 21, 38, 97
Gideon, 14, 98, 99
Gillingham, Susan, 18, 41, 107, 162
Glatt-Gilad, David A., 37
Goldingay, John, 13, 15, 29, 40, 56, 77, 79, 102, 110, 130, 135, 157
Goliath, 119
Gottwald, Norman K., 59, 67, 138
Grant, Jamie A., 50, 141
Gregory of Nyssa, 104
Grossman, Maxine L., 28

Halevi, Judah, 23
Hallo, William W., 25
Haman, 98
*Hamilton*, 73
*Hamlet*, 52
Hammurabi, 61
Hardin, Carmen S., 136
Hass, Andrew, 77
Hayes, Elizabeth, 75
Hayes, John H., 3
Hays, Christopher B., 94, 96
Hazael of Damascus, 59, 97
Heard, R, Christopher, 124, 132
Herbert, George, 23

Herman, David, 155
Herod, 97
Hess, Richard S., 116
Hezekiah, 5, 14, 104
Hibbard, J, Todd, 32
Hiebert, Robert J, V., 102
Hill, Andrew E., 165
Hoffmeier, James K., 90
Holladay, William, 23
Hopkins, Denise Dombkowski, 102
Hosea, 31
Hossfeld, Frank Lothar, 110, 116
Howard, David M., Jr., 21, 163
Howard, Thomas, 7
Human, Dirk, 30, 93
*Hunger Games, The*, 101
Hurowitz, Victor Avigdor, 30, 79
Hurvitz, Avi, 30, 79
Hushai, 122
Hutton, Jeremy M., 34
*Hymn to the Aten*, 25, 35

Ibn Ezra, 66
*Inferno*, 93
Isaac, 87
Isaiah, 5, 31, 32
Ishtar, 25

Jacobson, Rolf A., 20, 39, 45, 53, 62, 67, 75, 88, 130, 136, 145, 156, 162
Jasper, David, 77
Jay, Elisabeth, 77
Jeremiah, 6, 68, 104, 142
Jeroboam II, 31
Jerusalem, 5, 12, 17, 20, 21, 31, 33, 35, 59, 64, 72, 89, 91, 92, 94, 95, 96, 100, 108, 111, 113, 116, 117, 119, 120, 124, 127, 142, 146, 147, 148, 150, 152, 160, 166
Jesse, 19, 152
Joab, 94
Job, 36, 50, 68
Johnson, Vivian L., 127
Johnston, Philip S., 21, 49, 50
Johnstone, William, 3
Jonathan, 29, 119
Jones, Christine Brown, 106
Jordan River, 34, 76, 120

Joseph, 28, 84, 87, 88, 89, 94
Joshua, 67, 87

Kadesh, 27, 30
Keck, Leander E., 29
Kedar, 110
Keel, Othmar, 97
Kim, Hyun Chul Paul, 32
Koh, Yee Von, 104
Kolbet, Paul R., 156
Korah, 49, 106, 118, 132, 140, 147, 148, 151, 152, 153, 156
Kraus, Hans-Joachim, 6
Kselman, John S., 64
Kugel, James, 77

Lebanon, 25, 27, 30, 136
Lee, Archie C, C., 91
Levenson, Jon 35
Leviathan, 24, 32, 33, 34, 35, 36, 42, 159
Lewis, C, S., 10
Linafelt, Tod, 77
Litan, 32
Longman, Tremper III, 138, 153
*Lord of the Rings*, 157
Luther, Martin, 6

Machinist, Peter, 15
Magery, Dennis R., 52
Mandolfo, Carleen, 58
Marduk, 13, 37, 38, 39, 41
Maré, Leonard P., 95
Mays, James L., 30, 52, 55, 84, 95, 110, 124, 128, 132
McCann, J, Clinton, Jr., 29, 66, 72, 79, 86, 102
Melchizedek, 168
Mendelssohn, Felix, 123
Menken, Maarten J, J., 169
Mephibosheth, 29
*Merchant of Venice*, 80
Meshech, 110, 117
Mesopotamia, 25, 26, 28, 48
Meyers, Carol L., 64
Michal, 127
Midianites, 14, 98, 99
Miller, J, Maxwell, 3

Miller, Patrick D., 31, 72, 104, 132
Milton, John, 79
Mitchell, David C., 20, 106
Mizar, Mt., 149
Mordecai, 98
Moses, 61, 82, 90, 106, 147, 160, 161, 162, 163
Moyise, Steve, 169
Mozart, 123
Muffs, Yochanan, 30

Nathan, 100, 118, 123, 127
Nehushtan, 14
Nile River, 4, 40, 80, 90, 93
Noah, 30
Norris, Kathleen, 157

O'Connor, Michael P., 64
O'Day, Gail R., 4
Og of Bashan, 11
Ogden, Graham S., 96

Pardee, Dennis, 31
Parrish, Steven, 161
Paul, Shalom M., 30, 79
Pavan, Marco, 157
Persia, 5, 6, 32, 166
Peter, 59
Petersen, David L., 4
Pharaoh, 4, 34, 76, 81, 89, 104
Philistines, 56, 118, 157
Pietersma, Albert, 102
Plank, Karl A., 111
Pongratz-Leisten, Beate, 15
Pope Pius VI, 53
Pritchard, James B., 25
Purcell, Richard Anthony, 168

Raabe, Paul R., 149
Radak, 66
Red Sea, 4, 14, 34, 76, 81, 83
Rendtorff, Rolf, 132
Roberts, Ryan, 31, 132
Rome, 33
*Romeo & Juliet*, 7
Ross, Allen P., 12, 39, 109, 126

Saleska, Timothy E., 107

Samuel, 119
Sanchez, Edesio, 118
Sarah, 4
Sargon, 52
Satterthwaite, Philip E., 116
Saul, 29, 118, 119, 127, 128, 129, 130
Savran, George, 94, 97
Schaefer, Konrad, 17, 53, 124
Schipper, Bernd U., 24
Schwartz, Baruch J., 30, 79
Sennacherib, 53
Shakespeare, 7, 8, 80
Shiloh, 84, 85
Shimei, 120
Sinai, 4, 5, 163, 168
Smith, Mark S., 25, 27, 32, 37, 41
Solomon, 4, 20, 21, 29, 39, 48, 52, 64, 114, 115, 116, 119, 133, 155
Sommer, Benjamin D., 28, 29
*Sophie's Choice*, 158
Soskice, Janet Martin, 10
Spurgeon, Charles H., 130
*St, Paul*, 123
Steinbeck, John, 101
Strawn, Brent A., 103
Stulman, Louis, 142
Styron, William, 157
Sumerians, 7
Sweeney, Marvin A., 13
Syria, 25, 36, 149

Tanner, Beth LaNeel, 20, 39, 45, 53, 62, 67, 75, 88, 130, 136, 145, 156, 157, 162
Terrien, Samuel L., 26, 42, 67, 92, 163
Thucydides, 74
Tiamat, 37, 39
Tigay, Jeffrey H., 30, 37, 79
Tigris River, 40, 93
Tolkien, J, R, R., 157
Troxel, Ronald L., 52
Tucker, W, Dennis, Jr., 111, 141
Tull, Patricia K., 4
Tyre, 157

Ugarit, 25, 36
Ur of the Chaldeans, 166

Vaillancourt, Ian J., 18, 168

Vandals, 33
Vanderhooft, David S., 37
Venter, Pieter M., 30
Ventura, Tirsa, 118
Vos, Cas J, A., 30

Wallace, Robert E., 20, 162, 169
Waltner, James H., 130
*Wasteland, The*, 74
Weiser, Arthur, 40, 149
Wenham, Gordon J., 59, 98, 116, 141, 163
Whybray, Norman, 21
Wiggins, Steve A., 30, 94
Williams, Michael J., 37

Williams, Tyler F., 102
Willis, John T., 32
Wilson, Gerald H., 20, 49, 63, 103, 107, 139, 142, 145, 150, 163, 169, 172
Witt, Andrew, 108
Wittman, Derek E., 138

Younger, K, Lawson, Jr., 25

Zedekiah, 89
Zenger, Erich, 20, 98, 110, 116, 139, 169
Zernecke, Anna Elise, 24
Zion, 2, 16, 17, 46, 84, 85, 92, 94, 95, 97, 111, 117, 137, 149, 153, 156, 160, 163

Printed in the USA/Agawam, MA
May 3, 2024

865425.002